To Sam,
whose good heart
is the source
and center
of my happiness

Special thanks to Robert Cornfield,
Diane Reverand, Jennifer Katz, Lilyan Alberts,
and all the enthusiastic cooks and tasters
who shared in the process of creating
500 Low-Fat Fruit and Vegetable Recipes

500 Low-Fat
Fruit and Vegetable
Recipes

500 Low-Fat
Fruit and Vegetable
Recipes

THE ONE-STOP SOURCE
FOR HEALTHFUL,
GREAT-TASTING MEALS

(previously published as
The Garden Variety Cookbook)

SARAH SCHLESINGER

VILLARD BOOKS　NEW YORK　1995

Villard Books is a registered trademark of
Random House, Inc.

This work was originally published by Villard Books in 1992
under the title *The Garden Variety Cookbook*.

Library of Congress Cataloging-in-Publication data is
available.

ISBN: 0-679-76173-X

DESIGNED BY BARBARA MARKS

Manufactured in the United States of America on
acid-free paper

9 8 7 6 5 4 3 2

First Paperback Edition

Contents

Diet and health are matters that vary greatly from individual to individual. Be sure to consult your physician about your personal needs before beginning any diet program. Consultation with a medical professional is particularly important if you are under medical care for any illness or are taking medication.

500 Low-Fat
Fruit and Vegetable
Recipes

The Health Story

We're all familiar with the old adage "An apple a day keeps the doctor away!" But how many bananas, pineapples, sweet potatoes, kiwis, and red peppers will it take to help us fight cancer, heart disease, diabetes, high blood pressure, osteoporosis, and obesity? According to the National Academy of Science's National Research Council and the U.S. Department of Agriculture we should be eating between five and nine half-cup servings of fruits and vegetables a day —double the quantity that most of us now are consuming.

The growing body of scientific research suggesting the amazing powers of fruits and vegetables to protect us from cancer and other chronic diseases has prompted health officials to encourage us to include more of these treasures from the garden and the orchard in our daily diets.

In April of 1991, the Physicians' Committee for Responsible Medicine, a Washington-based nonprofit organization active in health and research policy, issued a report that dramatically illustrated the increasingly important role of fruits and vegetables in the fight against disease. The Committee asked the Federal Department of Agriculture to replace the four traditional food groups—meat, fish, and poultry; dairy products; grains; and fruits and vegetables—with a radical new grouping of foods: fruits; vegetables; grains; and legumes. The 3,000-member physician's group believes that meat and dairy products should play a far less central role in the American diet. They suggest that we should be eating 3 or more servings of fruit every day; 3 or more servings of vegetables; 5 servings of whole grains; 2 or 3 servings of legumes; and small quantities of meat and dairy products as options.

Dr. Colin T. Campbell, the director of the China Health Project, a study of diet and health in China, supports this position, explaining that project findings strongly suggest a diet that is 80 to 90 percent plant food.

The fruit and vegetable message is simple but vital to our health and well-being. By increasing our intake of delicious fruits and vegetables, we can take a giant step forward in fighting life threatening diseases and promoting optimum health for ourselves and our families.

The benefits of a high-fiber, low-fat diet rich in fresh fruits, vegetables, natural grains, and legumes, and containing specific vitamins and minerals, include lower cholesterol and reduced risks of heart disease, obesity, diabetes, high blood pressure, gall bladder disease, and certain forms of cancer.

In addition to protecting us against disease, this diet of choice for the 1990's can boost the energy we have available for work, exercise, pleasure, and creative endeavors, as well as make us trim and fit.

500 Low-Fat Fruit and Vegetable Recipes is a guide to launching an offensive attack against disease by making fruits and vegetables a significant part of every meal and snack time. By following the Fruit and Vegetable eating plan, you can painlessly and deliciously integrate 5 to 9 servings of fruits and vegetables a day into an anticancer, antihypertension, heart-healthy diet.

The emphasis in *500 Low-Fat Fruit and Vegetable Recipes* is not on what you have to give up, but on what you can add to your diet to strengthen your body and its antidisease defenses. The Fruit and Vegetable recipes will help you discover new ways of enjoying forty fabulous good-for-you foods that can not only nourish you, but protect you for a lifetime.

HOW FRUITS AND VEGETABLES FIGHT DISEASE

Fruits and vegetables are rich in vitamins A, C, and E; beta carotene, the coloring agent in orange-colored plants and dark green vegetables, which the body converts to vitamin A; and selenium. These nutrients have antioxidant properties that appear to make them effective in fighting cancer and other diseases. Antioxidants are substances that prevent cell damage from a form of oxygen released during physiological processes. Antioxidants defend the body against the damaging effects of highly reactive substances called free radicals that form in the body during normal metabolism or are acquired from environmental sources such as air pollution or cigarette smoke. Free radicals create chain reactions that can damage healthy cell membranes that protect tissues against attack by carcinogens. They may also change some potentially harmful substances into outright carcinogens. Free-radical damage may be a factor in promoting chronic diseases, including atherosclerosis, high blood pressure, inflammatory diseases such as rheumatoid arthritis, emphysema, Alzheimer's disease, Parkinson's disease, and perhaps even aging itself. Recent findings also suggest that free radicals can alter cholesterol that is circulating into the kind of cholesterol that clogs arteries and leads to heart attacks and strokes.

FRUITS AND VEGETABLES FIGHT CANCER

- Vitamin C may inhibit production of nitrosamines, substances produced in the body that are associated with cancer of the mouth, esophagus, stomach, and bladder.
- The National Research Council (NRC) states that there is strong evidence that a low intake of beta carotene contributes to an increased risk of lung cancer. A number of studies also suggest that beta carotene may protect against cancer of the colon, stomach, prostate, cervix, mouth, and skin.
- Significant quantities of an antioxidant compound called glutathione, which can deactivate at least 30 cancer-causing agents in laboratory experiments, are present in broccoli, spinach, and parsley.
- A carotenoid, called lycopene, which gives tomatoes, strawberries, cranberries, and watermelon their crimson color, may inhibit cancer in humans.
- Cruciferous vegetables, such as broccoli, Brussels sprouts, cabbage, cauliflower, and turnips, are especially protective against cancers of the stomach and intestine. These vegetables are rich in substances called indoles that deactivate carcinogens and block them from damaging cells. Indoles may inactivate estrogen, which can promote some cancers, particularly breast cancer.
- Since cancer is linked to high fat consumption and excessive caloric intake, diets rich in fruits and vegetables are cancer-protective because they are low in fat and calories.
- Fiber found in fruits and vegetables also has a cancer-protective function as it is thought to make bowel movements bulkier and faster moving. As a result, cancer-causing substances are diluted and spend less time in the body. Fiber also insulates the bowel wall from potential carcinogens. High-fiber diets may reduce the incidence of breast, uterine, and ovarian cancer.

FRUITS AND VEGETABLES FIGHT HEART DISEASE AND HIGH BLOOD PRESSURE

- Increased fruit and vegetable consumption has been found to be a valuable protection against diseases of the circulatory system. Nutrients found in fruits and vegetables, including soluble fiber, pectin, calcium pectate, alum, calcium, vitamin E, and vitamin C, are instrumental in the prevention of elevated cholesterol levels and the development of heart disease.

- Researchers at the Cleveland Clinic Foundation recently reported that a diet rich in antioxidant vegetables may be heart-protective because free radicals appear to contribute to the development of heart disease by causing cholesterol to be deposited in the arteries.

- Scientists at Tufts University in Boston discovered that a group of people who consumed more than 300 milligrams of vitamin C a day had higher-density lipoprotein (HDL) levels, which are thought to protect against heart disease. These results appear to be related to the fact that vitamin C is involved in the conversion of cholesterol for its removal from the body. This finding was reinforced when the National Institute on Aging found that participants in the ongoing Baltimore Longitudinal Study on Aging who had high blood levels of protective HDL cholesterol also had high levels of vitamin C in their blood.

- Vitamin C helps to build tough connective proteins, such as those found in blood vessel walls, and regulates the fat levels in the blood in three different pathways.

- Reporting on the Physician's Health Study, a 10-year study examining the effects of beta carotene, Dr. Charles Hennekens reported to the American Heart Association in November, 1990, that men with previous cardiovascular problems who take supplements of beta carotene have only about half the risk of stroke, heart attack, and death from cardiovascular disease as men not taking the supplements.

- The Lifestyle Heart Trial, conducted by Dr. Dean Ornish of the Preventive Medicine Research Institute in Sausalito, California, reported in 1990 that people with blocked coronary arteries who adhere to a strict vegetarian diet consisting primarily of fruits, vegetables, legumes, and grains, who engage in mild exercise, and practice stress-reduction techniques can reverse the blockage.

- Fruits and vegetables rich in potassium, including winter squash, spinach, sweet potatoes, Brussels sprouts, raw carrots, zucchini, peas, and cauliflower, as well as avocado, watermelon, banana, cantaloupe, orange, and pear, may contribute to lowering blood pressure. Potassium is a natural diuretic and helps remove sodium from the body. A high potassium intake protects against cholesterol buildup and helps keep arteries clear. A 1987 study at the University of California at San Diego concluded that a potassium-rich diet decreases the risk of stroke by 40 percent.

FRUITS AND VEGETABLES FIGHT OBESITY

- Fruits and vegetables are a key aspect in most weight control programs that stress replacing fat in the diet with high-fiber foods.

FRUITS AND VEGETABLES FIGHT DIABETES

- Recently developed diets for diabetics stress complex carbohydrates and high-fiber choices with emphasis on fruits and vegetables.

FRUITS AND VEGETABLES FIGHT CATARACTS

- Antioxidant vitamins found in fruits and vegetables may help prevent cataracts by stopping free radicals from damaging the lens of the eye.

FRUITS AND VEGETABLES FIGHT OSTEOPOROSIS

- Vegetables high in calcium can help in maintaining bone density and staving off osteoporosis. A Chinese study published in May, 1990, concluded that dairy calcium is not needed to prevent osteoporosis. The Chinese, who get all of their calcium from vegetables and consume half the calcium we do in America, rarely get osteoporosis, according to the study. Calcium may also play a role in cancer prevention. Broccoli, kale, parsley, and watercress are good vegetable sources of calcium.

FRUITS AND VEGETABLES PROTECT AND ENHANCE THE SKIN

- Fruits high in vitamins A and C are essential in keeping the skin moist and supple. Vitamin C is also crucial to the chemical reaction that forms collagen, a protein that is part of the support structure of the skin.

The
500 LOW-FAT FRUIT AND VEGETABLE RECIPES
Eating Plan

To take advantage of the health benefits of eating fruits and vegetables, you need to revise your diet to include a minimum of 5 to 9 servings of your choice of the forty fabulous low-fat fruits and vegetables every day. A fruit serving is a medium fruit; a half-cup of a cooked fruit; a half-cup of fruit juice; or a quarter-cup of dried fruit. A vegetable serving is 1 cup of raw vegetables; a half-cup of a cooked vegetable; or 1 cup of juice.

- Eat at least 3 servings of vegetables:

Choose 1 from the high vitamin C group.

Asparagus	Cauliflower	Peas
Broccoli	Spinach	Sweet potatoes
Brussels sprouts	Green bell peppers	Tomatoes
Cabbage	Red bell peppers	

Choose 1 from the high vitamin A group.

Asparagus	Dark leafy greens	Pumpkin
Broccoli	(romaine lettuce,	Sweet potatoes
Carrots	chicory, endive,	Tomatoes
	watercress, kale)	Winter squash
	Red bell peppers	

Choose 1 from the moderate/high fiber group.

Asparagus	Corn	Peas
Broccoli	Eggplant	Spinach
Brussels sprouts	Green beans	Winter Squash

Be sure 1 of your vegetable choices is a cruciferous vegetable several times a week.

Broccoli	Cauliflower	Turnip
Brussels sprouts	Kale	Watercress
Cabbage		

- Eat a minimum of 2 servings of fruit a day.

Be sure that at least one is from the high vitamin C/beta carotene group.

Apricots	Kiwi	Papaya
Avocado	Lemons	Pineapple
Blueberries	Limes	Raspberries
Cantaloupe	Oranges	Strawberries
Cranberries	Nectarines	Tangerines
Grapefruit	Mangoes	Watermelon

Choose 1 or 2 from the moderate/high fiber group.

Apples	Cantaloupe	Raspberries
Avocado	Honeydew	Strawberries
Bananas	Pears	Watermelon
Blackberries		

- At least 1 of your 5 servings every day should be from the following list of power-packed foods that offer the benefits of high fiber, vitamin A, and vitamin C.

Asparagus	Cauliflower	Spinach
Broccoli	Dark leafy greens	Strawberries
Brussels sprouts	Cantaloupe	Sweet Potatoes
Cabbage	Green bell peppers	Tomatoes
Carrots	Red bell peppers	Winter Squash

While I have stressed these forty fruit and vegetable choices because of their particular nutritional profiles, many of the recipes that follow include other fruit and vegetable choices as well. As you start to incorporate more fruits and vegetables into your overall eating plan, you should think in terms of emphasizing the forty choices, but also enjoying as wide a variety of produce as you have access to in your local markets. Many stores are now carrying a selection of exotic imported fruit and vegetable choices in addition to broadening their selection of domestic produce.

Your personal taste or lifestyle may make it more desirable for you to eat your 5 to 9 servings of produce in a different configuration than the one I am suggesting. For instance, you may prefer to eat 5 to 9 servings of vegetables a day. While it is certainly to the benefit of your health to eat 5 to 9 servings of produce a day regardless of your specific choices, keep in mind that the diets recommended by all of the major health organizations do advocate including a variety of both vegetables and fruits in your diet. By following the plan I have suggested, you will be getting a wide range of nutrients each day. By broadening your choices of foods, you will also keep your daily menu more appealing.

Make your 5 to 9 servings of fruits and vegetables a day part of an eating plan that follows the guidelines of the National Academy of Sciences, the National Cancer Institute, and the American Heart Association by cutting back on fat, eating more fiber, reducing cholesterol, and eating more whole-grain foods.

Focus on eating the correct number of calories to maintain or reach your ideal weight, developing an exercise program, and avoiding processed foods that contain excessive quantities of sugar, sodium, additives, and preservatives.

Getting Started

Here's a complete guide to buying the ingredients you'll be using in your Low-Fat Fruit and Vegetable recipes. The goal of the recipes is to provide at least ½ cup of fruits and/or vegetables per serving. The recipes are designed to be low in fat, cholesterol, and sodium.

While meat, poultry, seafood, and dairy food are included in many of the recipes, they are limited in portion size or introduced in a low-fat form. Meat, poultry, and seafood are suggested in 4-ounce servings.

Mild, light-flavored olive oil is suggested as the oil of choice, due to its high monounsaturated fat content. Canola oil is an acceptable substitute.

Some of the recipes include ingredients containing alcohol, but a nonalcoholic alternative is always offered.

Limited quantities of sugar and other sweeteners are used in some fruit recipes. You may wish to avoid or modify these recipes if you are on a sugar-restricted diet.

SHOPPING FOR RECIPE INGREDIENTS

- Buy "choice" or "good" graded beef, including lean, well-trimmed chuck, loin, and round.
- Buy ground beef (chuck or round) with no more than 10 percent fat.
- Buy nonfat or low-fat whole-grain, French or Italian bread and rolls. Buy whole-wheat pitas. Buy egg roll wrappers, which are now available in the refrigerator case in many supermarkets.
- Buy chicken broth that has a reduced salt content or low-sodium chicken bouillon.
- Buy nonfat or low-fat cheeses. Shop for those made from skim milk products that are low in fat, cholesterol, and sodium.
- Buy nonfat or 1% low-fat cottage cheese. Whirl it an electric blender and use it as a substitute for sour cream. Buy nonfat or low-fat cream cheese.
- Buy nonfat or part-skim ricotta cheese, which has almost half the calories of regular ricotta.
- Buy Parmesan cheese by the pound to grate yourself or buy freshly

grated Parmesan cheese for a flavor far superior to the preservative-laden types packaged in jars.

- Buy large fresh eggs, but limit egg yolk consumption to 2 a week in all foods. If you are particularly concerned about cholesterol, substitute a nonfat brand of egg substitute for the eggs in the Low-Fat Fruit and Vegetable recipes.
- Buy skim milk, 1% milk, and low-fat buttermilk. Skim milk is strongly suggested if you are concerned about the amount of fat you are consuming. Avoid 2% milk, which has almost as much fat as whole milk.
- Buy skinned white meat poultry, which has a lower fat content than dark meat.
- Buy low-fat ground turkey with a fat content under 7 percent.
- Buy canned or fresh crab meat; buy fresh shrimp, scallops, and fish.
- Buy natural brown rice as its bran layer can help to lower cholesterol.
- Buy white albacore tuna that is packed in either water or olive oil. Buy canned sardines and canned salmon.
- Buy nonfat or low-fat plain yogurt.
- Buy liquid or tub, diet or reduced-calorie margarine that contains less than 1 gram of saturated fat per tablespoon for general cooking. Buy regular stick margarine that contains less than 2 grams of saturated fat per tablespoon for baking.
- Buy nonfat or reduced-calorie mayonnaise and Dijon mustard.
- Buy all-fruit preserves sweetened only with fruit juice.
- Buy nonhydrogenated natural peanut butter with no added fats, stabilizers, salt, or sweeteners. If the oil rises to the top, stir it back in.
- Buy fresh parsley. It will chop very finely if it is thoroughly dried with a dish towel before chopping.
- Buy dry-roasted unsalted peanuts, walnuts, and almonds. Walnuts and most other nuts will keep for 1 month at room temperature and for 3 months in the refrigerator. They can also be frozen for 6 to 12 months. Frozen nuts do not need to be thawed before using.
- Buy dark seedless raisins.
- Buy dry-roasted unsalted sesame and sunflower seeds.
- Buy unbleached all-purpose flour.
- Buy canned fruit packed in unsweetened water or juice. Buy canned vegetables packed without added salt.
- Buy frozen fruit packed with no sugar added. Buy frozen vegetables packed without added salt.

- Buy old-fashioned rolled oats.
- Buy low-sodium (or no salt added) staples, such as canned tomatoes and tomato paste.
- Buy low-sodium canned kidney beans and chick-peas.
- Buy green and ripe olives. Be sure to rinse them well to get rid of salty brine before serving.
- Buy monounsaturated mild, light-flavored olive oil and extra-virgin olive oil, or canola oil instead of oils heavy in saturated or polyunsaturated fats. Refrigerate opened containers of olive oil. The oil will become cloudy and solidify, but it will clear and liquefy when it is returned to room temperature.
- Buy fresh gingerroot. To store, wrap the entire root in aluminum foil and keep it in the freezer. Peel the end and grate as needed. Frozen gingerroot will keep for months. Chunks of the root can also be refrigerated for several months in a jar filled with dry sherry.
- Buy fresh or canned chile peppers. Jalapeño peppers are dark green, have thick flesh, and are about 2 to 3 inches long. The jalapeño chile is very hot. Serrano peppers are green to red in color. They are thinner than jalapeño peppers and are about 1 inch long. Chopped jalapeño peppers can also be found in glass jars in the produce department of your food market.
- Buy fresh garlic.
- Buy fresh or dried herbs and spices. Dried herbs will be more flavorful if you crush them by rubbing them between your fingers as you use them. Store dried herbs out of direct sunlight and in jars or tins rather than cardboard boxes. They will keep a long time if tightly covered in a dark cool cabinet. As they age, herbs can lose flavor and you may need to add more than a recipe indicates. It is a good idea to replace red herbs, such as crushed red pepper and curry powder, after a year of storage. Low-Fat Fruit and Vegetable recipes frequently call for dried basil leaves; ground cinnamon and stick cinnamon; ground ginger; ground cloves; ground allspice; dried rosemary leaves; dried thyme leaves; dried dillweed; black pepper; white pepper; chili powder; cayenne pepper; ground cumin; dried tarragon leaves; bay leaves; and paprika.
- Buy curry powder, which is actually a blend of different herbs and spices that vary according to the country of origin. Varieties can differ in intensity of flavor, so use carefully. Curry flavor becomes stronger in a dish that stands or is kept refrigerated and then reheated.
- Buy soy sauce in a "lite" or low-sodium variety, which has 40 percent less sodium than traditional soy sauce.

- Buy hot pepper sauce if you like your foods hot and spicy.
- Buy granulated sugar, brown sugar, reduced-calorie maple syrup, and honey. If you choose to buy sugar substitutes, be aware of their particular chemical compositions and any resulting health implications.
- Buy red wine vinegar, apple cider vinegar, and white wine vinegar.
- Buy low-sodium crackers and no-salt potato chips, pretzels, and corn chips.
- Buy low-sodium sparkling and nonsparkling mineral water. Buy pure fruit juices, such as apple juice, pineapple juice, and pear nectar, with no sugar added. Some recipes call for dry sherry or white wine. Buy nonalcoholic wines for cooking if you are avoiding alcohol. (Fruit juices may also be substituted for wine.)
- In addition to the 40 main fruits and vegetables, the recipes frequently call for scallions; onion; red onion; celery; zucchini; yellow squash; peaches; plums; grapes; potatoes; fresh mushrooms; radishes; cucumbers; horseradish; bean sprouts; watercress; lima beans; and leeks.

SHOPPING FOR FRUITS AND VEGETABLES

While experts maintain that the benefits of eating fruits and vegetables far outweigh any potential risk from pesticides, increased consumption of fresh produce inevitably raises the issue of chemicals in our food supply.

Surveys show that 8 out of 10 Americans see pesticide residues on food as a serious threat to health. Growing public concern about pesticides has produced increased attention to the system of pesticide regulation and the three federal agencies that oversee the use of pesticides—the Environmental Protection Agency (EPA), the Food and Drug Administration (FDA), and the Department of Agriculture (USDA)—have stepped up efforts to work more effectively together. Grass-roots activism on pesticide-related issues is on the rise, and growers, large and small, are looking at ways to reduce pesticide use as well as experimenting with alternatives to pesticides.

Chemical manufacturers are taking a more active role in regulating themselves and many grocery chains and food producers now hire private laboratories to monitor fruits and vegetables to make sure pesticide residues fall far below federal limits.

In 1989, the National Academy of Sciences reported that farmers who apply few or no chemicals to their crops can be as productive as those who use pesticides and synthetic fertilizers and recommended changing federal subsidy programs that encourage overuse of agricultural chemicals.

While this increased awareness and concern about pesticides has positive implications for the future, the fact remains that currently more than 20,000 pesticide products, containing 600 active ingredients, are registered for use by the EPA. About 325 of the active ingredients are used on food crops, with a total of about 850 million pounds of active ingredients annually used on food and livestock-feed crops.

Pesticides are unquestionably toxic in large amounts. The federal regulatory system is responsible for making sure that the food supply is safe in terms of tiny amounts of pesticide residues that may remain on food, particularly raw products like fruits and vegetables. In 1988 the Food and Drug Administration analyzed over 18,000 samples of domestic and imported food and reported no residues on 61 percent of the raw foods tested. All but 4 percent of the samples in which residues were detected fell within legal limits set by the EPA. The FDA also conducts surveys to determine the amount of pesticides consumed from table-ready foods. The agency claims that the consumption of pesticide residues in the average American diet is less than 1 percent of what the World Health Organization says is acceptable.

If you are concerned about pesticide residues in the fruits and vegetables you buy, there are a number of steps you can take to minimize your exposure.

- Thoroughly rinse fruits and vegetables and scrub them before eating. While there are a number of commercial products that claim to wash the pesticides, hormones, and other chemicals off the skins of fruits and vegetables, you can get the same results by washing them in a pint of water to which you've added a few drops of dishwashing detergent. Be sure to rinse them thoroughly after using detergent. Scrubbing and rinsing will remove some pesticides from the surfaces of your produce, but no amount of washing will get rid of pesticides that are already inside the fruits and vegetables.
- You can peel fruits and vegetables, although some nutrients and fiber will be lost in the process. Remove outer leaves of leafy vegetables such as cabbage and lettuce.
- Look at labels of fruits and vegetables. Some growers are packaging their produce in plastic with a label that says the contents have been tested to meet government standards.

- Ask your produce manager where the fruits and vegetables in your market are from. Some industry critics believe that the risks are greater with imported produce, so you might want to choose domestic produce if you have a choice.
- Ask your produce manager if your supermarket chain has produce tested for pesticide residues.

You can also seek out a reliable supplier of organic produce—which means that the fruits and vegetables were grown naturally, without synthetic chemical pesticides or preservatives. But because most organic food is produced by small, unregulated farms, it is not always easy to be sure that the produce has been tested and is truly pesticide free.

While many supermarkets began selling organic produce in the late 1980's in reaction to growing publicity about the potential hazards of foods treated with pesticides, they have discovered that customers do not always support these efforts by buying the organic fruits and vegetables. Organic produce does not look as appealing as "regular" produce, and it can be as much as 30 percent more expensive due to higher production and handling costs. However, organic produce often has a better flavor.

Organic farming depends on the use of natural fertilizers and natural methods of controlling pests and is highly labor intensive. Fruits and vegetables not treated with pesticides after harvest to extend shelf life don't hold up as well. It also takes more man hours to keep organic produce presentable in the store, and there is more spoilage—all of which is costly.

If you are concerned enough about the pesticide issue to be willing to pay higher prices and accept a lower standard of appearance, find a health food store or supermarket with an organic produce department. Inquire about the sources of the produce and attempt to verify that it is truly organic. A list of the organizations certifying organic foods throughout the country can be obtained by writing to Americans for Safe Food, 1501 16th Street NW, Washington, D.C. 20036.

Another area of consumer concern in the marketing of fresh fruits and vegetables is produce waxing. Produce packers add a waxy, glossy coating to more than 30 fruits and vegetables that we find on our supermarket shelves. Waxed items include apples, cantaloupes, cucumbers, peaches, pineapples, eggplants, squash, tomatoes, and citrus fruits. These waxes are designed to seal in moisture and enhance the appearance of the fruits and vegetables. They are made from mineral derivatives such as paraffin, a petroleum derivative; vegetable derivatives; shellac; and animal by-products, such as rendered fat. For almost 20 years, the Federal Food and Drug Administration has required that a complete listing of the ingredients in these waxes be indicated on signs in supermarket produce sections. However, this law has not been enforced by the government. Recently, a number of state governments have begun enforcement attempts out of concern for the consumer's need to know if animal products are used in waxes for dietary and religious reasons. While the domestic produce industry claims to no longer use animal-based waxes, these products are frequently used in imported produce. If your supermarket is not posting this information and it is of concern to you, ask your produce manager to provide you with pertinent facts about wax ingredients used on the produce you buy.

Selecting and Storing the Fabulous Forty LOW-FAT Fruits and Vegetables

APPLES
Often called America's number one fruit because of their year-round availability and low calorie count, apples are 85–95 percent water. In addition to being a thirst quencher, they also act as a natural mouth freshener. One medium apple yields about 90 calories.

Although there are 300 varieties of apples grown in America, only twenty are cultivated in the major commercial orchards. When buying apples, look for those that are bruise-free and firm to the touch. A bruise or blemish on the skin means a decay spot in the flesh. Over-ripe apples will feel soft and the texture will be mealy or mushy. When the green of an apple is very dark, it is an indication that the apple is not fully mature. Such apples will be hard, sour, and have poor flavor. Underripe apples are fine for cooking. If you want to eat them raw, refrigerate them and allow them to ripen for a week or two. Apples differ in color depending on their variety as well as maturity. They may be bright green and red, solid vibrant red, golden-yellow, lemon-yellow or greenish-yellow. Some varieties become over-ripe and exhibit a mealy texture and a loss of flavor with even short exposure to warm temperatures. Larger apples should be very firm since they mature faster than small apples and become mushy sooner. Avoid apples with "russeting," a brown scab-like condition near the stem end.

After picking apples or buying them in a store, put them without delay in a cool place. Be sure to check for damaged or bruised apples and set those aside for immediate use. When keeping apples refrigerated, store them in perforated plastic bags or containers to prevent them from drying out. Apples stored at room temperature will dry out ten times faster than if they are refrigerated.

In the United States, apples are picked from June to December. After December, apples are coming to us from controlled storage and not direct from the orchard. From January to June, consumers are often limited to choosing from among the five best-keeping apples—Red Delicious, Golden Delicious, McIntosh, Rome Beauty, and Granny Smith. Storage apples are usually rinsed in a mild detergent and are often treated with chemicals to prevent dark spots from developing. The Red and Golden Delicious apples that are shipped from Washington state are usually coated with a vegetable wax to replace the natural wax removed during the washing process. Like wines, the quality of apples depends on many factors—latitude, terrain, weather, and growing methods. The background or undercast color of an apple changes from dark green to light green as it ripens and the surface turns a bright red or a deeper yellow.

The decision to buy a particular variety of apple should be determined by what you are planning to do with the fruit. If you plan to eat them raw, choose crisp, crunchy, juicy apples. Apples that you plan to cook should hold their shape and retain their flavor when baked.

To prepare apples for cooking, peel if desired and remove cores and slice into wedges. Apple corers and apple cutters, which divide the fruit into neat wedges, can make preparing apples quicker and easier. Since the inner color of apples turns brown quickly, dip slices or wedges in lemon juice and water to preserve the color.

TO FREEZE

Peel, core, and slice 3 pounds of apples (about 9 medium) into 1/4-inch slices. Soak in 1 gallon of water mixed with 2 tablespoons lemon juice. Bring a large pot of water to a boil and drop 1/3 of the apple slices in at a time. Blanch for 1 minute. Drain immediately. Place in single layers on baking trays and freeze. When frozen, place in plastic freezer bags, seal, and freeze. Three pounds of apples will produce 3 quarts of apple slices.

EQUIVALENTS

- 1 pound of apples yields 4 small, 3 medium, or 2 large apples
- 1 pound of apples yields 3 cups diced fruit
- 1 pound of apples yields 1 1/2 cups of applesauce
- 1 medium apple, cut into 1-inch cubes, equals 1 1/4 cups
- 1 medium apple, cut into julienne strips, equals 1 1/4 cups

- 2 medium apples equal 2 cups purée
- 2 medium apples, sliced, equal 3 cups
- 2 medium apples, diced, equal 2½ cups

APRICOTS

Several varieties of fresh apricots are available between late May and August. Their actual appearance is a strong indicator of good flavor. Choose apricots that look ripe and glowing and are on the firm side, since they will ripen at home. They should be smooth skinned and blemish free. Apricots range in color from pale yellow to a healthy golden-yellow. Watch out for traces of green that indicate the fruit is unripe. The stronger the color, the sweeter the apricot as a rule.

Apricots should be ripened at room temperature and refrigerated when ripe. When the fruit is soft to the touch, it is ready to eat. Apricots don't need to be peeled. Cut them in half and remove the pit or eat the fruit around the pit. Slice, chop, or purée for use in recipes. To remove apricot skins, plunge the fruit in boiling water for 30 seconds, then dip it in cold water. The skins can then be easily slipped off.

Apricots can be used as substitutes for peaches, plums, or nectarines in a variety of recipes.

Dried apricots, whole and chopped, are available year round. They store extremely well. Dried apricots should be soft and tender.

TO FREEZE

Bring 4 quarts of water to a rapid boil. Wash, halve, and pit the fresh apricots. Peel and cut into ¼-inch-thick slices. Blanch in boiling water for 1 minute. Chill in ice water for 30 seconds, drain, and dry. Freeze in freezer containers.

EQUIVALENTS

- 1 pound equals 10–12 apricots
- 1 pound of apricots yields 2 cups sliced fruit

ASPARAGUS

Asparagus is best cooked as close to harvesttime as possible since it loses its flavor and begins to become woody quickly. When selecting asparagus in the supermarket, try to buy loose stalks. Pick firm, straight green or creamy white spears with closed, compact tips or buds. Open heads with tiny sprouts between the leaves are a sign of age.

The optimum size for an asparagus stalk is ½ inch in diameter. If an asparagus stalk is thicker than your index finger, it will usually be very stringy. While very thin asparagus looks delicate, it often becomes stringy when cooked and can have a harsh flavor. Purchase spears of uniform thickness, either thick or thin, so that they will cook uniformly.

To store asparagus, refrigerate the spears, uncovered, and consume them as soon as possible. If you are not sure of their freshness, peeling asparagus stalks eliminates strings and can usually make the lower stalk as tender to eat as the tips.

To peel, simply cut off the white or pale green woody ends and pare with a vegetable peeler. Asparagus can be steamed, boiled, or stir-fried. Asparagus cookers, in which the stalks stand up in a basket immersed in boiling water, can be used or the stalks can simply be laid down in a frying pan, covered with boiling water, and cooked for 5–7 minutes, or until the tips droop.

TO FREEZE

Cut the asparagus stalks to the desired length, blanch in boiling water for 2 minutes, plunge in ice water for 2 minutes, drain, and pat dry. Freeze in moisture-proof containers for up to 10 months.

EQUIVALENTS

- 1 pound of asparagus equals 12–14 spears
- 1 pound of asparagus yields 2½ cups of cut-up asparagus
- Allow ½ pound per person

AVOCADOS
Fresh avocados are available at produce counters year round. It is essential to use them at the proper stage of ripeness to enjoy their fullest flavor.

When shopping for avocados, choose those with either smooth, green skins, or thick, pebbly, dark green skins that are free of bruises and damaged spots. If you plan to use the avocado within 24 hours, buy one that is soft but not mushy. If you plan to use it within several days, buy a harder one and allow it to ripen for 2 or 3 days. Soft avocados can be refrigerated for up to 5 days. Harder ones should be kept at room temperature. You can also place harder avocados in a paper bag or fruit-ripening bowl to speed the ripening process. Check on the fruit each day; when a wooden toothpick can be easily inserted in the stem end, the fruit is ready to be eaten.

Cut avocados immediately before using or serving. Using a sharp paring knife, cut the fruit in half lengthwise around the seed. Twist the 2 halves of the avocado in opposite directions and separate. Remove the seed with a spoon. The skin can be pulled off or slipped off with a paring knife. Since avocados discolor quickly when cut, dip the cut surfaces into a mixture of lemon juice and water to preserve the original color.

TO FREEZE

Freezing is not recommended for avocados.

EQUIVALENTS

- 2 small avocados weigh about 1 pound
- 2 small avocados yield about 1 cup mashed fruit

BANANAS

One banana is called a finger, a cluster of fingers is called a hand, and a stalk of hands is called a bunch or a stack. Bananas can be eaten raw or cooked, fresh or dried, green or ripe, hot or cold, alone or as part of another dish. The nutritional content of a banana changes as it ripens.

Bananas are best stored at room temperature (between 70 and 80 degrees) until they are ripe. Set them in a well-ventilated area out of direct sunlight. If you are using a glass or plastic container, try lining it with newspaper to prevent leaking or sweating, which can cause the fruit to spoil quickly. After they are ripe, bananas may be refrigerated for 3 or 4 days. If you refrigerate them before they are fully ripe, they may not ripen properly. Bananas should always be peeled and the strings from between the pulp and skin removed before they are eaten. Since bananas will discolor a few minutes after cutting, dip cut bananas into a mixture of water and lemon juice, orange juice, or grapefruit juice.

TO FREEZE

While bananas are sometimes frozen for brief periods of time to make frozen desserts, long-term freezing is not recommended.

EQUIVALENTS

- 1 pound of bananas yields 2 large or 3 medium-size bananas
- 1 pound of bananas yields 1 cup mashed or 1½ cups sliced fruit

BERRIES (Blackberries, Blueberries, Raspberries, and Strawberries)

When buying berries, avoid those that are very soft and show signs of mold or bruises. Buy berries to use within a day or two for the best flavor. Look for firm, plump berries with a healthy color. Blackberries should have a jet black color, and blueberries should be a deep blue. Strawberries should be firm, deep red, and have a green cap attached.

Store blackberries, blueberries, and raspberries unwashed in a shallow plastic container, covered with paper towels, in the refrigerator, to use within several days. Do not store raspberries in tin or aluminum containers or their red color may turn blue. Store strawberries in an open paper bag. Underripe strawberries can be stored at room temperature, covered with plastic wrap.

Gently wash all berries in a strainer or colander before serving and pat dry, discarding any that have gone bad. Wash before hulling to avoid losing any of the juices. Hull strawberries with a strawberry huller, but use a sharp paring knife for other berries. Try using an egg slicer to slice strawberries if you are in a hurry.

TO FREEZE

Blackberries   Arrange whole unwashed blackberries in a single layer in a shallow pan. Freeze solid. Transfer to freezer bags or containers leaving ½ inch of head space in bag or container, and store in freezer for up to 6 months. Thaw in bag or container and rinse before using.

Blueberries   Arrange whole unwashed blueberries in a single layer in a shallow pan. Freeze solid. Transfer to freezer bags or containers leaving ½ inch of head space in bag or container, and store in freezer for up to 6 months. Thaw in bag or container and rinse before using.

Raspberries   Arrange whole unwashed raspberries in a single layer in a shallow pan. Freeze solid. Transfer to freezer bags or containers leaving ½ inch of head space in bag or container. Store in freezer for up to 6 months. Thaw in bag or container and rinse before using.

Strawberries   Hull the berries and slice them or leave them whole. To freeze whole berries, arrange them in a single layer in a shallow pan. Freeze solid. Transfer to freezer bags or containers, leaving ½ inch of head space, and store in freezer. To freeze sliced or puréed berries, place directly in freezer containers and freeze. Thaw in their containers and rinse sliced strawberries before using in a recipe.

EQUIVALENTS

- 1 pound of fresh berries yields about 1 quart or 4 cups fruit
- 1 pint of fresh berries provides about 4 servings or 2½ cups of fruit

BROCCOLI

Select unwrapped broccoli or broccoli that has been wrapped to allow some air circulation. Look for a firm head with tightly closed buds. Avoid limp or loosely packed buds, which indicate an overmature, spongy, or pulpy texture. The buds may show a bluish-purple cast but should not be open to show yellow flowers. Do not store broccoli in tight plastic bags. Store in a perforated plastic bag or spray broccoli lightly with cold water and wrap in a damp kitchen towel. Store for 2–3 days in the refrigerator.

TO FREEZE

Wash and trim the broccoli and cut it into ¾-inch-thick pieces. Blanch for 3 minutes and plunge into cold water for 3 minutes. Drain, pat dry, and pack into freezer bags.

EQUIVALENTS

- A ½-pound bunch of broccoli yields 6 cups of trimmed pieces
- A 1½-pound bunch of broccoli yields 4 cups of cooked broccoli, or 4–5 servings

BRUSSELS SPROUTS

Shop for Brussels sprouts that have firm, tight heads that seem heavy for their weight. The core end should have a clean, white appearance. Brussels sprouts that are small, green, and firm will taste best. Avoid any with yellow or brown sprouts.

Store unwashed, in perforated plastic bags in the refrigerator for several days. Before cooking, remove any yellow or browned leaves and cut an X in the base of each sprout.

TO FREEZE

Blanch trimmed sprouts in boiling water for 4 minutes, then plunge into ice water for 4 minutes. Drain and place in freezer containers.

EQUIVALENTS

- ½ pound of medium sprouts yields 12–14 sprouts
- ½ pound of trimmed sprouts yields 2 cups, or 2–3 servings

CABBAGE

Cabbages should be heavy for their size, with crisp, fresh-looking leaves and no brown streaks or spots. Try to buy green cabbages with deep green leaves still attached. Red cabbages should have no black edges. Wrap cabbage tightly in plastic bags and store in a refrigerator crisper for 4–7 days. Don't cut or shred cabbage until you are ready to use it. Discard old or wilted leaves, then halve cabbage and remove the core. To retain the bright color of red cabbage, add lemon juice to the cooking water. Cabbage has about 18 calories a cup.

TO FREEZE

Cut a head into 2-inch chunks and blanch in boiling water for 3 minutes. Quickly plunge into ice water. Pat dry and pack in airtight freezer bags. To use, take chunks directly from freezer and simmer in broth or sauce until defrosted.

EQUIVALENTS

- 1 firm-headed 2-pound cabbage, trimmed, will yield 9–10 cups of sliced cabbage
- 1 firm-headed 2-pound cabbage, trimmed, will provide 5–6 cups of cooked cabbage
- Allow ¼ pound per person

CANTALOUPE

A good cantaloupe should seem heavy for its size. Weigh several that appear to be the same size and take the heaviest. A ripe melon should be firm but give slightly when pressed at the soft end. Ripe cantaloupe should also have a fragrant, musky scent. Melons should be free of dents and bruises and have dry rinds. Their outer color and shape should be uniform. The deeper the color of the flesh, the sweeter the melon will be. The netting on the rind should stand out in bold relief all over the outer surface. An overripe cantaloupe may feel sticky when you run your hands over it.

If the melon is slightly unripe, keep it at room temperature for 1–2 days. Refrigerate ripe melons to use within a few days.

Cut the melon in half with a sharp knife, if you are going to divide it into sections. Cut off the top if you are going to use it as a container. Scoop the seeds in a strainer over a bowl so no juice is wasted. Wrap melon in plastic wrap before refrigerating it in the crisper section since its odor tends to permeate other foods. Melon seeds can be dried and toasted in the oven.

TO FREEZE

Be sure the melon is very ripe. Halve and seed, scraping away pulp and strings. Use a melon-baller to scoop balls from the flesh. Pack the balls in freezer bags or containers, sprinkle with 1 teaspoon strained lemon juice, and seal tightly. Partially thaw before using.

EQUIVALENTS

- 1 pound of melon yields 1 cup of cut-up fruit

CARROTS
Shop for carrots that are small to medium in size. They should be bright orange and firm textured. Carrots that seem limp and are sprouting should be avoided.

Carrots can be sealed without their tops in perforated plastic bags in the refrigerator for several weeks.

When preparing carrots, scrub them and scrape the skin off if it seems tough.

TO FREEZE

Blanch sliced carrots for 2 minutes in boiling water, then plunge into ice water for 2 minutes. Drain, pat dry, and pack in freezer containers.

EQUIVALENTS

- 1 pound of carrots yields 4 cups shredded carrots
- 2 medium carrots (1/3 pound), shredded or sliced, yield 1 cup carrots
- Allow 1/4 pound per person

CAULIFLOWER
Choose cauliflower by size, weight, and color. Look for firm, compact white or ivory heads that are surrounded by tender, green leaves. Avoid brown spots.

A new product, broccoflower, has the shape and weight of a cauliflower but is the color of an underripe banana. It has a more moderate flavor and aroma than does white cauliflower and more vitamin C and twice as much beta carotene. Broccoflower can be steamed whole or cooked as florets.

Wrap cauliflower in perforated plastic bags and store, unwashed, in the refrigerator for 7 days.

You can cook trimmed, cored cauliflower whole or cut it into florets before cooking.

TO FREEZE

Blanch florets in boiling water with 1 teaspoon vinegar added for 3 minutes and plunge into ice water for 3 minutes. Drain and pack in freezer bags or containers.

EQUIVALENTS

- 1 pound of trimmed cauliflower yields about 4½ cups
- 1 medium head serves 4
- Allow ⅓ pound per person

CORN

Choose ears of corn with fresh, green husks with silk ends free from decay or worm injury. The ears should feel cool. The top of the cob should be round rather than pointed. The stem on fresh-picked corn is a damp, pale green. They should be filled with plump, milky kernels. When you press a thumbnail into a kernel, it should spurt milk. If the silk is brown and slightly dry, the corn is ripe. After 24 hours the stem turns opaque, chalky, and eventually brown.

The minute corn is picked, the sugar in its kernels begins to turn to starch and its quality begins to deteriorate. Keep ears in husks, unwashed, until ready to use. Store in the refrigerator and use as soon as possible. If husks have been removed, store in the refrigerator in perforated plastic bags. Never store corn at room temperature.

To remove corn silk, pull husks off and rub silk off under running water or scrape it away with a dry vegetable brush.

To remove kernels from the cob, hold the cob vertically and run a sharp knife down around its length.

TO FREEZE

Remove husks and silk. Blanch medium ears in boiling water for 6 minutes from the time water comes back to a boil. Plunge in ice water for 6 minutes. Drain and pack in freezer bags. You can also cut the kernels off after blanching and freeze them in freezer containers.

- 2 ears yield about 1 cup of kernels
- Allow 1 large or 2 small ears per person

CRANBERRIES
Raw cranberries offer more nutritional benefits than processed ones. The best cranberries are plump, firm, and lustrous. Avoid dull, sticky berries. The bright red varieties are tarter than the smaller, dark berries. Because of their tartness, most cranberry preparations require a sweetener, although it can be honey or maple syrup rather than sugar. Usually ½ cup sweetener to 1 pound of fresh berries is enough.

TO FREEZE
Fresh berries can be frozen in their original packages or repacked. If repacking, wash them and dry them well. Lay them on heavy-duty aluminum foil and place in the freezer. When they are frozen hard, pack them in freezer bags and tightly seal. It's not necessary to thaw frozen berries before cooking.

EQUIVALENTS
- 1 pound of cranberries yields 4 cups

DARK LEAFY GREENS

ROMAINE
Shop for crisp, colorful heads and put, unwashed and uncut, in a tightly closed plastic bag and refrigerate for up to 1 week. Don't store lettuce near melons, apples, or pears, all of which give off gases that can cause the lettuce to brown. Rinse in cool water before using. Pat or spin dry. Tear rather than cut with a knife.

TO FREEZE ROMAINE
Freezing is not recommended.

EQUIVALENTS
- 1 pound of romaine yields 20 leaves
- 1 pound of romaine yields 4–5 2-cup servings

CHICORY AND KALE

Shop for lively, green, tender leaves. Avoid any that look yellow or limp. Leaves that are too large may be bitter. Look for heads of chicory with a loose appearance, curly leaves, and ragged edges. Wrap in perforated plastic bags and refrigerate for about 1 week. Rinse well to get rid of grit before using.

TO FREEZE CHICORY AND KALE

Blanch in boiling water for 2 minutes, plunge into ice water for 30 seconds, and drain. Pack in freezer containers or bags.

EQUIVALENTS

- 1 pound of chicory or kale yields 8 cups

EGGPLANT

Since eggplant is very perishable, it is best to use it within a few days of purchase. Look for plump eggplants with very shiny skins that are firm to the touch and free of soft spots. Eggplants should feel heavy for their size. Bright green caps indicate freshness. The smaller the eggplant, the less bitter it will be.

Store eggplant in a cool place, or wrap in plastic wrap and store in the refrigerator for up to 2 days.

TO FREEZE

Freezing is not recommended except when eggplant is prepared as an ingredient in a recipe.

EQUIVALENTS

- 1 1/2 pounds of eggplant yield 4 servings
- 1/2 pound of peeled, chopped, or cubed eggplant yields 2 cups
- 1 pound of raw eggplant yields 1/2 pound of cooked

GRAPEFRUIT

When buying grapefruit, choose those with smooth skins, and a firm, round shape. Avoid fruit with rough or wrinkled skin, pointed stem ends that are flabby and springy to the touch, or soft spots. Scars, scratches, and discolorations should not affect quality. Thicker skins on grapefruit indicate a high concentration of nutrients in the fruit. The glossy look of many grapefruit results from a waxing treatment used to prevent loss of moisture. Red and pink varieties have a pink blush on their rinds. They are often sweeter and have fewer seeds than the white-fleshed varieties.

Grapefruit does not ripen after picking and its quality deteriorates with age. The longer the storage period, the greater the loss of juice and flavor. Store whole fruit in the crisper drawers of your refrigerator or in open containers on the shelves. Don't put them in airtight bags because mold develops quickly when air can't circulate freely.

Don't slice or peel grapefruit until you are ready to use it. Remove any white pith as it has a bitter flavor. After peeling, cutting, grating or shredding the fruit, refrigerate until serving time. If you wash the fruit after peeling it, do it quickly since vitamin C is water soluble. Other vitamins and minerals may also be leached away during prolonged washing.

TO FREEZE

Whole citrus fruit cannot be frozen, but you can freeze grapefruit slices or juice. To freeze grapefruit, cut into paper-thin slices or separate into sections; lay slices or sections on foil and freeze solid. Carefully transfer frozen grapefruit to a plastic freezer bag and freeze until needed.

EQUIVALENTS

- 1 medium grapefruit contains 6–8 ounces of juice
- 1 medium grapefruit yields 10–12 sections of bite-sized pieces
- 1 medium grapefruit contains 3–5 tablespoons of grated peel

GREEN BEANS

To test beans for freshness, break one between your thumb and forefinger. You should hear a distinct snapping noise. Buy loose beans, if possible, and select ones of the same size to promote even cooking. Buy thin beans without bulges. The skin should not feel tough or leathery. Avoid limp or spotted beans. Look for beans with good color, plumpness, and a fresh-looking velvety coat. Pods should be free of wrinkles. Heavy pods with well-defined beans inside are likely to be old and tough.

Refrigerate beans in perforated plastic bags in your vegetable crisper. Use within a few days.

TO FREEZE

Blanch in boiling water for 3 minutes, and chill in ice water for 3 minutes. Freeze in freezer bags.

EQUIVALENTS

- 1 pound of green beans yields 4 cups of cut-up beans
- 1 pound of green beans yields about 4 servings

HONEYDEW

Honeydew melons are pale white to yellow on the outside and are often sweeter than cantaloupes. Honeydews range from 5–10 inches in diameter. A good one should seem heavy for its size. Weigh several that appear to be the same size and take the heaviest. A ripe one should be firm but have a smooth depression at its stem end and a fragrant, musky scent at its blossom end. The melon should be free of dents and bruises, and have a dry rind. The skin should feel velvety and somewhat sticky; the outer color and shape uniform. If you shake the melon and hear seeds and juice moving around inside, it is overripe. The deeper the color of the flesh, the sweeter the melon will be.

If the melon is slightly unripe, keep it at room temperature for 1–2 days. Refrigerate ripe melons to use within a few days.

Cut the melon in half with a sharp knife, if you are going to divide it into sections. Cut off the top if you are going to use it as a container. Scoop the seeds in a strainer over a bowl so no juice is wasted. Wrap melon in plastic wrap before refrigerating it in the crisper section since its odor tends to permeate other foods. Melon seeds can be dried and toasted in the oven.

TO FREEZE

Be sure the melon is very ripe. Halve and seed, scraping away pulp and strings. Use a melon-baller to scoop balls from the flesh. Pack the balls in freezer bags or containers, sprinkle with 1 teaspoon strained lemon juice, and seal tightly. Partially thaw before using.

EQUIVALENTS

- 1 pound of honeydew yields about 1 cup of cut-up fruit

KIWIS

Kiwis are about the size of an extra-large chicken egg and have a sweet, juicy flavor. Their fuzzy brown exterior covers a jade green interior that is studded with edible black seeds. Look for firm round or oval-shaped kiwis that are free from bruises and skin breaks. Kiwis are ripe when the skin gives slightly if pressed. Underripe fruit continues to ripen off the vine. Put unripened kiwis in a plastic bag with an apple or two or a banana. The kiwis should be ready to eat in a few days. As soon as they are ripe, kiwis may be refrigerated for up to several days. Store away from other fruits to prevent overripening.

To prepare kiwis, trim their stem ends with a small paring knife and use a vegetable peeler to trim off the thin brown skin. If the skin proves hard to remove, dip the kiwis in boiling water for 30 seconds, then peel.

Kiwis can be quartered, sliced, chopped, or puréed.

TO FREEZE
Freezing is not recommended.

EQUIVALENTS
- 1 kiwi yields about ½ cup of cut-up fruit

LEMONS
When choosing lemons, buy those that have fine-textured, bright-yellow unblemished skin or those with a slight greenish tinge. Avoid light-weight fruits with coarse, green skin and mold or soft spots at the stem ends, which may indicate rot at the center of the fruit. The deeper yellow a lemon is, the less acidic it is likely to be. Choose lemons with thick skins and avoid those with soft, spongy patches.

Preserve the vitamin C content in lemons by storing them in the crisper drawers of your refrigerator or in open containers on the shelves. Don't put lemons in airtight plastic bags because mold develops quickly when air can't circulate freely.

Don't slice or peel lemons until you are ready to use them. After peeling, cutting, grating, or shredding the fruit, refrigerate until serving time. If you wash fruit after peeling, do it quickly. Vitamin C and other vitamins and minerals may be leached away during soaking.

To extract more of the juice, microwave lemons at 100% HIGH for 30 seconds before cutting and squeezing.

When you only need a few drops of lemon juice, use a thick needle or sharp skewer to puncture the skin at one end in several places. Squeeze the fruit until drops fall out. When you need to squeeze a whole lemon, first roll it over a hard surface with the palm of your hand to encourage the juice to flow more freely.

TO FREEZE

Although whole lemons don't freeze well, you can cut lemons into paper-thin slices, lay the slices on foil, and freeze them solid. Carefully remove the frozen slices to a plastic freezer bag and freeze until you need them. Frozen lemon slices can be added to drinks instead of ice cubes.

Lemon peel for use as zest can also be frozen and thawed with no loss of flavor or body.

EQUIVALENTS

- 1 medium lemon yields ¼–⅓ cup of juice
- 1 medium lemon yields 3–4 tablespoons of grated peel

LIMES
Choose limes with glossy fine-textured bright-green or yellow-tinged skins. Limes that have passed the yellowing stage and have dull brownish skins should be avoided.

Preserve the vitamin C content in limes by storing them in a cold or cool place. Store whole fruit in the crisper drawers of your refrigerator or in open containers on the shelves. Don't put limes in airtight plastic bags because mold develops quickly when air can't circulate freely.

Don't slice or peel limes until you are ready to use them. After peeling, cutting, grating, or shredding the fruit, refrigerate until serving time. If you wash fruit after peeling, do it quickly. Vitamin C is water soluble. Other vitamins and minerals may also be leached away during soaking.

To extract more of the juice, microwave limes at 100% HIGH for 30 seconds before cutting and squeezing.

TO FREEZE

Although whole limes don't freeze well, you can cut limes into paper-thin slices, lay the slices on foil, and freeze them solid. Carefully remove the frozen slices to a plastic freezer bag and freeze until you need them.

Lime peel for use as zest can also be frozen and thawed with no loss of flavor or body.

EQUIVALENTS

- 1 medium lime yields ¼–⅓ cup of juice
- 1 medium lime yields 3–4 tablespoons of grated peel

MANGOES

Mangoes are oval shaped and about the size of an apple. They have a greenish-yellow skin that blushes red all over when ripe. Inside, the orangy-yellow fruit surrounds a large, slender white seed. Mangoes can be substituted for peaches, papayas, and nectarines in recipes.

Shop for mangoes with reddish-yellow skin that seems fairly firm when gentle pressure is applied. Some mangoes turn yellow all over when they are ripe. They smell fragrant when ready to eat. Avoid very soft or bruised mangoes and green mangoes. A few brown spots on the skin are normal indicators of ripeness.

Store still-firm mangoes at room temperature. When it is soft to the touch, it can be stored in the refrigerator for up to 1 week. Don't cut mangoes until ready to serve them.

Peel mangoes with a sharp knife, then slice down the mango on one side of the seed as close to it as possible. Repeat with the other side. Trim off any remaining flesh from around the seed. Zip the skin off as you would for a banana.

TO FREEZE
Freezing is not recommended.

EQUIVALENTS
- 1 medium mango yields about ¾–1 cup of sliced fruit

NECTARINES

A nectarine is a smooth, plum-skinned variety of a peach. Nectarines have blushing golden-red, smooth skin and are round in shape. Their taste is somewhat sharper and richer than that of peaches. Nectarines are at their peak between mid-May and late September.

Nectarines come in both freestone, deep-red varieties with fruit that does not adhere to the pit, and semi-freestone, paler varieties with fruit that clings to the pit. Nectarines should be uniform in shape, with a creamy yellow skin and no green at the stem end. The blush on the skin does not indicate ripeness. Choose nectarines that yield to gentle pressure.

To ripen nectarines, place them in a brown paper bag or in a bowl with apples or other fruit. Check them daily. When they are ripe, refrigerate and use within a few days. To speed up peeling nectarines, bring a pot of water to a boil and remove from heat. Immerse nectarines in water for about 3 minutes, then peel. The easiest way to cut a nectarine is to run a small sharp knife down from the top to the bottom, cutting right through to the stone. Turn the nectarine slightly in your hand and make another cut so that the wedge falls out onto a plate. Continue in this manner all around the nectarine. Once the fruit has been cut, dip pieces in a mixture of lemon juice and water to prevent discoloration.

You can substitute nectarines for peaches, plums, or apricots in recipes.

TO FREEZE

Make a syrup by adding 3 cups sugar to 4 cups boiling water. Stir until dissolved. Chill. When the syrup is chilled, prepare an ascorbic-citric acid solution of 2 tablespoons of acid to 1 gallon of water. Peel the nectarines and slice them into the acid solution. Drain, rinse, and dry the slices. Pack them in freezer containers and cover with chilled sugar syrup, leaving ½ inch of head space. Seal tightly.

EQUIVALENTS

- 3 medium nectarines weigh about 1 pound
- 1 pound of nectarines yields 2 cups of sliced fruit and 1¾ cups of diced fruit

ORANGES

Navels and Valencias are the most familiar varieties of orange in the U.S., with most of them grown in Florida or California. The navel—named for the dimple at the bottom tip of the fruit—is also recognized by its distinctive pebbled skin. It is of medium size, sweet, seedless, easy to peel, and nicely sectioned. The Valencia is sweet, round in shape, and medium to large in size. Its skin is thinner and smooth or only slightly pebbled. The fruit is nearly seedless and very juicy.

Look for firm, heavy fruit with smooth skin. Very rough skin texture indicates unusually thick skin and scanty flesh. Dull dry skin and spongy texture indicate aging and a reduced eating quality. Avoid oranges with cuts or skin punctures, or soft, discolored, and weakened areas of skin around the stem end or bottom button. A ripe orange may not necessarily have orange skin. Oranges from areas where nights are warm tend to retain some green in the skin.

Store whole oranges in the crisper drawers of your refrigerator or in open containers on the shelves. Don't put them in airtight plastic bags because mold develops quickly when air can't circulate freely.

Don't slice or peel oranges until you are ready to use them. After peeling, cutting, grating, or shredding, refrigerate them until serving time. If you wash fruit after peeling, do it quickly. Vitamin C and other vitamins and minerals may be leached away during prolonged washing.

To extract more of the juice, microwave oranges at 100% HIGH for 30 seconds before cutting and squeezing. To remove the white membrane that clings to oranges, cover the unpeeled orange with boiling water and let stand for 5 minutes before peeling.

TO FREEZE

Although whole oranges don't freeze well, you can cut oranges into paper-thin slices, lay the slices on foil, and freeze them solid. Carefully remove the frozen slices to a plastic freezer bag and freeze until you need them.

Orange peel for use as zest can also be frozen and thawed with no loss of flavor or body.

EQUIVALENTS

- 1 medium orange yields 10–11 sections
- 1 medium orange yields about 5 teaspoons of grated peel
- 1 medium orange yields about 2/3 cup of combined pulp and juice
- 1 medium orange yields about 1/2 cup of bite-sized pieces and contains 1/3–1/2 cup of juice

PAPAYA

Papayas, shaped like elongated pears, are about 5–6 inches long, with one bulbous end that holds a cavity with round black seeds and juicy orange fruit. Papayas are available almost year round and have the taste of a rich, sweet melon, with a hint of peach flavor.

Select papayas that are at least half yellow and yield to gentle pressure. Look for bruise-free fruit with smooth, unwrinkled skin. Avoid very soft or bruised ones with a fermented aroma. Green papayas will ripen at home at room temperature, away from sunlight, in 3–4 days. Papayas are ripe when they yield to pressure when squeezed gently between the palms of the hands. Refrigerate ripe fruit and use within a week. If a ripening papaya should develop a soft spot, use it immediately.

As you cut a papaya in half, the yellowish-pink flesh parts easily and gray-black seeds spill out. Although the seeds are not often eaten, they are not harmful and can be used in dressings and as a garnish. You can either spoon the fruit from the papaya or peel the skin and slice the fruit thinly to serve. Most melon, peach, or nectarine recipes can be adapted to use ripe papaya instead.

TO FREEZE
Freezing is not recommended.

EQUIVALENTS
- 1 medium papaya weighs about 1 pound
- 1 medium papaya yields ¾ cup of cut-up fruit

PEAS (Garden, Snow Peas, and Sugar Snap Peas) Look for a bright color in fresh peas and crisp flesh with pods that snap, not bend. Old peas look spotted and limp.

Refrigerate unwashed peas in a plastic bag for 4 or 5 days.

To shell garden peas, snap off the top of the pod and pull the string down the side, pushing open the side seam in the process. The peas will pop out. Although the pods of sugar snap peas can be eaten, you still need to string both sides by snapping off the tip and pulling downward on the strings. Most snow peas need only their stem tips removed.

TO FREEZE GARDEN AND SNOW PEAS
Blanch shelled peas in boiling water for 2 minutes. Drain and immerse in ice water for 2 minutes. Drain. Pack loosely in freezer bags, making sure air is removed. Freeze.

TO FREEZE SUGAR SNAP PEAS
Blanch in boiling water for 2 minutes. Drain and immerse in ice water for 5 minutes. Drain. Place in a single layer on trays and freeze. Carefully transfer to freezer bags. Frozen sugar snap peas are best used in cooked dishes, as they will lose their crispness.

EQUIVALENTS

- 1 pound of unshelled garden peas yields 1 cup shelled
- 1 pound of snow peas yields 3 servings
- 1 pound of sugar snap peas yields 4–5 cups peas

PEARS

Pears are usually sold when firm and must be ripened at home. Avoid pears with soft spots near the stem or bottom ends and those with heavy bruises. If pears are very firm, ripen them at room temperature or place in a brown paper bag with a ripe apple until the pears are soft to the touch. Ripe pears yield slightly to finger pressure at the stem end. Store ripened pears in the refrigerator and use in a few days. Pears can be eaten out of hand or peeled, cored, and cut into slices or wedges. To keep cut pears from discoloring, as soon as they are peeled drop them into a mixture of water and lime, orange, or grapefruit juice.

TO FREEZE

Freezing is not recommended.

EQUIVALENTS

- 3 medium pears weigh about 1 pound
- 3 medium pears yield 2½ cups of diced pears
- 3 medium pears yield 1¾ cups of pear purée

BELL PEPPERS

(Green and Red) Buy plump, brilliantly colored well-shaped peppers with healthy-looking stems. Avoid those with soft spots, cracks, or soft stems. Peppers should look crisp and be firm. Refrigerate peppers up to several days in the crisper drawer. Red and yellow bell peppers will not keep as long as green peppers because of their high sugar content.

When preparing bell peppers, halve them from the stem to the base. Remove seedy core, stems, and white pith along ribs.

TO FREEZE

Remove cores, seeds, and stems, but do not blanch. Freeze in airtight freezer containers up to 6 months. Frozen peppers will lose their crispness.

- 3 large bell peppers weigh 1 pound
- 1 pound of peppers yields about 3–4 cups of sliced or chopped peppers

PINEAPPLES
When a pineapple is ripe, the inner leaves at the crown come out easily; the skin is orange or yellow with no traces of green; the base of the fruit should smell sweet; and the fruit should be heavy with juice. Under the tough heavy skin, the ripe fruit of a pineapple will yield slightly to finger pressure.

To peel a pineapple, first pull out the tuft of leaves at the top. With a serrated knife, take off a thin slice from the top and bottom of the pineapple. Holding it firmly on its base, cut the skin as far as the middle in thick, downward slices. Turn the pineapple upside down and cut off the rest of the skin in the same way. Halve, quarter, or slice the pineapple and core it. The hard, woody core running through the center of the pineapple must be cut out of halved or quartered fruit or stamped out of individual slices with a small plain round cutter.

TO FREEZE
Peel, core, and cut the pineapple into chunks. Make a syrup by adding 3 cups sugar to 4 cups boiling water. Stir until dissolved. Chill. When the syrup is chilled, prepare an ascorbic-citric acid solution of 2 tablespoons of acid to 1 gallon of water. Place the pineapple chunks in the acid solution. Drain, rinse, and dry the chunks. Pack them in freezer containers and cover with chilled sugar syrup, leaving ½ inch head space. Seal tightly.

EQUIVALENTS
- A medium (3-pound) pineapple yields 3 cups of cubed fruit

PUMPKIN
Shop for eating or sugar pumpkins. They are usually smaller in size than the decorative ones and weigh less than 7 pounds. They should be bright orange in color and still have their stems attached to prevent spoilage.

When storing a pumpkin, keep it for 1–2 months in a dry spot with temperatures in the 50–55 degree range. Pumpkin chunks keep in the refrigerator in a perforated plastic bag for a week.

If you're using the whole pumpkin, wash it well, cut a lid off the top, and scoop out the seeds and stringy pulp. If you want only the flesh, cut off the top and cut across the bottom so the pumpkin stands flat on the counter. Then cut the skin away, working your way around the pumpkin. Then simply halve the peeled pumpkin, scrape out the seeds, and proceed to use the pulp. Save the seeds to bake for a delicious snack.

TO FREEZE
Pumpkin can be frozen in freezer containers after it has been cooked and puréed.

EQUIVALENTS
- A 4-pound pumpkin yields 2 pounds raw flesh
- 1 pound of raw peeled pumpkin yields 4 cups of pumpkin chunks

RASPBERRIES See Berries.

SPINACH Buy fresh-looking dark green spinach with crisp leaves and thin stalks. If you must purchase spinach in a plastic bag, remove it from the bag and discard any damaged leaves. Refrigerate unwashed spinach uncovered or wrapped in a towel. The moisture in plastic bags can cause spinach to spoil quickly.

Careful cleaning is essential since spinach is very gritty. Dump unwashed spinach into a sink filled with warm water. Drain out water and clean sink. Rinse leaves separately under cold running water until spinach is completely free of grit. To stem spinach, fold the leaf in half lengthwise, and zip off the stem.

TO FREEZE
Clean and stem spinach. Blanch for 2 minutes in boiling water. Drain. Cool and pack in freezer containers.

EQUIVALENTS
- 2 pounds of fresh spinach yields 2 cups cooked spinach

STRAWBERRIES See Berries.

SWEET POTATOES

Although sweet potatoes are thought of as tubers, they are the roots of trailing vines belonging to the Morning Glory family. Look for unblemished, firm sweet potatoes with no soft spots or bruises. Types labeled yams or Louisiana yams are sweet, moist-fleshed varieties. Store raw sweet potatoes in a humid, well-ventilated spot with temperatures between 55 and 58 degrees. Wash well before cooking. Always drop peeled sweet potatoes in water immediately after peeling to prevent discoloration.

TO FREEZE

Freeze cooked mashed sweet potatoes in freezer containers.

EQUIVALENTS

- 1 pound (3 sweet potatoes) yields 1 cup of purée

TANGERINES

The fruit that we know as the tangerine is a mandarin variety called the Dancy. The Dancy and the Clementine are the most popular mandarins in America. They are medium in size, have a thin rind, orange-red flesh, and a medium number of seeds. Both feature easy peeling and are neatly sectioned, rich in flavor, and very juicy. Look for firm, deep-orange fruits. Avoid greenish fruits with cut or punctured skins or soft spots. Tangelos are a hybrid (a tangerine-grapefruit cross) with the same degree of sweetness but a slightly different flavor.

Store whole tangerines in the crisper drawer of your refrigerator or in open containers on the shelves. Don't put them in airtight plastic bags because mold develops quickly when air can't circulate freely.

Don't slice or peel tangerines until you are ready to use them. After peeling, cutting, grating, or shredding the fruit, refrigerate until serving time. If you wash fruit after peeling, do it quickly. Vitamin C, which is water soluble, and other vitamins and minerals may be leached away during soaking.

TO FREEZE

Although whole tangerines don't freeze well, you can cut them into paper-thin slices, lay the slices on foil, and freeze them solid. Carefully remove the slices to a plastic freezer bag and freeze until you need them.

- 1 medium tangerine yields ½ cup of sections

TOMATOES

The tomato is actually a fruit. It is classified as a berry because it is pulpy and contains numerous seeds. Look for tomatoes with good color and firm flesh. They should be well formed and free of bruises. Ripe tomatoes feel tender and are heavy in relation to their size. They have a full, red color. When fresh tomatoes are out of season, use canned tomatoes.

Ripe tomatoes will keep 2 or 3 days at room temperature. Do not refrigerate tomatoes unless necessary. Refrigerate only extra-ripe tomatoes you want to prevent from ripening further. Refrigerate them uncut and uncovered. Bring them back to room temperature before using.

Ripen green tomatoes by placing them in a closed brown paper bag with a ripe apple for several days.

Peel tomatoes by placing them in a strainer and pouring boiling water over them for 5 seconds. The peel will pull off easily. Tomatoes can also be immersed in boiling water for 45 seconds, then plunged into ice water for several seconds to stop their cooking before peeling.

TO FREEZE

Place whole or peeled tomatoes in plastic freezer bags and freeze. Use for cooking during the winter.

EQUIVALENTS

- 3 medium tomatoes weigh approximately 1 pound
- 3 medium tomatoes yield 1½ cups tomato pulp

TURNIPS

Turnips should be firm without any wrinkles, which indicate that the vegetable has lost moisture and will be spongy. Look for smaller turnips.

Turnips deteriorate quickly. Don't store them for more than a week in the refrigerator. Separate roots and greens before refrigerating.

TO FREEZE

Cooked, mashed, or puréed turnips can be frozen in freezer containers.

- 1 pound of trimmed turnips yields 4 cups of chopped turnips

WATERMELON

When a watermelon is ripe and ready it should sound dull, flat, and heavy. This will mean the juice, and flavor, will be at their peak. Also check the underside of the watermelon, the one that was resting on the ground during the growing period. A pale yellow color indicates a ripe, flavorful melon, while a white or greenish color can indicate that the melon was picked too soon. A shriveled stem also is a sign of ripeness. When buying cut watermelon, look for moist, brightly colored flesh.

Store whole watermelon at room temperature. Cut melon should be wrapped and refrigerated.

TO FREEZE

Be sure the watermelon is very ripe. Use a melon-baller to scoop balls from the melon flesh. Seed the melon balls. Pack the balls in freezer bags or containers, sprinkle with 1 teaspoon strained lemon juice, and seal tightly. Partially thaw before using.

EQUIVALENTS

- 1 pound of watermelon yields 1 cup of cut-up fruit

WINTER SQUASH (Acorn, Butternut, Hubbard)

Buy winter squash that is hard, heavy, and clean. Avoid squash that have cracks, soft spots, or decayed spots.

Store squash in a dry spot with low humidity with temperatures between 50 and 55 degrees.

TO FREEZE

Since winter squash keeps well, there is not much need to freeze it. However, you can freeze cooked winter squash in freezer containers.

EQUIVALENTS

- 1 pound of trimmed winter squash yields 2 cups of cooked squash

Basic
Cooking Techniques
for
Fruits and Vegetables

Any kind of cooking destroys the nutrients in fruits and vegetables. The amount of nutrient loss will depend on the freshness of the food when you bought it; how it was handled and stored; how long you cook it and at what temperature; and how much surface area is exposed to water and to air. To minimize nutrient loss:

- Cook foods as quickly as possible. Microwaving, steaming, and stir-frying are the quickest techniques. Cover pots to reduce cooking time.
- Don't buy precut produce and don't soak fruits or vegetables. Cook them whole and unpeeled if possible.
- Eat as many raw fruits and vegetables as possible.
- Use the nutrient-rich water left over from cooking fruits and vegetables to make soup.
- Shop frequently for fresh produce. Consider using frozen fruits and vegetables if this is not possible.

Grilling

Fruits and vegetables can be placed directly on the grill; arranged in an oiled hinged grilling basket; placed on an oiled piece of heavy-metal mesh; or threaded on skewers. They can also be wrapped in aluminum foil and steamed in their own juices, which is a good solution for grilling harder, longer-cooking vegetables.

Cooking times for grilling fruits and vegetables are hard to predict since the age, size, and shape of the vegetables and heat of the fire may vary greatly. Generally fruits and vegetables should be cooked over medium heat about 4–6 inches from the heat source. Be sure to monitor the grilling process carefully since all times suggested are approximate.

If you wish, you can baste vegetables with mild, light-flavored olive oil or a marinade of ½ cup mild, light-flavored olive oil or melted diet or reduced-calorie margarine, 2 tablespoons lemon juice, ½ teaspoon dried rosemary leaves, ½ teaspoon dried thyme leaves, 1 teaspoon Dijon mustard, and 1 clove garlic, minced.

Fruits can be basted with a mild, light-flavored olive oil or a marinade of ½ cup mild, light-flavored olive oil, melted diet or reduced-calorie margarine, 2 teaspoons brown sugar, and 1 teaspoon ground cinnamon or ground ginger.

APPLES

Remove the stems and wrap apples in squares of heavy-duty aluminum foil. Set apples on glowing coals for 10 minutes. After 10 minutes, turn apples over and cook for 10 minutes. Serve hot with maple syrup and teaspoons for scooping out the pulp.

To cook on skewers, thread apple quarters, rolled in melted diet or reduced-calorie margarine, and grill until lightly browned. Serve sprinkled with cinnamon.

APRICOTS

Halve and pit apricots. Brush with melted butter, oil, or marinade. Thread on skewers. Grill for 4–6 minutes or until tender.

ASPARAGUS

Trim tough ends from spears. Brush with olive oil and place diagonally across an oiled grill 4–6 inches from coals. Grill, turning frequently, until lightly browned and tender, about 5 minutes. The point of a knife should easily pierce stem end.

BANANAS

To cook on skewers, thread chunks, rolled in melted diet or reduced-calorie margarine, and grill until lightly browned. Roll in chopped walnuts.

BELL PEPPERS

Cut in half lengthwise, and seed. Grill until lightly charred on both sides.

To grill in foil, cut into chunks, dot with margarine or olive oil, and wrap up.

To cook on skewers, thread pepper chunks, baste with olive oil, and grill until cooked on all sides.

To grill whole peppers, place them on the grill, turning often, until skin is black all over. This should take about 10 minutes. Place grilled peppers in a plastic bag and set aside for 10 minutes, or until cool enough to handle. Remove peppers from bag and peel off skin under cold running water. Remove seeds and stems. Slice peppers into ½-inch-wide strips. Serve grilled peppers with a squeeze of lemon juice or a grating of Parmesan.

BROCCOLI

Brush broccoli florets with olive oil. Grill for 6–8 minutes, turning frequently until florets are touched with charred spots.

BRUSSELS SPROUTS

Blanch and drain Brussels sprouts. Toss with olive oil. Thread onto skewers. Place skewers on an oiled grill 4–6 inches from the coals. Turn several times until browned, about 5 minutes.

CANTALOUPES

Cut melon into ½-inch-thick wedges. Skewer wedges in groups of 4. Push 3 skewers through each group, pushing one skewer through the middle, a second 1 inch to the right, and a third 1 inch to the left. Brush with melted margarine, oil, or marinade. Grill 4–6 inches from heat until melon is hot and streaked with brown.

CARROTS

Place small whole carrots or carrot slices or sticks in foil and dot with margarine or olive oil. Grill for approximately 45 minutes. If you blanch carrots before grilling, reduce cooking time to 20 minutes. When done, the outside of the carrots should be brown and the insides should be tender when pierced with a fork. Carrots can be basted during the last 5 minutes of grilling with glaze or barbecue sauce.

CORN

To grill corn in husks, pull leaves down, remove silk, and pull leaves back up around ears. Soak ears in water for 10 minutes. Grill, turning occasionally.

To grill corn in foil, remove husks and silk and brush with melted reduced-calorie margarine or olive oil. Sprinkle with herbs and minced garlic. Wrap in foil and roast on grill for 20 minutes, turning every 5 minutes. Sprinkle with grated Parmesan cheese before serving. You can also wrap cut corn kernels, dotted with butter or olive oil, in foil, and grill until hot.

EGGPLANT

Slice in half lengthwise. Don't peel. Brush with olive oil and place, cut side down, on the grill. Cook until golden brown. Turn over. Baste with olive oil and cook until just tender. Very small eggplants can be cooked whole. Larger eggplant can also be sliced for grilling. If eggplant is more than 3 inches in diameter, you can cut the slices in half. To grill slices, drizzle with olive oil and grill for 10–15 minutes until golden brown outside and tender inside when pierced with the tip of a knife.

To cook in foil, cut into chunks, dot with reduced-calorie margarine or olive oil and herbs, and seal foil. Grill, checking for doneness after 20 minutes. Serve grilled eggplant with grated pepper and lemon juice or tomato sauce and chopped black olives.

GREEN BEANS

Brush raw green beans with olive oil. Grill, rolling them with tongs to expose all sides to the heat, for 5–10 minutes or until touched with charred spots.

GRAPEFRUIT

Cut grapefruit into ¼-inch-thick rounds. Brush rounds with olive oil and cook on oiled grill, turning once, until lightly browned inside, about 3–4 minutes.

HONEYDEW

Cut melon into ½-inch-thick wedges. Skewer wedges in groups of 4. Push 3 skewers through each group, pushing one skewer through the middle, a second 1 inch to the right, and a third 1 inch to the left. Brush with melted margarine, oil, or marinade. Grill 4–6 inches from heat until melon is hot and streaked with brown,

MUSHROOMS

Toss very large fresh mushrooms in olive oil. Place mushroom caps, stem down, on oiled grill 4–6 inches from the coals. Grill until edges are browned, about 3–5 minutes. Turn and grill until caps of mushrooms are golden brown.

NECTARINES

To cook on skewers, thread nectarine slices, which have been brushed with oil, melted butter, or marinade. Grill until lightly browned. Sprinkle with cinnamon or minced red onion and fresh basil.

RED ONION
SPANISH ONION

Remove skin, and cut in half lengthwise. Brush with olive oil and place on grill, cut side down. When charred, turn and baste with more oil. Grill until charred. Total cooking time will be about 15 minutes. Scrape char before serving.

To cook in foil, dot sliced onions with reduced-calorie margarine or olive oil, and wrap.

To cook on skewers, thread onion chunks and baste with olive oil. Grill, turning, until charred. Serve grilled onions sprinkled with thyme, red wine vinegar, or cayenne pepper.

ORANGES

Cut large unpeeled oranges into ¾-inch-thick slices or cut small oranges in half. Brush with olive oil and grill 4–6 inches from heat for 5–10 minutes or until streaked with brown.

PAPAYAS

Peel papayas. Cut into quarters. Remove seeds. Brush with melted margarine or olive oil. Grill, turning until hot, for about 5–8 minutes or until streaked with brown.

PEARS

Halve and core unpeeled pears. Brush cut surfaces with oil and vinegar. Grill, turning and basting with oil and vinegar, until tender, about 3–5 minutes.

PINEAPPLE

Combine ¼ cup lemon juice, 2 tablespoons honey, and ¼ teaspoon cayenne pepper in a saucepan and heat until honey has melted. Brush pineapple slices with olive oil. Grill ½-inch-thick slices for 3 minutes. Turn and grill for 3 minutes more. Spoon lemon-honey sauce over them and serve.

POTATOES
SWEET POTATOES

Wrap large potatoes in foil and bury in coals. Allow 45–60 minutes. Dot sliced potatoes or small whole new potatoes with margarine or olive oil. Wrap in foil and bury in coals. Allow approximately 45 minutes.

You can also grill parboiled chunks or slices of potato or sweet potato brushed with olive oil on skewers.

STRAWBERRIES

Dip large berries in orange juice and place on oiled grill 6 inches from heat, turning carefully, for about 5 minutes. Berries should be hot and slightly browned.

ZUCCHINI and YELLOW SQUASH

Cut squash in half lengthwise. Brush with olive oil. Place, cut sides down, on grill and cook until lightly browned. Turn, brush, and cook until tender.

To cook in foil, dot chunks of squash with reduced-calorie margarine or oil and wrap. Check after 20 minutes.

To cook on skewers, thread whole small squash and brush with olive oil. Grill, turning, until tender. Serve with diced tomatoes, part-skim mozzarella, olive oil, and chopped fresh parsley.

WINTER SQUASH

Wrap chunks of winter squash, dotted with margarine or olive oil, in foil and cook for 45 minutes.

TOMATOES

Place halved large tomatoes on the grill, cut sides down, brush with oil, and grill until seared. Turn, brush, and grill until tender.

To cook in foil, dot cherry tomatoes with margarine or olive oil and wrap. Heat through.

To cook on skewers, thread plum tomatoes on skewers and brush with margarine or olive oil. Grill, turning, until tender.

MIXED GRILLED VEGETABLE AND/OR FRUIT COMBINATIONS

Grilling a mixture of different vegetables and/or fruit on skewers or in foil packets does not always produce satisfactory results since they may not cook at the same rate. Another alternative is to cook an assortment of vegetables on separate skewers or in separate foil packets and combine them for serving.

To grill vegetables and/or fruit on skewers:
1. Use flat-edged skewers rather than round ones.
2. Cut vegetables and/or fruit into 1-inch chunks.
3. Combine vegetables and/or fruit of consistent cooking times.
4. Arrange vegetables and/or fruit on skewers using firmer foods such as onions and peppers to support more fragile ones like tomatoes and mushrooms.

5. Marinate skewered vegetables and/or fruit briefly in olive oil or marinade. Grill 4–6 inches from hot coals until all vegetables and/or fruits are soft but not charred.

To grill vegetables and/or fruit in packets:
Prepare a medium fire. Grill packets 4–6 inches from the coals.

To grill 4–6 servings in one package:
Fold a 30-inch long sheet of heavy-duty aluminum foil in half to create a double thickness. Place vegetables and/or fruit to be grilled in the center of the packet. Sprinkle with olive oil, black pepper, and herbs if desired. Fold edges of foil over to seal securely. To serve, slit packet in the center.

To grill in individual serving-size packets:
Cut 1 heavy-duty aluminum foil sheet 10 inches long for each serving. Divide vegetables and/or fruit among the packets. Sprinkle with olive oil, black pepper, and herbs if desired. Fold edges of foil over to seal securely. Unwrap to serve.

Guide to timing foil-wrapped vegetables and/or fruit:
Single-serving tomato packets: 20 minutes
Single serving eggplant packets: 20 minutes
Foil-wrapped corn: 15–20 minutes
Six servings of mixed tomatoes, squash, and onion in one packet: 30 minutes
Single-wrapped potatoes: 45–60 minutes
Single-wrapped sweet potatoes: 45–60 minutes
Single-serving carrot packets: 30 minutes
Six servings of apple slices in one packet: 20 minutes

POSSIBLE SERVING COMBINATIONS FOR GRILLED VEGETABLES AND/OR FRUIT

Since the vegetables and/or fruit in these combinations take varying amounts of time to grill, be sure to grill them separately and then combine them at serving time.
- Red and green bell peppers; mushrooms; sweet onions; zucchini; cherry tomatoes; eggplant
- Summer squash; zucchini; cherry tomatoes; mushrooms
- Corn; tomatoes; carrots; bell peppers; broccoli
- Asparagus; yellow squash; carrots; corn; mushrooms

- Brussels sprouts; cherry tomatoes; yellow bell peppers; celery; sweet potatoes
- Apples; pears; bananas; oranges
- Pineapple; nectarines; strawberry; grapefruit
- Winter squash; bananas; pineapple; carrots; green beans
- Zucchini; nectarines; red bell pepper; red onion
- Yellow bell peppers; apples; Brussels sprouts; potatoes
- Pears; sweet potatoes; apples; celery; broccoli
- Pineapple; red bell pepper; zucchini; tomatoes; green beans

You can store grilled vegetables and/or fruit in the refrigerator in containers with lids or large zipper-locked bags. Add ½ cup olive oil and 1 clove garlic, crushed, to each container or bag of grilled vegetables.

Grilled vegetables can be used in omelets, salads, and a variety of main dishes.

Steaming

To steam vegetables and/or fruit bring ¾–1 inch of water to a boil in a steamer. Place vegetables or fruit in steamer basket or colander and cover steamer. Steam according to times given below.

Seasoning suggestions follow each food. You can also season steamed vegetables and/fruit with your choice of:

Sesame seeds	Onion powder	Dried thyme leaves
Nutmeg	Dried tarragon leaves	Fresh chopped
Toasted bread	Dried marjoram	parsley
crumbs	leaves	Chives
Chopped egg white	Dried dillweed	Ground cinnamon
Black pepper	Ground cloves	Ground allspice
Ground ginger	Caraway seeds	Olives
Curry powder	Celery seeds	Toasted chopped
Dried basil leaves	Cumin	nuts
Dried oregano leaves	Chili powder	Grated cheese
Garlic powder	Paprika	

Use a small quantity of mild, light-flavored olive oil on your steamed vegetables instead of high-fat butter or margarine.

APPLES (peeled and cored)   10–12 minutes
- Sprinkle with ground cinnamon and grated orange peel.

ASPARAGUS (medium stalks, whole)   4–8 minutes
- Serve hot with fresh lemon or lime juice.
- Sprinkle with almonds or pine nuts.

BROCCOLI FLORETS (stems ⅜-inch thick)   6–12 minutes
- Serve hot with fresh lemon or lime juice.
- Sprinkle with almonds or minced garlic and chopped cherry tomatoes.

BRUSSELS SPROUTS (medium, whole)   10–15 minutes
- Serve hot with fresh lemon or lime juice.
- Sprinkle with black pepper or grated Parmesan cheese.

CABBAGE (green, 1 pound, cut into wedges)   8–10 minutes
- Serve sprinkled with dried dillweed or caraway seeds.
- Top with tomato sauce or reduced-calorie sour cream and cider vinegar.

CARROTS (whole)   10 minutes
CARROTS (thinly sliced)   4–8 minutes
- Serve with fresh lemon juice, minced scallions, and dried basil, thyme, or mint.
- Sprinkle with pecans or almonds.
- Sprinkle with black pepper and grated Parmesan cheese.
- Toss with honey, lemon juice, and grated fresh gingerroot.

CAULIFLOWER (florets)   5–9 minutes
- Sprinkle with lemon juice and chopped fresh parsley.
- Sprinkle with almonds.

CORN (shucked, whole)   5–7 minutes
- Spread with reduced-calorie margarine or mild, light-flavored olive oil. Sprinkle with dried basil leaves, oregano leaves, dried dill leaves, snipped chives, or ground cumin.

EGGPLANT (1 pound, cut in half lengthwise)   13 minutes
EGGPLANT CHUNKS   5–8 minutes
- Sprinkle with grated Parmesan cheese and sautéed chopped onion and minced garlic.
- Top with chopped fresh tomatoes and part-skim mozzarella cheese.
- Sprinkle with curry powder.

GREEN BEANS (whole fresh or frozen, cut in 5-inch lengths) 4–12 minutes
- Serve with fresh lemon or lime juice.
- Sprinkle with walnuts.

GREEN PEAS   (shelled)   5–7 minutes
- Serve with dried mint leaves and grated orange peel.
- Sprinkle with almonds, chopped fresh parsley, or grated Parmesan cheese.
- Sprinkle with cumin.

NECTARINES   (peeled and pitted)   10–12 minutes
- Sprinkle with ground cinnamon and grated lemon peel.

NEW POTATOES   (2 inches in diameter)   15–18 minutes
- Sprinkle with lemon juice.
- Top with low-calorie cottage cheese and chives.

PEARS   (peeled and cored)   10–12 minutes
- Sprinkle with ground cloves or ground ginger.

PEPPERS   (bell, red, or green cut, in ½-inch strips)   4–5 minutes
- Top with chopped tomatoes.

PUMPKIN   (cut in 1-inch chunks)   15–20 minutes
- Sprinkle with fresh lemon or lime juice or olive oil.
- Sprinkle with ground ginger or nutmeg.
- Sprinkle with sesame seeds, sunflower seeds, or pumpkin seeds.

SNOW PEAS   4–5 minutes
- Sprinkle with sesame oil and sesame seeds.
- Top with minced water chestnuts and bamboo shoots.

SWEET POTATOES   (cut in 1-inch chunks)   12–15 minutes

WHOLE SWEET POTATOES   (6 ounces)   35 minutes
- Sprinkle with lemon or lime juice.
- Top with chopped fresh parsley or chives.
- Sprinkle with chopped peanuts or pecans.

SPINACH   (whole or halved leaves)   4–6 minutes
- Sprinkle with olive oil and minced garlic.
- Sprinkle with fresh lemon juice.
- Sprinkle with sesame oil, soy sauce, and toasted sesame seeds.

SUMMER SQUASH   (zucchini, yellow crookneck, whole, 7 inches long)
10–15 minutes
- Serve cut in chunks with fresh lemon juice and dried basil leaves or oregano leaves.
- Top with grated Parmesan cheese.

TURNIPS   (white, medium, 3 ounces each)   20–25 minutes
- Sprinkle with black pepper and dried thyme leaves.

WINTER SQUASH   (cut in 1½-inch chunks)   15–20 minutes
- Sprinkle with ground ginger or nutmeg.
- Sprinkle with fresh lemon juice.

Stir-Frying

Because of the high heat and short cooking time involved in stir-frying, vegetables maintain their bright color, crisp texture, and flavor when cooked in this manner. To stir-fry, place a wok or heavy skillet over high heat. Add 1 tablespoon of either mild, light-flavored olive oil or canola oil and 5 cups of vegetables. Add water or low-salt chicken broth. Cover and complete cooking. Follow directions below for individual vegetables.

ASPARAGUS: Cut asparagus into ½-inch diagonal slices. When wok is hot, add 1 tablespoon oil and 5 cups of asparagus slices and stir-fry for 1 minute. Add 2 tablespoons of liquid. Cover. Cook for 2 minutes.

GREEN BEANS: Cut beans into 1-inch lengths. When wok is hot, add 1 tablespoon oil and 5 cups of cut beans and stir-fry for 1 minute. Add 4 tablespoons of liquid. Cover. Cook for 4–7 minutes.

BROCCOLI: Cut broccoli stalks and florets into ¼-inch pieces. When wok is hot, add 1 tablespoon oil and 5 cups of broccoli and stir-fry for 1 minute. Add 3 tablespoons of liquid. Cover. Cook for 3 minutes.

CABBAGE: Shred cabbage. When wok is hot, add 1 tablespoon oil and 5 cups of cabbage and stir-fry for 1 minute. Add 2 tablespoons of liquid. Cover. Cook for 3–5 minutes.

CARROTS: Cut carrots into ¼-inch-thick slices. When wok is hot, add 1 tablespoon oil and 5 cups of carrots. Stir-fry for 1 minute. Add 2 tablespoons of liquid. Cover. Cook for 3–5 minutes.

CAULIFLOWER: Cut florets into ¼-inch slices. When wok is hot, add 1 tablespoon oil and 5 cups of cauliflower. Stir-fry for 1 minute. Add 3–4 tablespoons of liquid. Cover. Cook for 4–5 minutes.

PEPPERS: Cut bell peppers into 1-inch squares. When wok is hot, add 1 tablespoon oil and 5 cups of peppers. Stir-fry for 1 minute. Add 2–3 tablespoons of liquid. Cover. Cook for 3–5 minutes.

SPINACH: Chop spinach. When wok is hot, add 1 tablespoon oil and 5 cups of spinach. Stir-fry for 30 seconds. Cover. Cook for 3–5 minutes.

TURNIPS: Cut peeled turnips into ¼-inch-thick slices. When wok is hot, add 1 tablespoon oil and 5 cups of turnips. Stir-fry for 1 minute. Add 4–5 tablespoons of liquid. Cover. Cook for 4–5 minutes.

POSSIBLE COMBINATIONS FOR STEAMED VEGETABLES AND/OR FRUIT

Since the foods in these combinations take varying amounts of time to steam, be sure to steam them separately and then combine them at serving time.

- Asparagus; corn; eggplant; green beans with toasted bread crumbs sautéed in olive oil
- Broccoli; carrots; cauliflower; red bell peppers with dried oregano leaves
- Brussels sprouts; new potatoes; summer squash with chopped fresh parsley
- Cabbage; carrots; corn; new potatoes with pepper and caraway seeds
- Green bell pepper; onion; asparagus and grated reduced-calorie cheddar cheese
- Eggplant; carrots; mushrooms and dried basil leaves
- Carrots; green beans; zucchini; onions; new potatoes and ground ginger
- Pumpkin; green beans; corn and ground cumin
- Spinach; red bell pepper; yellow crookneck squash and paprika
- Cauliflower; peas and ground ginger
- Eggplant; zucchini; green pepper and olives
- Turnips; carrots; broccoli with grated Parmesan cheese
- Winter squash; green beans with ground nutmeg and white pepper
- Turnip and pumpkin with dried thyme leaves
- Sweet potato; apple; snow peas and ground ginger
- Try mixing and matching steamed vegetables with the sauces that begin on page 270

You can make a quick dinner with steamed vegetable combinations by adding chopped cooked chicken or turkey; cooked lean ground beef or ground turkey; cooked shrimp or chopped cooked fish fillet; flaked cooked tuna or salmon; or steamed shucked clams. Flavor with wine; vegetable stock; low-salt chicken broth; tomato sauce; or reduced-calorie sour cream. Serve over pasta or brown rice. Top with grated Parmesan cheese; shredded reduced-calorie Swiss or cheddar cheese; or shredded part-skim mozzarella.

Blanching

Blanching, which is also called parboiling, is an important technique in cooking with vegetables. Basic blanching technique is to immerse whole or cut vegetables for a few minutes in boiling water, then plunge them into cold water. This will stop their cooking and set their colors.

ASPARAGUS: Place asparagus in an oval stovetop casserole ¾ full of boiling water. Partially cover until water returns to a boil. Uncover, reduce heat, and cook for 4 minutes. Place pot in sink and run cold water into it. Drain asparagus and pat dry.

BROCCOLI: Bring a large pot of water to a boil. Add 1 bunch of broccoli stems and florets, cut into 1½-inch pieces. Cover pot until water returns to a boil. Boil, uncovered, for 3–5 minutes or until broccoli is tender but still crunchy. Plunge into cold water, drain, and pat dry.

BRUSSELS SPROUTS: Bring a large pot of water to a boil. Add medium-size Brussels sprouts and return to a boil. Cook for 5–8 minutes. Plunge in cold water, drain, and pat dry.

CABBAGE: Bring a large pot of water to a boil. Add cabbage wedges and return water to a boil. Cook for 6–9 minutes. Plunge into cold water, drain, and pat dry. Squeeze out as much moisture as possible.

CARROTS: Bring a large pot of water to a boil. Add whole carrots and return water to a boil. Cook 8 minutes or until just tender. Chill in cold water, drain, and pat dry. Thinly sliced carrots will cook in 1–2 minutes and carrot logs will cook in 3–4 minutes.

CAULIFLOWER FLORETS: Bring a large pot of water to a boil. Add 1 teaspoon of lemon juice to keep cauliflower white. Drop in florets and return water to a boil. Cook 3–6 minutes or until just tender. Plunge in cold water, drain, and pat dry.

EGGPLANT: Bring a large pot of water to a boil. Add sliced or cubed eggplants and return water to a boil. Cook 1–2 minutes or until just tender. Plunge in cold water, drain, and pat dry.

GREEN BEANS: Boil 4 quarts of water in a large pot. Add 1 pound of beans. Cover pot until water returns to a boil. Uncover and boil for 3–5 minutes until beans are tender but still crisp. Plunge into cold water, drain, and pat dry.

GREEN PEAS: Boil 4 quarts of water in a large pot. Add 2½ cups shelled green peas or snow peas and return water to a boil. Shelled green peas will cook in 2–4 minutes; snow peas in 1 minute. Plunge in cold water, drain, and pat dry.

PUMPKIN: Bring a large pot of water to a boil. Add 1½- to 2-inch pumpkin chunks. Return water to a boil and cook for 8 minutes. Plunge in cold water, drain, and pat dry.

SPINACH: Bring a large pot of water to a boil. Add spinach, bit by bit, to keep water boiling. When water reaches a second rolling boil, cook spinach for 2–5 minutes. Let cold water run into the pot, drain, squeeze spinach to remove moisture.

WINTER SQUASH: Peel winter squash and cut into chunks. Place in a saucepan and barely cover with water. Cover pan and bring water to a boil. Reduce heat and cook for 5 minutes or until tender. Plunge in cold water, drain, and pat dry.

Using the Recipes

You will find three different recipe formats in *500 Low-Fat Fruit and Vegetable Recipes.*

EASY ACCESS: THE BASICS

QUICK TAKES

AT YOUR LEISURE

Easy Access selections are designed to allow you to build your own recipes using fruits and vegetables you have on hand. Quick Takes are recipes that are quick to assemble with fresh ingredients or leftovers, have few steps, or are quick to cook. The Fabulous Forty Fruits and Vegetables appear in capital letters in the Quick Takes sections. At Your Leisure recipes, while still simple, take a bit longer and often involve a few more steps.

The
500 LOW-FAT FRUIT
AND VEGETABLE
Recipes

Breakfast and Lunch

Breakfast

EASY ACCESS: THE BASICS

Basic Omelets: Vegetable Omelets and Fruit Omelets   Basic Crêpes
Basic Fruit Griddle Cakes   Basic German Vegetable Pancake
Basic Hot Oatmeal with Fruit   Pure and Simple Fruit with Yogurt
Basic Breakfast Fruit Salads

QUICK TAKES

Fruit Salad Bagels   Carrot-Nut Bagels   Strawberry Waffle Sandwiches
Orange-Pecan Waffles   Pineapple Plus Muffins
Single-Serving Fruit and Nut Muesli   Carrot-Cinnamon Oatmeal
Vegetable Home Fries   Nectarine French Toast
Cottage Cheese Pear Open Faces   Citrus Sundae
Honeyed Fruit and Raisins   Sautéed Apple Rings   Chicken-Apple Hash
Apricot Whirl

AT YOUR LEISURE

Fruit Porridge   Oat Waffles with Cinnamon-Fruit-Raisin Sauce
Personal Pineapple Pancake   Oven Pancake with Fruit Sauce
Pear-Raisin French Toastwiches   Apple Vegetable Frittata
Good Morning Salad

I n order to include 5–9 servings of fruits and vegetables in your daily diet, you need to find creative ways to incorporate them in your breakfast and lunch plans. This chapter is designed to get you thinking about new ways to use fruits and vegetables in your morning and midday meals.

Breakfast Fare

EASY ACCESS: BASIC OMELETS

When you're preparing an omelet for breakfast or lunch, plan to include a fruit or vegetable filling. Filling ingredients should be pre-cooked and warm.

VEGETABLE OMELETS

(Serves 3)

INGREDIENTS
6 egg whites and 2 egg yolks
4 tablespoons skim or low-fat milk
¼ teaspoon black pepper
1 cup chopped, sliced, or diced raw, sautéed or steamed
    vegetables (see possibilities below)
1 clove garlic, minced, or 1 tablespoon chopped
    scallions
1–2 tablespoons mild, light-flavored olive oil or diet or
    reduced liquid or tub margarine containing not
    more than 1 gram of saturated fat per tablespoon

1. Mix egg whites, egg yolks, milk, and black pepper together lightly with a fork.
2. Combine vegetables and garlic or scallions.
3. Preheat a nonstick skillet or omelet pan over low heat until thoroughly hot. Add oil or margarine.
4. When oil or margarine sizzles, add eggs. Using a fork or spatula, draw egg mixture from sides to the middle of the pan. Repeat until the mixture is set.

5. When eggs are lightly scrambled on top, spread vegetable mixture evenly across the omelet's surface.

6. Fold the omelet over and transfer to a serving platter.

VEGETABLE FILLING POSSIBILITIES

Sautéed red bell pepper; green bell pepper; mushrooms; zucchini

Sautéed spinach; mushrooms; cayenne pepper

Steamed broccoli; carrots

Sautéed tomato; onion; green bell pepper; dried basil leaves; grated Parmesan cheese

Steamed fresh or frozen green peas; onion; parsley; tomato; cooked chicken

Sautéed tomato; green bell pepper; olives; cooked potato; dried thyme leaves

Sautéed low-fat ground turkey; green bell pepper; tomato; mushrooms

Steamed asparagus tips; red bell pepper

Sautéed fresh, frozen, or canned corn kernels; green bell pepper; shredded reduced-fat cheddar cheese

Avocado; shredded reduced-fat Monterey Jack cheese; tomato

FRUIT OMELETS

(Serves 3)

INGREDIENTS

6 egg whites and 2 egg yolks

4 tablespoons skim or low-fat milk

¼ teaspoon black pepper

1 cup chopped, diced, or sliced fruit (see possibilities below)

2 tablespoons orange juice

1 tablespoon honey

1–2 tablespoons mild, light-flavored olive oil or diet or reduced liquid or tub margarine, containing not more than 1 gram of saturated fat per tablespoon

1. Mix egg whites, egg yolks, milk, and black pepper together lightly with a fork.

2. Combine fruit, juice, and honey.

3. Preheat a nonstick skillet or omelet pan over low heat until thoroughly hot. Add oil or margarine.

4. When oil or margarine sizzles, add eggs. Using a fork or spatula, draw egg mixture from sides to the middle of the pan. Repeat until the mixture is set.

5. When eggs are lightly scrambled on top, spread fruit mixture evenly across the omelet's surface.

6. Fold the omelet over and transfer to a serving platter. Top with additional fruit.

FRUIT FILLING POSSIBILITIES

Warmed sliced strawberries
Sautéed bananas
Warmed sliced nectarines or peaches
Warmed pineapple; dried mint; lemon zest
Sautéed apple; onion; mango
Warmed fresh or frozen raspberries; honey; chopped walnuts
Warmed fresh or frozen blackberries; honey
Warmed bananas; apples; oranges; dried mint
Warmed apricots and kiwis
Warmed bananas; cantaloupe; reduced-calorie shredded Swiss cheese
Warmed bananas; papaya; reduced-calorie shredded Monterey Jack
    cheese

BASIC CRÊPES

(4 servings, 2 crêpes each)

Crêpes are a great base for fruit and vegetable servings for breakfast or lunch. They can be served with a topping on the surface; folded over, or stacked like a cake with filling between the layers.

INGREDIENTS
1 cup unbleached all-purpose flour
Pinch of salt
2 eggs
1¼ cups skim or low-fat milk
1 tablespoon melted diet or reduced liquid or tub
    margarine, containing not more than 1 gram of
    saturated fat per tablespoon
1 tablespoon mild, light-flavored olive oil

1. Sift flour and salt into a bowl.

2. Make a well in the center and add eggs and 2 tablespoons of milk. Beat with a wooden spoon.

3. Slowly add remaining milk until the batter bubbles.

4. Stir in margarine.

5. Lightly oil a 7-inch crêpe pan with olive oil. Place over high heat.

6. Pour in 2–3 tablespoons crêpe batter and tilt pan so batter covers the bottom thinly and evenly.

7. Cook for 1 minute until the crêpe is lightly browned on the bottom.

8. Turn with spatula and cook on the second side for 30 seconds. Transfer to a plate and keep crêpes warm until serving.

9. Repeat until batter is used.

10. Top with one of the chopped, sliced, or diced vegetable or fruit combinations below.

TOPPING POSSIBILITIES

Sautéed onion and green bell pepper; fresh or canned tomatoes, grated Parmesan cheese

Sautéed red bell pepper; tiny cooked shrimp; shredded reduced-fat cheddar cheese

Sautéed low-fat ground turkey; celery; onion; fresh, frozen, or canned corn; tomatoes; chili powder

Steamed fresh or canned asparagus tips; parsley; chives; grated Parmesan cheese

Steamed spinach; sautéed onions; paprika; grated Parmesan cheese

Steamed green peas; shredded canned salmon; lemon juice; sautéed onion; grated Parmesan cheese

Warmed fresh or juice-packed canned pineapple; watercress

Warmed bananas; honey; chopped walnuts; lemon juice; nutmeg

Warmed fresh or frozen raspberries; honey

Warmed oranges; lemon juice; honey

Warmed apricots; lemon juice; all-fruit orange marmalade

Warmed puréed apples or applesauce; raisins; lemon juice; cinnamon

Warmed puréed apples or applesauce; blackberries

Warmed canned pears; slivered almonds; all-fruit raspberry jam

Simmered cranberries; maple syrup; chopped walnuts; grated lemon zest

NOTE: Crêpes can be prepared in advance and stored in the refrigerator for 5–6 days. They can be stacked and wrapped in aluminum foil or plastic bags. Reheat them quickly by cooking in a lightly greased pan for 30 seconds on each side. They can also be frozen for up to 6 months. Stack them between pieces of waxed paper and wrap in foil or plastic bags. They can be thawed at room temperature for 3 hours or overnight in the refrigerator.

BASIC FRUIT GRIDDLE CAKES

(2 servings)

INGREDIENTS
1¼ cups unbleached all-purpose flour
1 tablespoon sugar
1 tablespoon baking powder
¼ teaspoon salt
1¼ cups skim or low-fat milk
1 egg
1 tablespoon mild, light-flavored olive oil
1 cup sliced or chopped fruit (see possibilities below)

1. In a medium bowl combine flour, sugar, baking powder, and salt. In a separate bowl combine milk, egg, and oil. Stir wet ingredients into dry ingredients just until well mixed.
2. Add fruit to the batter.
3. Lightly oil a griddle or large skillet over medium heat.
4. Spoon ⅓ cup of batter on the the griddle for each griddle cake. Cook until bubbles appear on the top and the bottom is light brown.
5. Turn and cook on the second side for 2 minutes until browned.
6. Serve with remaining fruit as a topping.

FRUIT TOPPING POSSIBILITIES

Fresh or frozen blueberries; strawberries; raspberries; blackberries
Fresh or frozen peaches or nectarines
Apples
Mango or papaya
Fresh or canned apricots
Fresh cranberries
Bananas
Canned solid-pack pumpkin
Fresh or canned pears

BASIC GERMAN VEGETABLE PANCAKE

(4 servings)

This easy oven pancake can be served with a variety of vegetable toppings.

INGREDIENTS
1 tablespoon mild, light-flavored olive oil
4 egg whites and 2 egg yolks
⅓ cup unbleached all-purpose flour
⅓ cup skim or low-fat milk
¼ teaspoon salt
1 cup sautéed or steamed, chopped, diced, or sliced
     vegetable topping (see possibilities below)

1. Preheat oven to 450 degrees. Heat oil in a heavy 9-inch skillet with an oven-safe handle over medium heat. Tilt skillet to oil sides and bottom of pan.
2. Beat eggs in an electric mixer at medium speed until they are fluffy. Lower speed and beat in flour, milk, and salt.
3. Pour egg mixture into the skillet. Bake for 20 minutes or until the pancake puffs and is lightly golden.
4. Remove from oven. The center will fall, leaving a hollow for the vegetable topping.
5. Spoon topping over pancake and serve at once.

VEGETABLE TOPPING POSSIBILITIES
Sautéed red and green bell peppers; minced garlic
Sautéed steamed broccoli; carrot; onion
Steamed asparagus tips; carrot; scallions
Sautéed tomatoes; zucchini; fresh, frozen, or canned corn kernels; dried
    thyme leaves
Sautéed tomatoes; steamed green beans; dried basil leaves
Sautéed spinach; red bell pepper; grated Parmesan cheese
Sautéed turnips; carrots; green bell pepper
Sautéed eggplant; tomatoes; zucchini; onion; dried basil leaves
Steamed chopped cauliflower; tomatoes

BASIC HOT OATMEAL WITH FRUIT

(4 servings)

A bowl of heart-healthy oatmeal topped with fruit is a great way to start the morning.

INGREDIENTS
3 cups water
1 cup rolled oats
¼ teaspoon salt (optional)
¼ cup raisins
⅛ teaspoon ground cinnamon
2 cups chopped fruit topping (see possibilities below)
Skim or low-fat milk

1. Bring water to a boil in a large saucepan.
2. Stir in oats and salt. Lower heat and cook for 3 minutes.
3. Remove pan from heat.
4. Add raisins and cinnamon. Cover and let stand for 12–15 minutes.
5. Top each serving with ½ cup fruit and milk.

FRUIT TOPPING POSSIBILITIES

Apples and blackberries
Mangos and blueberries
Pears and strawberries
Nectarines and raspberries
Bananas and walnuts

PURE AND SIMPLE FRUIT WITH YOGURT

(4 servings)

INGREDIENTS
3 cups chopped or sliced chilled fruit (see possibilities below)
8 ounces plain nonfat or low-fat yogurt
2 teaspoons ground cinnamon

1. Dish fruit into 4 chilled dishes.
2. Top with a dollop of yogurt.
3. Sprinkle with cinnamon.

FRUIT POSSIBILITIES

Fresh or frozen blueberries
Fresh or frozen raspberries
Fresh or frozen blackberries and fresh or canned nectarines or peaches
Fresh or frozen strawberries and blackberries
Kiwis; mangoes; and papayas
Seeded tangerines and bananas
Navel orange sections; bananas; and apples
Fresh or canned pears; kiwis; red grapes
Fresh or canned apricots; pears; peaches; dark sweet cherries
Chopped fresh or juice-packed canned pineapple and apricots
Apples; raisins; maple syrup

BASIC BREAKFAST FRUIT SALADS

Fruit salad for breakfast is a quick and easy way to start the day off with a delicious, nutritious wallop. Make a big bowl of fruit salad the night before and have it ready for a hurried morning. Serve it over cereal or sprinkled with rolled oats and nuts.

POSSIBILITIES

Diced cantaloupe; sliced strawberries; blueberries; sliced bananas; dried mint
Diced honeydew; sliced raspberries; navel orange sections; lime juice; honey
Diced watermelon; blueberries; sliced peaches; sliced apricots
Blackberries; tangerine sections; halved red grapes
Diced cantaloupe; pitted cherries; halved green grapes; diced pineapple
Pineapple chunks; diced honeydew; apple chunks; pear chunks; sliced banana; honey; cinnamon
Blueberries; sliced strawberries; navel orange sections
Nectarine sections; sliced raspberries; pink grapefruit sections; sliced pears
Navel orange sections; chopped apples; chopped pears; chopped apricots; cinnamon; ginger
Diced honeydew; pineapple chunks; navel orange sections; sliced kiwis; sliced strawberries; sliced raspberries
Navel orange sections; pink grapefruit sections; sliced bananas; sliced avocados; halved red grapes
Pineapple chunks; sliced strawberries; sliced papaya; diced honeydew; diced cantaloupe

Orange sections; blueberries; diced honeydew; sliced strawberries

Pineapple chunks; peach slices; seeded tangerine sections; sliced bananas; chopped yellow apples

Diced pineapple; sliced bananas; sliced kiwis; sliced strawberries; sliced apricots

Sliced mangoes; sliced peaches; diced pineapple; sliced papaya; sliced kiwi; sliced banana

Chopped cranberries; chopped apples; pear chunks; navel orange sections; red grapes; sliced bananas

Strawberries; white grapefruit sections; navel orange sections.

QUICK TAKES

FRUIT SALAD BAGELS: Spread nonfat or low-fat cream cheese or cottage cheese on toasted sesame bagels and sprinkle with cinnamon. Top with thin slices of BANANA, HONEYDEW, and PEACH.

CARROT-NUT BAGELS: Spread natural peanut butter on toasted pumpernickel bagels. Press slices of CARROT into the peanut butter.

STRAWBERRY WAFFLE SANDWICHES: Toast frozen waffles. Spread one waffle with plain low-fat yogurt and sliced STRAWBERRIES. Top with another waffle.

ORANGE-PECAN WAFFLES: Serve waffles topped with thick rounds of ORANGE sprinkled with reduced-calorie maple syrup, cinnamon, and ground pecans.

PINEAPPLE PLUS MUFFINS: Spread a toasted whole-grain English muffin with low-fat cream cheese. Spoon juice-packed canned crushed PINE-APPLE on both sides and sprinkle with cinnamon. Broil for 4 minutes.

SINGLE-SERVING FRUIT AND NUT MUESLI: Mix 3 tablespoons rolled oats with ¼ cup water. Set the oats aside for 15 minutes. Chop a small PEACH, several STRAWBERRIES, and an APPLE. Stir 1 tablespoon milk, 1 tablespoon honey, and 1 tablespoon lemon juice into the oats. Add the fruit and 1 tablespoon chopped nuts.

CARROT-CINNAMON OATMEAL: Place 2 medium CARROTS, scrubbed and shredded, and 4 cups water in a medium saucepan. Bring to a boil. Reduce heat. Add ½ cup seedless raisins and simmer for 4 minutes or until the carrots are soft. Add ⅔ cup oat bran; 1⅓ cups old-fashioned rolled oats; and ½ teaspoon ground cinnamon. Simmer, stirring constantly, for 5 minutes. Serve with warm low-fat milk and reduced-calorie maple syrup. (4 servings)

VEGETABLE HOME FRIES: Preheat oven to 400 degrees. Heat 3 tablespoons mild, light-flavored olive oil in a heavy skillet. Add 3 medium

POTATOES, peeled and thinly sliced, ½ pound CARROTS, peeled and sliced, 1 medium onion, thinly sliced, and ½ GREEN BELL PEPPER, seeded and diced. Sauté for 10 minutes or until crisp and tender. Transfer to a baking pan and bake for 30 minutes. (4 servings)

NECTARINE FRENCH TOAST: Top French toast with fresh nectarine or peach sauce. Mix 6 fresh NECTARINES or PEACHES, pitted and sliced, with 1 teaspoon brown sugar, ¾ cup nonfat or low-fat plain yogurt, and 2 tablespoons reduced-calorie maple syrup.

COTTAGE CHEESE PEAR OPEN FACES: Preheat broiler and spread 1 cup low-fat cottage cheese on 4 slices whole-grain bread. Spoon unsweetened juice-packed canned PEARS over cottage cheese and sprinkle with cinnamon. Broil until cottage cheese is hot. Serve at once.

CITRUS SUNDAE: Layer ⅓ cup granola, several spoonfuls nonfat or low-fat plain yogurt or low-fat cottage cheese, and sections of GRAPEFRUIT and navel ORANGES or other fruit in a tall sundae glass. Repeat layers.

HONEYED FRUIT AND RAISINS: Place 2 large GRAPEFRUIT, peeled and separated into sections, 2 APPLES, cored and chopped, 2 BANANAS, peeled and cut into ½-inch slices, 4 tablespoons seedless raisins, ½ cup apple juice, and 2 tablespoons honey in a medium saucepan. Simmer over low heat for 10 minutes until the fruit is warmed through. (4 servings)

SAUTÉED APPLE RINGS: Cut 4 APPLES into ¼-inch-thick rings. Heat 3 tablespoons mild, light-flavored olive oil in a large skillet over medium heat. Cook the apple rings until they begin to soften. Turn and cook on the other side. Sprinkle with brown sugar. Cook for 1 more minute. (4 servings)

CHICKEN-APPLE HASH: Heat 3 tablespoons mild, light-flavored olive oil in a skillet over medium heat. Sauté ½ cup finely chopped onion and ½ teaspoon dried rosemary leaves for 3 minutes. Stir in 4 cups diced cooked potatoes, 1 cup diced cooked chicken, 1 diced APPLE. Cook until browned. Sprinkle with chopped fresh parsley. (4 servings)

APRICOT WHIRL: Place 1 cup drained canned APRICOT halves or fresh apricot halves, 2 egg whites, and ¾ cup orange juice in the container of a blender. Blend until smooth.

AT YOUR LEISURE

FRUIT PORRIDGE

Apples, bananas, and lemon peel make this morning cereal a special event.

YIELD: *4 servings*
PREPARATION TIME: *10 minutes*
COOKING TIME: *10 minutes*

2 apples, cored and chopped
2 bananas, peeled and cut into 1-inch slices
1 teaspoon finely grated lemon rind
½ cup nonfat or low-fat plain yogurt
1⅓ cups old-fashioned rolled oats
3 cups water
4 teaspoons honey

1. Place apples, 1 banana, and lemon rind in the workbowl of a food processor or in a blender and process until smooth.
2. Pour the apple mixture into a medium saucepan with the yogurt, oats, and water. Bring to a boil, reduce heat, and simmer for 10 minutes.
3. Stir in honey and top with remaining banana slices.

VARIATION
- Add 2 tablespoons sunflower seeds or sesame seeds.

OAT WAFFLES WITH CINNAMON-FRUIT-RAISIN SAUCE

Hot waffles are topped with an apple, pear, raisin, and cinnamon combination. Try using this sauce over low-fat frozen yogurt, too.

YIELD: *4 servings*
PREPARATION TIME: *10 minutes*
COOKING TIME: *20 minutes*

FRUIT SAUCE
2 cups apple juice
2 tablespoons cornstarch
1 tablespoon mild, light-flavored olive oil
2 apples, cored and sliced
1 pear, cored and sliced
½ cup seedless raisins
½ teaspoon ground cinnamon
¼ teaspoon vanilla extract

WAFFLES
1 whole egg and 2 egg whites
1½ cups skim or low-fat milk
¼ cup mild, light-flavored olive oil
1½ cups unbleached all-purpose flour
1 cup quick rolled oats
1 tablespoon baking powder

1. To make the sauce, combine ½ cup of apple juice and cornstarch in a small pan and cook over medium heat, stirring. Bring to a boil and cook for 1 minute. Remove from heat.
2. Heat olive oil in a skillet over medium heat. Sauté apple slices and pear slices for 3 minutes.
3. Stir in raisins, cinnamon, vanilla, and the rest of the juice. Bring sauce to a boil and add the cornstarch-apple mixture. Cook, stirring, until thickened.
4. To make the waffles, in a large bowl mix eggs, milk, and olive oil.
5. Add flour, oats, and baking powder. Mix again.
6. Heat lightly oiled waffle iron until hot. Cook waffles until lightly browned and steam has stopped rising.
7. Serve waffles with fruit sauce.

PERSONAL PINEAPPLE PANCAKE

If you're making a quick breakfast for yourself, try this baked pancake with a terrific fruit topping.

YIELD: *1 serving*
PREPARATION TIME: *10 minutes*
COOKING TIME: *10 minutes*

PINEAPPLE SAUCE
¾ cup unsweetened juice-packed canned pineapple
     chunks, cut into small pieces
1 teaspoon lemon juice
⅛ teaspoon ground ginger
¼ teaspoon ground cinnamon

PANCAKE
1 egg
⅓ cup unbleached all-purpose flour
¼ teaspoon ground cinnamon
⅛ teaspoon ground nutmeg
½ teaspoon honey
¼ teaspoon vanilla extract
½ cup skim or low-fat milk
2 tablespoons mild, light-flavored olive oil

1. To make the sauce, place pineapple, lemon juice, ginger, and cinnamon in the workbowl of a food processor or in a blender, and purée. Set aside.
2. To make the pancake, preheat oven to 375 degrees. Mix egg, flour, cinnamon, nutmeg, honey, vanilla, and milk.
3. Heat olive oil in an 8-inch ovenproof skillet or shallow casserole.
4. Pour batter into skillet or casserole and immediately place in oven. Bake for 10 minutes or until "set" and lightly browned. The center of the pancake will be softer and will not rise as high as the sides.
5. Slide your pancake onto a serving dish and fill the center with pineapple sauce. Enjoy!

VARIATIONS
▪ Substitute 1 ripe medium nectarine, peeled and chopped, or ¾ cup fresh or frozen strawberries for the pineapple.

OVEN PANCAKE WITH FRUIT SAUCE

Baked pancakes are served with a nonfat or low-fat cottage cheese or low-fat sour cream filling and topped with a sauce packed with blueberries, strawberries, and kiwi. Baked pancakes can be served either warm or cooled. They can also be made ahead and reheated.

YIELD: *4 servings*
PREPARATION TIME: *20 minutes*
COOKING TIME: *20 minutes*

FRUIT SAUCE
1½ cups apple juice
2 tablespoons cornstarch
1 teaspoon vanilla extract
3 kiwis, peeled and cut into wedges
1 cup fresh or frozen and thawed unsweetened blueberries
1 cup fresh or frozen and thawed unsweetened strawberries

PANCAKE
4 egg whites and 2 egg yolks
1 cup skim or low-fat milk
⅓ cup unbleached all-purpose flour
1 teaspoon sugar
¼ teaspoon salt
¾ cup nonfat or low-fat cottage cheese or sour cream

1. To make the sauce, combine apple juice and cornstarch in a small pan and cook over medium heat, stirring. Bring to a boil and cook for 1 minute.
2. Add vanilla, kiwi wedges, blueberries, and strawberries. Simmer for 5 minutes. Remove from heat.
3. To make the pancake, preheat oven to 425 degrees. Beat eggs in a large bowl until they are fluffy. Continue beating as you add milk, flour, sugar, and salt.
4. Divide the batter between 2 lightly oiled glass pie plates.
5. Bake for 15 minutes. The batter will rise during baking. When the pancakes are "set" and lightly browned, remove from oven and place one pancake on a serving dish.
6. Spread the pancake with the cottage cheese or sour cream. Top with second pancake.
7. Spoon fruit sauce over the pancake. Cut into 4 wedges and serve.

PEAR-RAISIN FRENCH TOASTWICHES

These morning sandwiches are a warm, crunchy delight. Try substituting other fruit combinations for the pear-raisin mixture.

YIELD: *4 servings*
PREPARATION TIME: *10 minutes*
COOKING TIME: *15 minutes*

PEAR-RAISIN FILLING
2 tablespoons seedless raisins
1 tablespoon apple juice
3 tablespoons mild, light-flavored olive oil
3 pears, peeled, cored, and thinly sliced
½ teaspoon ground cinnamon
1 teaspoon sugar

1 egg yolk and 2 egg whites
½ teaspoon ground cinnamon
¼ teaspoon ground nutmeg
¼ teaspoon ground ginger
½ cup skim or low-fat milk
8 slices firm-textured bread

1. To make the pear-raisin filling, combine the raisins and the apple juice in a small bowl and set aside.
2. Heat olive oil in a skillet over medium heat. Sauté pears for 5 minutes. Add raisins, cinnamon, and sugar. Cook for 5 minutes or until pears are slightly tender.
3. Remove pears from skillet with a slotted spoon and set aside.
4. Beat the eggs, cinnamon, nutmeg, ginger, and milk together in a shallow bowl.
5. Place 1 slice of bread on a wide spatula and top the bread with ¼ of the pear slices. Top with another slice of bread.
6. Lower the sandwich into the egg mixture on the spatula, lift the sandwich out and let it drain. Lower the sandwich still on the spatula onto a lightly oiled griddle or skillet and grill until golden brown on each side, turning carefully.
7. Repeat Steps 5 and 6 for each sandwich, keeping cooked sandwiches warm until serving.

APPLE-VEGETABLE FRITTATA

Frittatas can be filled with a variety of fruit and vegetable combinations. In addition to the ones that follow, try filling frittatas with new potatoes, red or green bell peppers, green beans, cherry tomatoes, zucchini, fresh herbs, and pesto sauce.

YIELD: *4 servings*
PREPARATION TIME: *20 minutes*
COOKING TIME: *15 minutes*

6 egg whites and 2 egg yolks
½ cup skim or low-fat milk
¼ teaspoon black pepper
2 teaspoons mild, light-flavored olive oil
2 apples, peeled, cored, and thinly sliced
½ cup thinly sliced scallions
½ cup sliced fresh mushrooms, rinsed and dried
½ cup chopped green bell pepper
1 clove garlic, minced
½ cup shredded nonfat or part-skim mozzarella cheese
    (optional)

1. Preheat oven to 400 degrees. Beat eggs, milk, and pepper in a large bowl.
2. Heat olive oil in a skillet or casserole over medium heat. Sauté apples, scallions, mushrooms, green pepper, and garlic for 5 minutes. Reduce heat to medium-low.
3. If using cheese, sprinkle it over the apple mixture in the skillet.
4. Pour egg mixture over apple mixture in skillet. Tilt skillet to allow some of the egg mixture to run under the apple mixture. Cook for 4 minutes or until egg mixture is "set" and the bottom of the frittata is lightly browned.
5. Remove from skillet, cut into 4 wedges, and serve.

VARIATIONS
- Substitute 1 10-ounce package frozen chopped spinach, thawed and well drained, for the apples and ⅓ cup Parmesan cheese for the mozzarella. Serve topped with red pepper rings.
- Substitute 1 cup steamed chopped broccoli and ½ cup steamed diced carrots for the apples. Add 2 tablespoons Dijon mustard to the egg mixture.

- Instead of adding the cheese in Step 3, wait until the frittata has "set." Then sprinkle the cheese on top of the frittata and broil it for 1 minute 6 inches from the heat or until cheese melts. Be sure to use an ovenproof skillet or remove frittata to an ovenproof dish before broiling.

GOOD MORNING SALAD

If you're looking for a breakfast alternative, why not try a morning fruit salad for a quick and easy change of pace? Substitute a cup of any fruit that's in season and you'll have a year-round formula for a great start.

YIELD: *1 serving*
PREPARATION TIME: *10 minutes*

⅓ cup sliced fresh or frozen and thawed unsweetened strawberries
⅓ cup sliced fresh or unsweetened juice-packed or water-packed canned peaches
⅓ cup sliced bananas
½ cup nonfat or low-fat cottage cheese
2 tablespoons plain nonfat or low-fat yogurt
2 tablespoons toasted old-fashioned rolled oats
4 romaine lettuce leaves, rinsed and torn in bite-sized pieces

1. Combine strawberries, peaches, bananas, cottage cheese, yogurt, and oats in a small bowl.
2. Arrange lettuce leaves in a serving bowl and top with fruit mixture.

VARIATION
- Substitute chopped walnuts or almonds for the oats.

Lunch

EASY ACCESS: THE BASICS

Basic Vegetable Melts   Basic Pita Sandwiches
Basic Cottage Cheesewich   Basic Vegetable Pizza

QUICK TAKES

Dilled Apple-Tuna French Twists
Almond with Cantaloupe Chicken Sandwiches
Beef and Salad Sandwiches   Salmon-Vegetable Salad Sandwiches
Roast Beef and Orange Sandwiches
Chicken, Avocado, and Spinachwiches
Turkey, Cottage Cheese, and Pineapple Specials
Greek Salad Sandwiches   Peanut Butter Plus Sandwiches
Lunchtime Shish Kabobs   Vegetable Tortillas
Strawberry-Nectarine Ricotta Pizza

AT YOUR LEISURE

Grilled Chicken Citrus Sandwiches   Ratatouille Heroes
Open-Faced Turkey Apple Melts   Veggie-Fish Sandwiches

Lunch Fare

EASY ACCESS

Instead of thinking of fruits and vegetables as afterthoughts and condiments at lunchtime and snacktime, try making them a featured ingredient using the recipes that follow as your guide.

BASIC VEGETABLE MELTS

(4 servings)

Serve these sandwiches bubbling hot from the broiler with a salad for a quick, nutritious meal. Melts are a great way to use up leftover steamed vegetables.

> ### INGREDIENTS
> 2 cups steamed or sautéed chopped vegetables (see
>   possibilities below)
> 1/4 teaspoon dried thyme leaves
> 1/8 teaspoon black pepper
> 4 slices whole-grain bread
> 3/4 cup nonfat or low-fat shredded cheese

1. Preheat broiler.
2. Sprinkle vegetables with thyme and black pepper.
3. Lightly toast the bread.
4 Spoon vegetables onto toasted bread and cover with shredded cheese.
5. Place on a broiling pan and heat under broiler until cheese melts.

VEGETABLE POSSIBILITIES

Broccoli and carrots
Cauliflower and red bell pepper
Eggplant; green bell pepper; and tomatoes
Asparagus and yellow summer squash
Spinach and mushrooms
Green beans; carrots; and mushrooms
Tomatoes and mashed avocado

BASIC PITA SANDWICHES

Pita pockets make a handy container for an endless array of fruit and vegetable combinations. Toast large whole-wheat pita pockets and stuff them with one of the following combinations.

PITA FILLING POSSIBILITIES

Chopped blanched broccoli florets; chopped raw carrots; chopped blanched snow peas; chopped blanched green beans; chopped blanched asparagus; chopped cucumber; halved cherry tomatoes; watercress; olive oil; red wine vinegar.

Chopped cooked chicken breast; shredded zucchini; tomato; romaine lettuce; reduced-calorie mayonnaise.

Shredded cabbage; shredded fresh spinach; shredded carrots; shredded rare lean roast beef; brown mustard.

Chopped cooked chicken breast; diced celery; diced onion; diced apple; chopped green pepper; curry powder.

Chopped cooked chicken breast; pineapple chunks; white pepper; watercress.

Cooked chicken breast; chopped blanched asparagus tips; chopped red bell pepper; walnuts; chopped parsley; lemon juice; olive oil.

Chopped cooked chicken breast; chopped apple; chives; chopped black olives; diced green pepper.

Flaked canned red salmon; ripe olives; diced avocado; orange sections.

Cooked turkey breast; chopped fresh spinach; seeded tangerine chunks.

Chopped tomato; mashed cooked beans; romaine lettuce; diced avocado; shredded low-fat cheddar cheese.

Chopped rare roast beef; chopped nonfat or low-fat Swiss cheese; shredded red cabbage; sliced radishes; shredded carrots; paprika; red wine vinegar; reduced-calorie mayonnaise.

Tiny shrimp; chopped blanched snow peas; bean sprouts; chopped scallions; chopped green pepper; sesame oil.

Tiny shrimp; diced celery; diced green bell pepper; chopped onion; pineapple chunks; romaine lettuce.

Tuna salad; chopped red bell pepper; romaine lettuce; nectarine sections.

Tuna fish; chopped scallions; chopped parsley; chopped tomatoes; chopped cucumbers; chopped green bell pepper; sliced radishes; watercress.

Chopped tomatoes; shredded nonfat or low-fat mozzarella cheese; dried basil; chopped turkey breast; romaine lettuce. Tuna fish; halved cherry tomatoes; sliced egg whites; blanched chopped green beans; black olives.

Tuna fish; chopped almonds; chopped apple; diced celery; curry powder; lemon juice.

Tuna fish; diced celery; crushed pineapple; chopped green bell pepper; ground ginger.

Diced avocado, diced papaya; diced kiwi; sliced banana; alfalfa sprouts; sunflower seeds; honey; lemon juice; olive oil.

Diced avocado; chopped scallions; ripe olives; sliced egg whites; sliced tomatoes; diced celery; nonfat or low-fat cheddar cheese; romaine lettuce.

Nonfat or low-fat mozzarella cheese; spinach leaves; sliced red onion; sliced tomato; reduced-calorie mayonnaise.

Diced low-fat Swiss cheese; spinach leaves; alfalfa sprouts; halved cherry tomatoes; green peas; shredded carrot; shredded zucchini; chopped parsley; olive oil; lemon juice.

Peanut butter; honey; sliced bananas; chopped walnuts; romaine lettuce.

Peanut butter; crushed pineapple; sunflower seeds.

Peanut butter; grated carrots; raisins.

Peanut butter; grated apple; apple butter; romaine lettuce.

Spinach leaves; sesame seeds; melon chunks; sliced water chestnuts.

Shredded red cabbage; shredded carrots; shredded nonfat or low-fat Swiss cheese; chick-peas; black olives.

Broccoli florets; sliced water chestnuts; sliced black olives; oil and vinegar.

BASIC COTTAGE CHEESEWICH

(1 serving)

Nonfat or low-fat cottage cheese makes a super go-with for fruit and vegetables. The combination is calcium- and nutrient-rich.

To make a cottage cheesewich, spread ¼ cup low-fat cottage cheese on a slice of whole-grain, raisin, sunflower, corn, rye, or oatmeal bread. Top with one of the following combinations:

TOPPING POSSIBILITIES

Chopped apricots; toasted walnuts; and chopped watercress

Crushed pineapple; toasted almonds; diced celery; romaine lettuce

Grated carrots; slivered green bell peppers; chopped scallions; ground cumin

Sliced bananas; toasted sunflower seeds; and sliced kiwis

Chopped apples; diced celery; walnuts

Chopped tomatoes; slivered green bell pepper; grated carrots
Sliced chicken; sliced strawberries
Sliced turkey; blueberries

BASIC VEGETABLE PIZZA

INGREDIENTS
Ready-made 12- or 14-inch pizza crust (available in the
    refrigerator case at your supermarket)
1 tablespoon mild, light-flavored olive oil
1 small onion, diced
1 clove garlic, minced
1 8-ounce can tomatoes
3 tablespoons tomato paste
½ teaspoon dried basil leaves
½ teaspoon dried oregano leaves
⅛ teaspoon cayenne pepper
Cornmeal
3 cups nonfat or low-fat shredded mozzarella cheese
2½ cups steamed or sautéed chopped, sliced, or diced
    vegetables (see possibilities below)

1. Heat olive oil in a medium saucepan over medium heat. Add onion
and garlic and stir until tender.
2. Add tomatoes with liquid, tomato paste, basil, oregano, and cayenne. Heat to boiling, stirring to break up tomatoes. Reduce heat to
low. Cover partially and simmer for 15 minutes.
3. Preheat oven to 425 degrees. Brush pizza pan with oil. Sprinkle
with cornmeal. Place pizza shell on pan.
4. Sprinkle half of cheese over pizza crust. Top with tomato sauce.
Sprinkle with remaining cheese. Add vegetable topping.
5. Follow baking direction on pizza crust package or bake on bottom
rack of oven for 25 minutes or until crust is golden or crisp.

VEGETABLE TOPPING POSSIBILITIES
Sautéed green bell pepper; red bell pepper; broccoli
Sautéed mushrooms; chopped cauliflower; shredded carrots
Sautéed red bell pepper; fresh, frozen, or canned corn kernels
Sautéed spinach; mushrooms
Steamed asparagus tips; carrots; yellow summer squash

Sautéed green bell pepper; zucchini; mushrooms; eggplant
Steamed Brussels sprouts; fresh, frozen, or canned corn kernels; cauliflower
Sautéed mushrooms; eggplant; onions
Sautéed red bell pepper; sautéed yellow bell pepper; red onion;
    mushrooms; zucchini.

NOTE: The sauce and toppings can also be used on individual bases
    like halved English muffins or pita rounds.

QUICK TAKES

DILLED APPLE-TUNA FRENCH TWISTS: Combine 6 tablespoons reduced-calorie mayonnaise, 1 clove garlic, minced, and 1 teaspoon dried dillweed in a medium bowl. Stir in a 6½-ounce can white albacore tuna, packed in olive oil or water, drained and flaked, 1 large APPLE, cored and chopped, ½ cup chopped celery, and ½ cup chopped scallions. Halve 4 French rolls and top with 4 large ROMAINE lettuce leaves. Top with tuna-apple salad and remaining roll halves.

ALMOND WITH CANTALOUPE CHICKEN SANDWICHES: Combine 2 tablespoons nonfat or low-fat plain yogurt, 2 tablespoons reduced-calorie mayonnaise, 1 clove garlic, minced, ½ teaspoon black pepper and ⅛ teaspoon cayenne pepper in a medium bowl. Stir in 1 cup chopped cooked chicken breast, 1 cup diced CANTALOUPE, ½ cup chopped almonds, and 1 tablespoon lemon juice. Halve 4 whole-grain French rolls and top with 4 large ROMAINE lettuce leaves. Top with chicken-melon salad and remaining roll halves.

BEEF AND SALAD SANDWICHES: Combine 1 cup chopped red CABBAGE, ½ cup cooked CORN kernels, ¼ cup chopped GREEN BELL PEPPER, ¼ cup chopped TOMATO, ¼ cup chopped scallions, 1 tablespoon Dijon mustard, and 1 teaspoon red wine vinegar in a medium bowl. Halve 4 submarine rolls. Spread ¼ of the cabbage mixture on half of the rolls. Top each half with 2 slices of roast beef or turkey breast. Cover with tops of the rolls.

SALMON-VEGETABLE SALAD SANDWICHES: Cut 4 crusty rolls in half and remove the soft inside dough. Sprinkle each of the rolls with ½ teaspoon each of vinegar and olive oil. Crumble the insides of the rolls and add to a medium bowl with 1 cup chopped ripe TOMATOES, 1 cup seeded chopped GREEN BELL PEPPER, ½ cup sliced radishes, ½ cup minced onion, ½ cup chopped cucumber, 2 cloves garlic, minced, ½ cup canned salmon, drained and flaked, 1 teaspoon dried basil leaves, ½ teaspoon black pepper, 2 hard-boiled egg whites, chopped, 1½ tablespoons red wine vinegar and 3 tablespoons mild, light-flavored olive oil. Toss the salmon mixture and place ¼ of it on 4 roll halves. Cover with tops of the rolls and press closed.

ROAST BEEF AND ORANGE SANDWICHES: Spread 4 crusty sandwich rolls with reduced-calorie mayonnaise. Arrange ¾ pound rare lean roast beef on rolls. Sprinkle with black pepper. Top with sections from 2 ORANGES, peeled, and ¼ pound fresh SPINACH leaves. Top with thin slices of red onion. Cover with tops of the rolls. (You can substitute turkey breast for the roast beef.)

CHICKEN, AVOCADO, AND SPINACHWICHES: Spread sunflower or rye bread with reduced-calorie mayonnaise. Sprinkle with curry powder. Top with slices of peeled AVOCADO, cooked chicken breast, fresh SPINACH leaves, and a piece of bread.

TURKEY, COTTAGE CHEESE, AND PINEAPPLE SPECIALS: Combine ¾ cup nonfat or low-fat cottage cheese and ½ teaspoon poppy seeds. Spread on toasted whole-grain bread. Top with a slice of PINEAPPLE, a slice of turkey, and another slice of toasted whole-wheat bread.

GREEK SALAD SANDWICHES: Combine 1 clove garlic, minced, ½ cup mild, light-flavored olive oil, 2 tablespoons red wine vinegar, 1 teaspoon dried oregano leaves, ½ cup chopped cucumber, 1 small onion, minced, 1 GREEN BELL PEPPER, seeded and chopped, 1 TOMATO, chopped, 8 chopped black olives, 3 ounces crumbled feta cheese in a bowl. Top slices of hearty whole-grain bread with ROMAINE lettuce leaves. Top with Greek salad and another piece of bread.

PEANUT BUTTER PLUS SANDWICHES: Spread oatmeal bread with natural peanut butter and top with sliced PEARS.

LUNCHTIME SHISH KABOBS: Thread chunks of nonfat or low-fat cheese, cooked chicken or lean beef, PINEAPPLE chunks, cherry TOMATOES, and GREEN BELL PEPPER pieces on skewers.

VEGETABLE TORTILLAS: Heat 1 tablespoon mild, light-flavored olive oil in a skillet over medium heat. Sauté 1 small zucchini, diced, 6 mushrooms sliced, 1 TOMATO diced, and 1 GREEN BELL PEPPER, seeded and diced until vegetables are soft. Stir in ½ cup blanched BROCCOLI florets, ½ cup canned CORN kernels, 1 teaspoon ground cumin, and 1½ cups shredded nonfat or low-fat cheese. When cheese has melted, remove skillet from heat. Serve with warm tortillas and Tomato Salsa (page 272).

STRAWBERRY-NECTARINE RICOTTA PIZZA: Bake a ready-made 12- or 14-inch pizza crust according to directions on the package. Brush with olive oil and top with 3 NECTARINES, peeled, thinly sliced, and tossed with 1 tablespoon lemon juice, 1 KIWI, peeled and thinly sliced, 1 pint STRAWBERRIES, hulled and thinly sliced, ¼ pound nonfat or low-fat ricotta cheese, and ½ cup chopped walnuts.

AT YOUR LEISURE

GRILLED CHICKEN CITRUS SANDWICHES

A pita pocket stuffed with grilled chicken, orange slices, and chicory offers a convenient way to get an additional serving of citrus and dark leafy greens.

YIELD: *4 servings*
PREPARATION TIME: *15 minutes + 1 hour marinating time*
COOKING TIME: *15 minutes*

1 tablespoon lime juice
4 tablespoons mild, light-flavored olive oil
1 teaspoon ground cumin
1 teaspoon chili powder
2 whole boneless, skinless chicken breasts, cut in half
   and pounded ¼-inch thick
4 whole-wheat pita pockets
1 medium red onion, peeled and sliced paper thin
2 large seedless oranges, peeled and each cut into
   4 slices
Half a small head of chicory, cut up.

1. Combine the lime juice, 2 tablespoons of olive oil, cumin, and chili powder. Place chicken in a bowl and pour the lime juice-olive oil marinade over it. Cover and marinate in the refrigerator for 1 hour.
2. Remove chicken and heat the 2 remaining tablespoons olive oil in a skillet over medium heat. Sauté chicken until lightly browned, about 7 minutes on each side.
3. Fill the pitas with red onion, orange slices, and chicory. Put 1 piece of grilled chicken in each pita.

RATATOUILLE HEROES

This robust Mediterranean sandwich makes a great supper when served with a mixed green salad and fruit dessert.

YIELD: *4 sandwiches*
PREPARATION TIME: *20 minutes*
COOKING TIME: *35 minutes*

1/3 cup mild, light-flavored olive oil
1/2 pound mushrooms, rinsed, dried, and sliced
1 large onion, diced
2 cloves garlic, minced
1 teaspoon dried oregano leaves
1 teaspoon dried basil leaves
1 teaspoon dried thyme leaves
1 medium eggplant, diced
3 cups chopped fresh or canned tomatoes
1 yellow squash, diced
1 green bell pepper, seeded and diced
1/2 teaspoon black pepper
4 crusty Italian or French rolls, halved horizontally
3/4 cup grated Parmesan cheese

1. Heat olive oil in a skillet over medium heat. Sauté mushrooms, onion, garlic, oregano, basil, and thyme for 5 minutes or until onion is soft.
2. Add the eggplant and the tomatoes. Cook over high heat for 3 minutes. Reduce heat and simmer for 15 minutes.
3. Preheat oven to 350 degrees. Add yellow squash, green pepper, and black pepper to eggplant mixture. Simmer for 10 more minutes.
4. Lightly toast rolls in oven on a baking sheet covered with aluminum foil. Remove rolls from oven. Leave 4 halves on the baking sheet and set aside the other 4 halves.
5. Top the 4 halves on the baking sheet with the ratatouille. Sprinkle with Parmesan cheese. Return baking sheet to oven for 8 minutes. Remove, top with remaining roll halves, and serve.

OPEN-FACED TURKEY APPLE MELTS

Apples are a surprise ingredient in this Dijon-accented hot turkey sandwich.

YIELD: *6 servings*
PREPARATION TIME: *10 minutes*
COOKING TIME: *5 minutes*

6 slices whole-grain bread
Dijon mustard
6 slices roast or smoked turkey
4 medium apples, cored and cut into 1/8-inch-thick slices
6 slices nonfat or low-fat cheddar cheese

1. Preheat oven broiler.
2. Spread bread with mustard. Top with turkey slices.
3. Place 3 apple slices on each sandwich. Top with a slice of cheese.
4. Broil until cheese melts and browns slightly. Serve at once.

VEGGIE-FISH SANDWICHES

Broiled fish fillets are topped with cabbage, radishes, and scallions in a yogurt sauce. Serve with Fruit Salad Shakes (page 98).

YIELD: *4 servings*
PREPARATION TIME: *15 minutes*
COOKING TIME: *8 minutes*

2 cups thinly sliced green cabbage
4 tablespoons chopped radishes
2 tablespoons nonfat or low-fat plain yogurt
1 tablespoon reduced-calorie mayonnaise
2 tablespoons chopped scallions
4 4-ounce fish fillets
1 teaspoon paprika
1 clove garlic, minced
1/4 teaspoon black pepper
4 large crusty whole-wheat rolls, halved

1. Preheat oven broiler. Combine cabbage, radishes, yogurt, mayonnaise, and scallions in a medium bowl and set aside.

2. Sprinkle fish fillets with paprika, garlic, and black pepper.

3. Broil fish for 4 minutes. Turn and continue broiling until fish flakes when fork-tested.

4. Place ¼ of cabbage mixture and 1 broiled fish fillet on each roll.

Drinks

EASY ACCESS: THE BASICS

Frozen Yogurt Fruit Soda   Fruit Milk Shake   Fruit Yogurt Shake

QUICK TAKES

Tangerine-Kiwi Chiller   Apple-Blueberry-Banana Shake
Fruit Salad Shake   Banana-Raspberry Shake   Veggie Cocktail
Cranberry-Cantaloupe Cooler   Banana-Papaya Shake
Watermelon Fizz   Watermelon-Raspberry Drink   Citrus Shake
Four Fruit Shake   Papaya-Banana Shake   Strawberry-Banana Drink
Strawberry-Pear Frosty   Strawberry-Papaya Drink
Carrot-Pineapple Drink   Mango-Orange Shake   Fresh Tomato Juice
Pineapple-Strawberry Party Punch   Gazpacho Cooler   Russian Fruit Tea

Drinks based on fruits and vegetables make great snacks, add flavor when served with meals, and can even be used to stand in for dessert.

The following recipes take full advantage of both seasonal fruits and vegetables, such as strawberries and fresh tomatoes, and more frequently available choices, such as pineapple, bananas, and oranges. Whenever possible use the best-tasting ripe fruits and vegetables and chill them before incorporating in a drink recipe. To keep a drink chilled while it is being served, pour it into a pitcher and set the pitcher in a larger bowl filled with ice.

Freeze extra fruit that is on the verge of overripening for use in frozen drinks.

Frozen fruit drinks can be placed in the freezer for thirty minutes before serving. If you store them in the freezer for any longer, they will become quite icy.

Fruit can also be frozen in cubes and used as a garnish for fruit juices and other beverages. Freeze whole strawberries, raspberries, or cherries with stems in ice-cube trays using part of a fruit drink mixture or fruit juice. If you're preparing a fruit drink to serve from a punch bowl, you can use muffin tins for ice-cube trays. These "jumbo" cubes won't melt as quickly as regular-sized ones.

For pure-fruit ice cubes, purée 3 cups of sliced pears, nectarines, plums, or peaches and 1 tablespoon of lemon juice in the workbowl of a food processor or in a blender. Pour into an ice-cube tray and freeze. Serve with sparkling mineral water, seltzer, or fruit drinks.

Tomato juice can be frozen in ice-cube trays. Serve the cubes with chilled vegetable drinks.

EASY ACCESS: THE BASICS

FROZEN YOGURT FRUIT SODA

(4 servings)

INGREDIENTS
1½ cups diced fruit (see possibilities below)
2½ cups fruit juice (see possibilities below)
4 scoops nonfat or low-fat fruit-flavored frozen yogurt

1. Divide the fruit into 4 tall glasses.

2. Pour the fruit juices into a pitcher and stir.

3. Pour the juice over the fruit in the glasses.

4. Top each glass with a scoop of frozen yogurt and serve immediately.

FRUIT AND JUICE POSSIBILITIES

Diced navel orange and pineapple chunks with pineapple and grapefruit juices. Yogurt flavor: Peach.

Diced apricots and mangoes with orange and papaya juices.
Yogurt flavor: Pineapple.

Blueberries and watermelon balls with orange and grape juices.
Yogurt flavor: Blueberry.

Strawberries and sliced nectarines with apple juice and peach nectar.
Yogurt flavor: Strawberry.

FRUIT MILK SHAKE

(4 servings)

INGREDIENTS
2 cups diced fresh, frozen, or canned fruit (see
possibilities below)
2 cups skim or low-fat milk
2 tablespoons honey
12 ice cubes, cracked

1. Place fruit, milk, and honey in the workbowl of a food processor or in a blender and purée.

2. Add ice gradually and blend until smooth.

FRUIT POSSIBILITIES

Apples and apricots
Pears and blackberries
Nectarines and blueberries
Strawberries and cantaloupe
Bananas and honeydew

FRUIT YOGURT SHAKE

(2 servings)

INGREDIENTS
1 cup cracked ice
1 cup nonfat or low-fat yogurt
2½ cups sliced fruit (see possibilities below)

Place ice, yogurt, and fruit in the workbowl of a food processor or in a blender and process until smooth.

FRUIT POSSIBILITIES
Strawberries and kiwis
Nectarines and raspberries
Pineapple and banana
Papaya and orange
Apples and cranberries
Cantaloupe and mango

QUICK TAKES

TANGERINE-KIWI CHILLER: Place 2 large TANGERINES, peeled, seeded, and separated into sections, 2 KIWIS, peeled and sliced, 2 BANANAS, peeled and cut into 1-inch slices, and 1 cup orange juice in a blender and purée.

APPLE-BLUEBERRY-BANANA SHAKE: Place 2 cups apple juice, ½ cup unsweetened frozen BLUEBERRIES, thawed, 1 large BANANA, cut into 1-inch slices, and 1 cup nonfat or low-fat plain yogurt in a blender and purée.

FRUIT SALAD SHAKE: Place 3 BANANAS, peeled and cut into 1-inch slices, 3 APPLES, cored and cut into chunks, 3 PEARS, cored and cut into chunks, 3 cups orange juice, and 6 tablespoons raisins in a blender or the workbowl of a food processor and process until smooth. Pour into glasses and serve immediately.

BANANA-RASPBERRY SHAKE: Place 2 cups frozen RASPBERRIES, thawed, 2 ripe BANANAS, peeled and cut into 1-inch slices, 4 cups skim or low-fat milk, and ¼ teaspoon vanilla extract in a blender or the workbowl of a food processor and process until smooth.

VEGGIE COCKTAIL: Place 2 celery stalks with leaves, 1 cup fresh or frozen GREEN PEAS, 2 CARROTS, scrubbed and chopped, 2 cups water, ¼ teaspoon black pepper, ¼ teaspoon dried dillweed, and 2 cups nonfat or low-fat plain yogurt in a blender or the workbowl of a food processor. Purée.

CRANBERRY-CANTALOUPE COOLER: Place 2 cups CANTALOUPE chunks, ½ cup orange juice, ¼ cup fresh CRANBERRIES, ¼ cup cranberry juice, 3 tablespoons honey, and ½ cup nonfat or low-fat plain yogurt in the workbowl of a food processor and blend for 30 seconds until smooth. Pour into glasses and serve immediately.

BANANA-PAPAYA SHAKE: Place 1 cup mashed PAPAYA, 2 cups water and 2 tablespoons lemon juice in a blender. Purée. Add 3 medium ripe BANANAS, sliced, and continue to purée until smooth.

WATERMELON FIZZ: Place 2 cups cubed seeded WATERMELON in a blender and purée. Strain into a pitcher, discarding the pulp. Repeat with 2 more cups cubed seeded watermelon. Add 3 teaspoons lemon juice to the watermelon juice in the pitcher. Pour the watermelon-lemon juice into 4 glasses. Add ½ cup low-sodium sparkling mineral water or seltzer and 5 ice cubes to each glass.

WATERMELON-RASPBERRY DRINK: Place 1 cup seeded WATERMELON chunks, 1 cup fresh RASPBERRIES, 8 STRAWBERRIES, and ½ cup orange juice in a blender and purée.

CITRUS SHAKE: Place 2 seedless ORANGES, peeled and separated into sections, 2 TANGERINES, peeled, separated into sections, and seeded, 1½ cups skim or low-fat milk, and 1 tablespoon brown sugar in a blender and purée. Pour into 4 tall glasses.

FOUR FRUIT SHAKE: Place 1 cup apple juice, 1 APPLE, peeled, cored, and sliced, 6 STRAWBERRIES, 1 BANANA, and ½ PAPAYA peeled and seeded, in a blender and purée.

PAPAYA-BANANA SHAKE: Place 1 cup orange juice, 1 PAPAYA, peeled, seeded, and sliced, and 1 BANANA in a blender and purée.

STRAWBERRY-BANANA DRINK: Combine 1 cup fresh apple juice, 8 medium STRAWBERRIES, and 1 medium BANANA in the workbowl of a food processor or in a blender. Blend until smooth.

STRAWBERRY-PEAR FROSTY: Place 2 cups frozen STRAWBERRIES, 1 large PEAR, cored and chopped, and 12 ice cubes, cracked, in a blender. Repeat with 2 more cups Strawberries, another pear, and 12 more ice cubes. Pour into chilled glasses.

STRAWBERRY-PAPAYA DRINK: Combine 1 cup pineapple juice, 1 small ripe PAPAYA, seeded, peeled, and sliced, 8 STRAWBERRIES, and 1 BANANA in a blender. Purée.

CARROT-PINEAPPLE DRINK: Place 2 cups pineapple juice, 1 cup diced raw CARROT, 2 tablespoons lemon juice and ¼ teaspoon dried basil leaves in a blender or the workbowl of a food processor. Process until smooth.

MANGO-ORANGE SHAKE: Place 1 cup orange juice, 2 cups cubed MANGO, and 1 frozen BANANA in a blender and purée.

FRESH TOMATO JUICE: Place 1 quart peeled ripe TOMATOES, cut in quarters, ¼ cup chopped fresh parsley, 1 scallion, chopped, and ¼ teaspoon black pepper in a blender and process until smooth. Chill before serving.

PINEAPPLE-STRAWBERRY PARTY PUNCH: Purée 2 pints STRAWBERRIES, hulled, 4 peaches, sliced, and 2 6-ounce cans frozen pineapple juice concentrate in a blender. Gradually add 24 cracked ice cubes and blend until smooth. Pour blended fruit mixture into a punch bowl. Add 4 cups low-sodium sparkling mineral water or seltzer and garnish with sliced strawberries. Ladle into glasses.

GAZPACHO COOLER: Place 3 cups low-sodium tomato juice, chilled, 1 cup chopped fresh or canned TOMATO, 2 tablespoons chopped celery, 2 tablespoons chopped cucumber, 2 tablespoons lemon juice, 2 tablespoons chopped onion, 2 tablespoons chopped GREEN BELL PEPPER, 2 tablespoons chopped RED BELL PEPPER, 2 tablespoons chopped fresh parsley, and 2 cloves garlic, minced, in the workbowl of a food processor or in a blender and process until smooth. Serve in short glasses and garnish with slices of lime. Pass hot pepper sauce.

RUSSIAN FRUIT TEA: To make one serving, pour ⅔ cup hot brewed herbal tea into a teacup. Stir in 1 teaspoon honey, and 1 APPLE, cored and finely diced. Let tea stand for several minutes. Eat fruit with a spoon and sip the tea. Try mixing and matching peaches, grapes, pears, or oranges with your favorite herbal tea flavors.

Appetizers

EASY ACCESS: THE BASICS
Basic Yogurt Dip for Vegetables and Fruit   Fresh Vegetable Dip   Fruit Dip
Baked Vegetable Egg Rolls   Fruit Kabobs

QUICK TAKES
Apple Antipasto   Apple Canapés   Maple-Pineapple-Mango Bites
Raisin-Fruit Canapés   Spiced Pineapple   Gingered Oranges
Papaya Guacamole   Marinated Vegetables   Stuffed Avocados
Spinach Pesto–Stuffed Celery   Citrus Vegetable Guacamole Dip
Carrot Dip   Curried Apple Dip with Fall Fruit Platter   Tomato Bruschetta
Vegetable Nachos

EASY ACCESS: THE BASICS

BASIC YOGURT DIP FOR VEGETABLES AND FRUITS

INGREDIENTS
1 cup nonfat or low-fat plain yogurt
2 teaspoons lemon juice
1 Easy Access Dip Add-On (see possibilities below)
Vegetables or fruit dippers (see possibilities below)

1. Blend yogurt, lemon juice, and your choice of Easy Access Add-On.
2. Use as a dip for your choice of fruits and vegetables in.

EASY ACCESS DIP ADD-ON POSSIBILITIES

2 teaspoons Dijon mustard
$1/2$ teaspoon curry powder
$1/2$ teaspoon dried basil leaves
1 teaspoon crushed sesame seeds
$1/2$ teaspoon finely minced garlic
$1/2$ teaspoon paprika
$1/2$ teaspoon ground ginger

VEGETABLE DIPPER POSSIBILITIES

When serving raw vegetable dippers, wash vegetables thoroughly, then dry them and chill overnight wrapped in damp paper towels inside sealed plastic bags. The following vegetables can be served raw:
Strips of green bell pepper
red bell pepper
yellow bell pepper
zucchini and yellow summer squash rounds, sticks, and spears
broccoli and cauliflower florets
celery stalks
carrot sticks
romaine or spinach leaves
snow peas
cherry tomatoes
green, pole, or wax beans, whole or cut into 3-inch lengths

Belgian endive spears
fennel sticks
scallions
jicama rounds or sticks
kohlrabi rounds or sticks
mushroom caps or halves
sweet onion rings or strips
Vidalia onion rings or strips
red or white radishes, whole or cut into sticks or rounds
sugar snap peas
and canned water chestnut slices

When serving blanched vegetables for dippers, prepare by adding them to a large pot of boiling water and cooking only until they are barely crisp-tender. Remove at once with a slotted spoon to chill in a bowl of ice water. Drain well before serving. The following vegetables can be served blanched:
Asparagus
green, pole, or wax beans, whole or cut into 3-inch lengths
broccoli florets
Brussels sprouts
carrot sticks
cauliflower florets
scallions
kohlrabi rounds or sticks
yellow onion rings or strips
rutabaga sticks
snow peas
and sugar snap peas

When serving new potatoes as dippers, boil them in a saucepan in enough water to cover for about 20 minutes or until just tender. Drain, cool, and slice into ¼-inch rounds.

FRUIT DIPPER POSSIBILITIES

Core large red apples and pears and cut crosswise into thick slices. Dip the slices in lemon juice and cut into bite-size wedges
Peel, separate into sections, and seed oranges, tangerines, and grapefruit
Cut bananas, cantaloupes, honeydews, nectarines, peaches, mangoes, papayas, and pineapples into wedges or chunks
Hull strawberries. Place large berries and grapes on wooden picks

FRESH VEGETABLE DIP

INGREDIENTS
1 cup steamed chopped fresh vegetables, well drained
(see possibilities below)
4 tablespoons minced onion
1 tablespoon minced horseradish
¼ cup reduced-calorie mayonnaise
1½ cups nonfat or low-fat plain yogurt
½ teaspoon hot pepper sauce
4 cups fresh vegetable chunks or strips (see possibilities below)

1. Combine the steamed chopped vegetables, onion, horseradish, mayonnaise, yogurt, and pepper sauce in a medium bowl.

2. Serve at once or refrigerate, covered, for several hours.

3. Place dip in the center of a large platter and surround with vegetables for dipping.

CHOPPED VEGETABLE POSSIBILITIES
Spinach, broccoli, cauliflower
Green or red bell peppers
Eggplant
Green beans
Zucchini
Yellow summer squash

VEGETABLE DIPPER POSSIBILITIES
Broccoli and cauliflower florets
Bell pepper strips
Zucchini or yellow squash strips
Carrots
Celery
Whole steamed green beans
Cherry tomatoes
Asparagus spears

FRUIT DIP

INGREDIENTS
¾ cup crushed fruit or berries (see possibilities below)
½ cup finely chopped walnuts
½ cup brown sugar
1½ cups nonfat or low-fat cream cheese, softened
1¾ cups nonfat or low-fat plain yogurt
4 cups fruit dippers (see possibilities below)

1. Combine crushed fruit, chopped walnuts, and brown sugar in a medium bowl.
2. Blend softened cream cheese and low-fat yogurt until smooth.
3. Add cream cheese mixture to fruit mixture in bowl and stir until combined.
4. Cover and chill until ready to serve.
5. Place the bowl in the center of a large platter and serve surrounded by the whole fruit.

CRUSHED FRUIT POSSIBILITIES

Strawberries
Blueberries
Bananas
Pineapple
Apples
Apricots
Nectarines
Peaches
Pears

FRUIT DIPPER POSSIBILITIES

Strawberries
Banana chunks
Pineapple chunks
Apple slices
Apricot halves
Nectarine slices
Peach slices
Mango chunks
Papaya chunks
Pear slices
Orange segments

BAKED VEGETABLE EGG ROLLS

(8 rolls)

INGREDIENTS
3 to 4 tablespoons mild, light-flavored olive oil
3 scallions, minced
1 slice fresh gingerroot, minced
1 clove garlic, minced
4 cups minced steamed vegetables and/or cooked meat,
    poultry or seafood (see possibilities below)
1 tablespoon light soy sauce
8 7-inch chilled egg roll skins

SAUCE
¼ cup light soy sauce
1 tablespoon Dijon mustard
½ teaspoon sugar
1 teaspoon rice vinegar
1 teaspoon minced scallion

1. Heat 3 tablespoons of the olive oil in a large skillet or wok over medium heat. Add scallions, gingerroot, and garlic and stir-fry for 30 seconds.

2. Add vegetables and/or cooked meat, poultry, or seafood and soy sauce. Stir to blend flavors and heat through.

3. Transfer to a colander to drain as dry as possible.

4. Chill drained filling for at least 30 minutes.

5. After filling is chilled, prepare egg rolls. Lay 1 chilled egg roll skin out on the counter with one point toward you. Put about ¼ cup of filling across the middle of the egg roll skin. Fold bottom point of skin over filling. Tuck bottom point under filling. Fold side corners over, forming an envelope shape. Roll up egg roll toward remaining corner. Moisten point with water and press firmly to seal. Make egg rolls with remaining skins and filling in same manner.

6. Brush egg rolls with remaining oil. Set rolls on a baking sheet and bake until burnished, about 7 minutes on each side.

7. To make the sauce, combine soy sauce, mustard, sugar, vinegar, and scallion.

8. Serve egg rolls with the dipping sauce.

NOTE: The amount of filling needed to fill 8 egg rolls will fill 36 wonton wrappers. Egg roll skins and wonton wrappers—squares of noodle dough—may be found at many supermarkets and at Oriental grocery stores.

VEGETABLE AND/OR COOKED MEAT, POULTRY, OR SEAFOOD POSSIBILITIES

Broccoli; water chestnuts; red bell pepper; chicken
Asparagus; bamboo shoots; mushrooms; shrimp
Spinach; bean sprouts; yellow summer squash; pork
Green beans; celery; carrots; scallops

FRUIT KABOBS

(4 servings, 2 skewers each)

INGREDIENTS
KABOBS
5 cups 1-inch fruit chunks (see possibilities below)
¼ cup lemon juice
8 large whole strawberries, hulled
8 small skewers

SAUCE
1 cup nonfat or low-fat plain yogurt
3 tablespoons natural peanut butter
¼ cup orange juice
1 teaspoon honey
1½ teaspoons grated fresh gingerroot

1. Place fruit chunks in a medium bowl. Sprinkle with lemon juice to prevent discoloration.
2. Thread skewers by placing a strawberry at the top of each one. Then alternate the threading of the other fruit chunks.
3. Arrange skewers on a tray or dish.
4. To make the sauce, combine yogurt, peanut butter, orange juice, honey, and ginger in the workbowl of a food processor or in a blender and process until smooth.
5. Serve skewers immediately with dipping sauce.

FRUIT POSSIBILITIES

Red apples; bananas; pineapple
Yellow apples; cantaloupe; nectarines
Pears; honeydew; apricots
Mango; banana; papaya

QUICK TAKES

APPLE ANTIPASTO: Arrange thin unpeeled slices of red and green APPLES, strips of GREEN BELL PEPPERS, sardines, black olives, stuffed olives, pickled onions, chunks of canned white albacore tuna, celery sticks, TOMATO wedges, and a mound of coleslaw attractively on a large platter. Surround with thin slices of whole-grain bread and accompany with cruets of wine vinegar and extra-virgin olive oil.

APPLE CANAPÉS: Use APPLES, cut crosswise into ¼-inch-thick slices, as a canapé base for cheese spreads.

MAPLE-PINEAPPLE-MANGO BITES: Serve PINEAPPLE and MANGO chunks, with forks, for dipping into a cup of reduced-calorie maple syrup.

RAISIN-FRUIT CANAPÉS: Cut raisin bread or raisin brown bread into small squares. Spread with nonfat or low-fat cream cheese and top with sliced STRAWBERRIES, thin APPLE slices, MANDARIN ORANGE sections, and halved grapes. Garnish with sliced almonds or chopped walnuts.

SPICED PINEAPPLE: Peel a small PINEAPPLE, quarter it lengthwise, and remove core. Cut pineapple quarter in half and slice into ¼-inch slices. Toss with ¼ teaspoon each of cinnamon, ginger, cloves, and allspice. Cover and refrigerate for 1 hour. Serve with toothpicks.

GINGERED ORANGES: Peel 4 seedless ORANGES and cut them into chunks. Place on a broiler pan. Sprinkle with 4 teaspoons brown sugar and 1 teaspoon ground ginger. Broil 5 minutes. Spoon oranges into a serving bowl and serve warm with toothpicks.

PAPAYA GUACAMOLE: Combine 2 AVOCADOS, peeled and diced, 1 PAPAYA, peeled, halved, seeded, and diced, 1 large TOMATO, diced, 1 red onion, diced, 2 cloves garlic, minced, 1 jalapeño pepper, seeded and minced, ¼ cup lime juice, 1 tablespoon ground cumin, and ½ teaspoon white pepper in the workbowl of a food processor or in a blender and process into a chunky paste.

MARINATED VEGETABLES: Place 4 cups whole fresh mushrooms, 2 cups CAULIFLOWER florets, and 3 CARROTS, cut into sticks, in a marinade of ⅓ cup red wine vinegar, ¼ cup extra-virgin olive oil, 2 tablespoons lemon juice, and 1 teaspoon sugar. Marinate at room temperature for 1 hour. Remove from the marinade with a slotted spoon. Line a serving platter with salad greens and arrange the vegetables on the greens.

STUFFED AVOCADOS: Fill pitted AVOCADO halves with a mixture of 12 ounces canned or fresh crab meat, 1½ cups diced unpeeled red

APPLES, ½ cup slivered toasted almonds, and ½ cup reduced-calorie mayonnaise, *or* a mixture of 6 ounces fresh or canned crab meat, ¼ teaspoon chili powder, 1 tablespoon virgin olive oil, 2 tablespoons lemon juice, ¼ pound chopped cooked ASPARAGUS, and ¼ cup chopped celery.

SPINACH PESTO–STUFFED CELERY: Combine 2 cups chopped fresh SPIN-ACH, 2 cloves garlic, ½ cup grated Parmesan cheese, ¼ cup chopped walnuts, and ¼ cup mild, light-flavored olive oil in the workbowl of a food processor or in a blender. Process until smooth. Stuff 8 celery stalks with the SPINACH pesto. Cut stalks into 3-inch pieces. Use leftover pesto to make a dip by mixing 4 tablespoons of it with ½ cup low-fat yogurt, 1 tablespoon grated Parmesan cheese, and ¼ teaspoon black pepper.

CITRUS VEGETABLE GUACAMOLE DIP: Cut 2 ripe AVOCADOS in half lengthwise. Remove pits and carefully scoop out pulp. Mash avocados with fork in a medium glass bowl. Put the juice of 2 medium oranges, the juice of 1 lemon, 1 tablespoon chopped scallion, and 1 tablespoon chopped parsley in the workbowl of a food processor or in a blender and process until liquefied. Add juice mixture to mashed avocados in bowl and mix. Add ¼ head red CABBAGE, coarsely chopped, 1 cup CAULIFLOWER florets, chopped, ½ cup chopped GREEN BELL PEP-PER, 2 large ripe TOMATOES, coarsely chopped, ½ teaspoon dried basil leaves, and ½ teaspoon dried thyme leaves to bowl and stir well. If refrigerating, place the pit from the avocado in the mixture and cover bowl with plastic wrap. (The pit will keep the mixture from turning brown.) Remove pit before serving. Garnish with cherry to-mato slices, ORANGE wedges, fresh parsley, or a dollop of nonfat or low-fat plain yogurt.

CARROT DIP: Boil CARROTS in a large pot of boiling water for 10–12 minutes or until very soft. Drain carrots and put in workbowl of a food processor or in a blender with 2 teaspoons paprika, 2 chopped cloves garlic, ½ teaspoon ground ginger, 1 tablespoon ground cumin, ¼ teaspoon black pepper, 3 tablespoons red wine vinegar, and 4 tablespoons mild, light-flavored olive oil. Purée. Serve garnished with black olives. Use BELL PEPPER strips for dippers.

CURRIED APPLE DIP WITH FALL FRUIT PLATTER: Combine 2 large red APPLES, peeled and sliced, ½ cup water, and 4 teaspoons lemon juice in a medium saucepan. Bring to a boil, reduce the heat, cover, and simmer for about 30 minutes or until the apples are tender. Mash apples, leaving some large chunks. Combine apples with ¼ cup honey, ¼ cup seedless raisins, and ½ teaspoon curry powder in a bowl. Mix well, cover, and chill for 1 hour. When ready to serve, mound 2 cups grapes in the center of a platter. Arrange alternating slices of 2 KIWIS, 2 BANANAS, 2 PEARS, 2 red APPLES and 1 green APPLE, cored and sliced, in a circle around the grapes. Sprinkle fruit with lemon juice and serve with curried dip.

TOMATO BRUSCHETTA: Preheat oven to 450 degrees. Cut 2 10-ounce loaves of Italian bread in half lengthwise; then cut crosswise into thirds. Combine 3 tablespoons chopped fresh parsley leaves, ⅓ cup olive oil, and 2 cloves garlic, finely minced, in a small bowl until well blended. Spread olive oil mixture over cut sides of bread. Spread ½ cup grated Parmesan cheese on waxed paper. Dip the oiled side of the bread slices in the cheese and shake off excess. Place bread slices in a shallow pan and bake for 5 minutes or until lightly browned. Combine 3½ cups diced ripe TOMATOES, 1 teaspoon dried basil leaves, and ½ teaspoon black pepper in a medium saucepan. Stir over medium heat for 4 minutes. Place bread on a platter and spoon tomato sauce over it.

VEGETABLE NACHOS: Place 4–6 cups drained cooked kidney or pinto beans in the workbowl of a food processor or in a blender and mash. Heat 1 tablespoon mild, light-flavored olive oil in a medium saucepan over medium heat. Mix in mashed beans and cook until the beans have absorbed the oil. Place ¾ cup fresh or canned TOMATOES, coarsely chopped and drained, 2 tablespoons tomato paste, 1 table-spoon finely grated onion, ¼ teaspoon black pepper, and 1 clove garlic, minced, in a second saucepan and bring to a boil. Simmer gently for 10 minutes. Preheat oven to 350 degrees. Add tomato sauce to beans in saucepan and simmer for 30 minutes. Spread 20 ounces low-sodium tortilla chips on a heatproof platter. Spread bean mixture over chips and top with 2 cups grated nonfat or low-fat cheese. Heat in oven for 15 minutes or until cheese is melted. Remove from oven and sprinkle with 1 cup thinly sliced broccoli florets, 1 cup thinly sliced CAULIFLOWER florets, 1 cup thinly sliced onions, 1 cup thinly sliced GREEN BELL PEPPER, 2 TOMATOES, thinly sliced, 2 AVOCA-DOS, thinly sliced, and 1 cup green olives, rinsed and thinly sliced.

Soups

EASY ACCESS: THE BASICS

Basic Multi-Vegetable Soup   Simple Puréed Soup
You-Choose-the-Vegetables Minestrone   Basic Cold Fruit Soup

QUICK TAKES

Hot Soups

Apple Cider-Squash Soup   Curried Apple-Turnip Soup
Butternut Fruit Bisque   Cabbage-Tomato Soup   Green Pea Soup
Orange, Carrot, and Tomato Soup   Pumpkin-Chicken Soup
Sweet Potato-Tomato Soup   Tomato Corn Soup
Quick Chicken-Vegetable Soup   Pure Vegetable Puréed Soup
Leftovers Soup   Asparagus-Lemon Soup   Spinach Soup

Cold Soups

Avocado-Tomato Soup   Blueberry Soup   Mango Bisque
Pear-Apple Soup   Strawberry Yogurt Soup   Cold Pea Soup
Cold Tomato Soup   Simple Blender Gazpacho for Two
Chunky Gazpacho for Four   Cold Vegetable Bisque
Curried Fruit and Vegetable Soup   Fruit Salad Soup   Very Berry Soup
Spicy Melon Soup

Hot Soups

Basic Vegetable Stock Base   Basic Chicken Broth   Eggplant Soup
Brussels Sprouts Soup   Broccoli-Potato Soup
Red Pepper and Pear Soup   Corn Chowder   Scallop-Vegetable Bisque
Vegetable Crab Soup

Cold Soups

Cold Cream of Pepper Soup   Fruit Gazpacho   Fruit Fantasy Soup

Soup tastes best when served at just the right temperature. To keep soup hot or cold, serve it in heated or chilled soup bowls. To heat bowls, run hot water over them for a few minutes. For family suppers or informal gatherings, serve soups that don't require a spoon in large mugs.

Chilled soups are the perfect choice for an invigorating and attractive appetizer or main dish on a steamy day when the thermometer is soaring sky high. Any of the colorful and cooling soups that follow can be an ideal solution for a hot-weather brunch, lunch, or dinner when served with sandwiches or salads. The excellence of cold soups depends on your using fresh ingredients of the highest quality available. Since chilling can mute seasonings, check flavors immediately before serving.

- Garnish soups with chopped fresh herbs, finely chopped raw vegetables, grated cheese, sunflower seeds, nuts, or chopped egg white, blanched pea pods, thin scallion slices, celery leaves, toasted sesame seeds, finely shredded lettuce, spinach or watercress leaves, popcorn, shredded nonfat or low-fat cheddar cheese, ¼ cup chopped fresh parsley with 2 tablespoons chopped lemon peel added, grated Parmesan cheese, finely chopped tomatoes, fresh chives, a dash of paprika, thin apple slices, raisins, scallion curls, sliced almonds, or diced red bell peppers.
- Drop a dollop of nonfat or lowfat yogurt or lowfat sour cream on each serving of a thick soup and gently swirl with a spoon.
- Top soup with homemade croutons. Prepare croutons in advance and store them in an airtight container at room temperature for 1 or 2 days. They can be reheated by placing on a baking sheet in a 350 degree oven for 5 minutes.

Sautéed Croutons

Heat 4 tablespoons mild, light-flavored olive oil in a skillet over medium heat. Sauté 2 cloves garlic, minced, for 1 minute. Stir in 2 cups whole-grain bread cubes. Sauté until lightly browned. Add the herbs and spices of your choice.

Baked Croutons

Toss bread slices in mild, light-flavored olive oil. Cut into cubes. Spread on an ungreased baking sheet and toast in a preheated 400 degree oven until brown and crisp.

EASY ACCESS: THE BASICS

BASIC MULTI-VEGETABLE SOUP

(4–6 servings)

INGREDIENTS

3 tablespoons mild, light-flavored olive oil
1 medium onion, chopped
½ cup chopped celery
1 medium carrot, scrubbed and sliced into ⅛-inch rounds
1 large potato, scrubbed and cut into ½-inch cubes
2 cups diced fresh or canned tomatoes
6 cups low-salt chicken broth
¼ teaspoon black pepper
1 teaspoon dried basil leaves
3 cups chopped, sliced, or diced vegetables (see
    possibilities below)

1. Heat olive oil in a large heavy soup pot over medium heat.
2. Add onion, celery, and carrot. Cook, stirring frequently, until vegetables are tender, about 10 minutes.
3. Add potato, tomatoes, broth, pepper, and basil. Bring to a boil, reduce heat, cover, and simmer for 20 minutes.
4. Add vegetables, cover, and simmer for 15 minutes or until vegetables are tender.

VARIATION

- Add 2 cups diced cooked chicken, turkey, lean pork, lean beef, or fish after vegetables have been simmering for 10 minutes.

VEGETABLE COMBINATION POSSIBILITIES

Cauliflower; green beans; shredded cabbage
Zucchini; green peas; cauliflower
Broccoli; corn; diced turnips
Spinach; red bell pepper; yellow summer squash
Red cabbage; lima beans; corn
Brussels sprouts; yellow wax beans
Green bell pepper; pumpkin; green beans
Sweet potato; cauliflower; zucchini
Eggplant; green bell pepper; corn
Turnips; green beans; peas
Green cabbage; diced turnips; zucchini; corn

SIMPLE PURÉED SOUP

(4 servings)

INGREDIENTS
2 tablespoons mild, light-flavored olive oil
¾ cup chopped onion
½ cup diced celery
1 cup water
2 cups low-salt chicken broth
3 cups diced vegetables (see possibilities below)
2 cups skim or low-fat milk
¼ teaspoon seasoning (see possibilities below)
2 scallions, green part only, thinly sliced, for garnish

1. Heat the olive oil in a heavy soup pot over medium heat. Sauté the onion and celery until tender but not browned, stirring often.
2. Add water, chicken broth, and vegetables. Bring to a boil, reduce heat to medium, and cook until vegetables are tender.
3. Place cooked vegetables and remaining liquid in a blender or in the workbowl of a food processor and purée.
4. Transfer purée to soup pot. Add milk and seasoning. Bring to a boil and turn off heat.
5. Garnish with chopped scallions and serve.

VEGETABLE AND SEASONING POSSIBILITIES

Cauliflower; potato; peas. Seasoning: Curry powder
Sweet potato; apple. Seasoning: Ginger
Turnip; pumpkin. Seasoning: Thyme
Kale. Seasoning: Nutmeg
Cabbage; potato. Seasoning: Caraway seeds
Cauliflower; peas. Seasoning: Curry powder
Winter squash. Seasoning: Nutmeg
Broccoli; turnips; carrots. Seasoning: White pepper
Asparagus. Seasoning: Dry mustard
Brussels sprouts. Seasoning: Nutmeg
Red bell peppers; eggplant; zucchini. Seasoning: Basil
Spinach; mushrooms. Seasoning: Cayenne pepper

YOU-CHOOSE-THE-VEGETABLES MINESTRONE

(4–6 servings)

INGREDIENTS
3 tablespoons mild, light-flavored olive oil
½ cup minced onion
⅓ cup chopped celery
1 clove garlic, chopped
½ teaspoon dried rosemary leaves
4 cups chopped vegetables (see possibilities below)
3 cups chopped fresh or canned tomatoes
3 cups low-salt chicken broth
¼ cup uncooked small pasta
2 tablespoons minced fresh parsley
⅓ cup grated Parmesan cheese

1. Heat olive oil in a heavy soup pot over medium heat. Sauté onion and celery for 10 minutes.
2. Stir in garlic, rosemary, vegetables, and tomatoes. Cook over medium heat for 5 minutes.
3. Add broth. Lower heat and simmer for 20 minutes.
4. Add pasta. Cook 10 more minutes or until tender.
5. Combine parsley and cheese. Pass with minestrone.

VEGETABLE POSSIBILITIES

Carrots; cauliflower; escarole
Broccoli; corn; green beans
Cabbage; zucchini; carrots
Eggplant; green beans; red bell pepper
Brussels sprouts; corn; carrots

BASIC COLD FRUIT SOUP

(5 servings)

INGREDIENTS

4 cups orange juice
1 cup skim or low-fat milk
3 cups nonfat or low-fat plain yogurt
2 tablespoons lemon juice
1 tablespoon honey
1/8 teaspoon ground cinnamon
1/8 teaspoon ground nutmeg
2 1/2 cups fresh, frozen and thawed, or canned fruit (see
     possibilities below)
1/2 teaspoon dried mint leaves

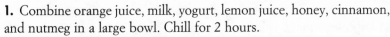

1. Combine orange juice, milk, yogurt, lemon juice, honey, cinnamon, and nutmeg in a large bowl. Chill for 2 hours.
2. Stir fruit into bowl, sprinkle with mint leaves, and serve.

FRUIT POSSIBILITIES

Diced apples and blackberries
Sliced nectarines and blueberries
Sliced apricots and strawberries
Diced cantaloupe and raspberries
Sliced bananas and seeded tangerine chunks

QUICK TAKES: HOT SOUPS

APPLE CIDER-SQUASH SOUP: Heat 4 tablespoons mild, light-flavored olive oil in a heavy soup pot over medium heat. Add 1 large APPLE, peeled, cored, and diced, 1 onion, sliced, and 1 medium zucchini and 1 medium yellow squash, both chopped. Sauté for 10 minutes. Add ½ cup apple cider, ½ teaspoon black pepper and ½ teaspoon ground nutmeg. Simmer, covered, for 15 minutes. Add 4 cups low-salt chicken broth and cook over low heat for 5 minutes. Purée the vegetable-broth mixture in the workbowl of a food processor or in a blender. Transfer to soup pot. Add ½ cup of nonfat or low-fat milk and heat for 5 more minutes. (4 servings)

CURRIED APPLE-TURNIP SOUP: Heat ¼ cup mild, light-flavored olive oil in a large soup pot over medium heat. Add 2 red onions, chopped, and cook for 8 minutes. Add 6½ cups low-salt chicken broth, 2 cups grated peeled APPLE, ¼ cup grated CARROT, ½ cup grated turnip, 2 tablespoons grated celery, ½ teaspoon curry powder, ¼ teaspoon black pepper, ⅛ teaspoon dried thyme leaves, ⅛ teaspoon ground cinnamon, and ⅛ teaspoon ground allspice. Bring to a boil. Lower heat and cover pot. Simmer for 25 minutes. (5–6 servings)

BUTTERNUT FRUIT BISQUE: Heat 3 tablespoons of mild, light-flavored olive oil in a large soup pot over medium heat. Add onion, chopped, and cook for 3 minutes. Stir in 1 large BUTTERNUT SQUASH, peeled, seeded, and cut into 1½-inch chunks; 2 APPLES, cut into chunks; 1 large PEAR, cut into chunks; and 3½ cups low-salt chicken broth. Add ¼ teaspoon dried thyme leaves, ¼ teaspoon black pepper, ⅛ teaspoon dried sage leaves, and ⅛ teaspoon ground nutmeg. Bring to a boil, lower heat, and simmer the mixture, covered, for 20 minutes. Transfer soup in batches to the workbowl of a food processor or to a blender and purée. Return to pot and stir in ¾ cup skim or low-fat milk. Add ⅛ teaspoon white pepper. Reheat, but don't allow to boil. Serve garnished with chopped walnuts. (5–6 servings)

CABBAGE-TOMATO SOUP: Sauté 3 tablespoons mild, light-flavored olive oil in a heavy soup pot. Sauté 1 onion, diced, and 8 cups shredded green CABBAGE. Cook until the cabbage is limp. Sprinkle ½ cup unbleached all-purpose flour over cabbage and mix well. Add 4 cups chopped fresh or canned TOMATOES, 2 cups tomato juice, 1 tablespoon caraway seeds, 2 cups low-salt chicken broth, 2 tablespoons honey, ¼ teaspoon black pepper, and the juice of 1 lemon. Simmer for ½ hour. Serve garnished with nonfat or low-fat sour cream. (6–8 servings)

GREEN PEA SOUP: Heat 2 tablespoons mild, light-flavored olive oil in a heavy soup pot over medium heat. Add 2 stalks celery, chopped, 1 clove garlic, minced, and 1 onion, chopped. Sauté for 5 minutes. Add 2 cups low-salt chicken broth, 3 cups fresh or frozen and thawed GREEN PEAS, and ⅛ teaspoon white pepper. Cover and simmer for 5 minutes. Pour soup into the workbowl of a food processor or a blender. Purée. Return to soup pot. Add ½ cup skim or low-fat milk and ⅛ teaspoon ground nutmeg. Heat and stir for 5 more minutes. (3–4 servings)

ORANGE, CARROT, AND TOMATO SOUP: Sauté 1 large onion, sliced, 3 CARROTS, sliced, and 1 stalk celery, sliced, in 3 tablespoons mild, light-flavored olive oil. Place sautéed vegetables in a blender with ¼ teaspoon black pepper and ¼ cup water and liquefy. In large saucepan add liquefied vegetables to 2½ cups TOMATO purée and ¾ cup orange juice. Heat. Serve garnished with ½ cup chopped fresh parsley. (2 servings)

PUMPKIN-CHICKEN SOUP: Cook 2 cups peeled cubed PUMPKIN in 6 cups low-salt chicken broth for 30 minutes or until tender. Add 2 cups cooked chicken and ½ teaspoon black pepper. Garnish with a dollop of nonfat or low-fat yogurt and serve with warm cornbread. (4 servings)

SWEET POTATO-TOMATO SOUP: Heat ¼ cup mild, light-flavored olive oil in a heavy soup pot over medium heat. Add 2 medium onions, chopped. Cook and stir for 4 minutes. Add 3 SWEET POTATOES, cut into ¾-inch chunks, and 6 cups low-salt chicken broth. Bring to a boil, lower the heat, cover, and simmer for 25 minutes. Stir in 2 TOMATOES, chopped, and ¼ teaspoon white pepper. Transfer soup to the workbowl of a food processor or to a blender and purée in batches. Return to pot and stir in ¼ cup orange juice and 1½ cups water. Reheat. (6 servings)

TOMATO CORN SOUP: Sauté 1 onion, chopped, in ¼ cup mild, light-flavored olive oil in a heavy soup pot over medium heat for 3 minutes. Stir in 6 tablespoons unbleached all-purpose flour, 1 teaspoon curry powder, and 1 tablespoon tomato paste. Slowly add 2 cups low-salt chicken broth. Stir until soup starts to boil. Reduce heat and simmer for 10 minutes. Add 1 cup nonfat or low-fat milk, 1½ cups fresh, frozen, or canned CORN kernels, 3 ripe or canned TOMATOES, chopped, ⅛ teaspoon black pepper, and 1 GREEN BELL PEPPER, seeded and chopped. Simmer for 5 minutes. (4 servings)

QUICK CHICKEN-VEGETABLE SOUP: Heat 4 cups low-salt chicken broth. Add ½ cucumber, thinly sliced, 4 mushrooms, thinly sliced, 1 cup shredded CABBAGE, 1 cup shredded SPINACH, 1 cubed TOMATO, and ½ cup cooked diced chicken. Bring to a boil, reduce heat, and simmer 5 minutes. (4 servings)

PURE VEGETABLE PURÉED SOUP: Place 2 cups chopped fresh vegetables (a mixture of onion, potato, and green and yellow vegetables works well), 2 cups water, ½ teaspoon dried basil leaves, ½ teaspoon dried thyme leaves, and ⅛ teaspoon black pepper in a heavy soup pot. Bring to a boil, stirring frequently. Reduce heat, cover, and simmer for 7–8 minutes. Transfer to the workbowl of a food processor or to a blender and purée until smooth. Stir in a few drops of mild, light-flavored olive oil and sprinkle with grated Parmesan cheese if desired. (2–3 servings)

LEFTOVERS SOUP: Place 1 cup cooked vegetables, ¼ onion, sliced, ¼ teaspoon dried basil leaves, ¼ teaspoon dried thyme leaves, and 1 cup low-salt chicken broth or skim or low-fat milk in the workbowl of a food processor or in a blender. Blend until smooth. Transfer to a double boiler and heat. Garnish with chopped fresh parsley before serving. (1–2 servings)

ASPARAGUS-LEMON SOUP: Place 1 pound ASPARAGUS, thinly sliced, ½ cup diced celery, ½ cup diced onion, and 3 cups low-salt chicken broth in a large saucepan over high heat and bring to a boil. Reduce heat. Cover and simmer 10 minutes or until asparagus is tender. Transfer to the workbowl of a food processor or to a blender and purée until smooth. Add ¼ cup skim or low-fat milk, 1 tablespoon lemon juice, ½ teaspoon grated lemon peel, and ¼ teaspoon white pepper. Process until blended. Return to saucepan and heat through. (4 servings)

SPINACH SOUP: Heat 2 tablespoons mild, light-flavored olive oil in a skillet over medium heat. Add 2 cloves garlic, minced, 4 medium leeks, scrubbed and sliced, 1 medium red onion, chopped, and 2 stalks celery, thinly sliced. Sauté for 10 minutes. Transfer the vegetables with a slotted spoon to a heavy soup pot. Add 6 cups low-salt chicken broth, 1 bay leaf, 3 tablespoons chopped parsley, ½ teaspoon dried tarragon leaves, ¼ teaspoon white pepper, and 1 pound fresh SPINACH, well washed and trimmed. Bring soup to a boil, reduce heat, and simmer, covered, for 20 minutes. Remove bay leaf. Transfer to the workbowl of a food processor or to a blender in batches and purée. Return to soup pot and stir in 1 cup skim or low-fat milk. Warm over low heat, but do not allow to come to a boil. (6 servings)

QUICK TAKES: COLD SOUPS

AVOCADO-TOMATO SOUP: Combine 8 medium TOMATOES, puréed, 2 tablespoons tomato paste, 1 cup low-fat buttermilk, and 1 tablespoon mild, light-flavored olive oil. Add 1 AVOCADO, mashed, 2 tablespoons lemon juice, and 2 tablespoons chopped fresh parsley. Refrigerate for 2 hours. Season with ¼ teaspoon white pepper. Garnish with diced cucumber and nonfat or low-fat plain yogurt. (4 servings)

BLUEBERRY SOUP: Place 1 pint BLUEBERRIES, 1½ cups water, ¼ cup sugar, ½ teaspoon ground cinnamon, and ¼ teaspoon ground cloves in a heavy soup pot. Bring to a boil, cover, and reduce heat. Stir blueberries with a wooden spoon several times, crushing them with the back of the spoon. Simmer for 10 minutes. Stir in 2 tablespoons lemon juice. Mix 1 tablespoon cornstarch with ¼ cup dry white wine or nonalcoholic white wine. Stir into the soup. Bring soup to boil for 1 minute. Chill and serve garnished with lemon slices. (4 servings)

MANGO BISQUE: Place 3 MANGOES, peeled, seeded, and cubed, in the workbowl of a food processor or in a blender with the juice of 4 limes, 1 cup nonfat or low-fat plain yogurt and 1 cup skim or low-fat milk. Process until smooth. Serve chilled. (4 servings)

PEAR-APPLE SOUP: Place 2 PEARS, cored and chopped, and 2 green APPLES, cored and chopped, in a saucepan with the juice of 1 lemon. Simmer, stirring, for 10 minutes. Transfer pears and apples to the workbowl of a food processor or to a blender and purée. Add 1 cucumber, peeled, seeded, and diced, and purée. Mix in ½ cup dry white wine or nonalcoholic white wine. Chill for 2 hours. (4 servings)

STRAWBERRY YOGURT SOUP: Combine 1 cup sliced hulled fresh STRAWBERRIES, 1 cup nonfat or low-fat plain yogurt, 2 tablespoons apple juice, and 1 tablespoon honey in the workbowl of a food processor or in a blender. Blend until smooth. Serve in chilled bowls. (2 servings)

COLD PEA SOUP: Heat 2 tablespoons mild, light-flavored olive oil in a heavy soup pot over medium heat. Sauté 1 onion, chopped, for 5 minutes. Add 4 cups low-salt chicken broth and bring to a boil. Add 2 cups frozen GREEN PEAS, 2 cups frozen lima beans, ¼ teaspoon dried mint leaves, and ¼ teaspoon black pepper. Lower heat, cover, and simmer for 10 minutes or until beans are tender. Transfer contents to the workbowl of a food processor or to a blender and add 1 cup nonfat or low-fat plain yogurt, and ¼ teaspoon curry powder. Purée. Chill before serving. (4–5 servings)

COLD TOMATO SOUP: Place 1 cup nonfat or low-fat plain yogurt, 2½ cups chopped fresh TOMATOES, 1 tablespoon mild light-flavored olive oil, 1½ tablespoons lemon juice, 1½ tablespoons vinegar, ⅛ teaspoon cayenne pepper, ½ teaspoon curry powder, 1½ tablespoons grated onion, 2 tablespoons minced fresh parsley in the workbowl of a food processor or in a blender and purée. Chill before serving. (2 servings)

SIMPLE BLENDER GAZPACHO FOR TWO: Place ½ small onion, chopped, 1 clove garlic, ½ GREEN BELL PEPPER, seeded and chopped, 3 ripe TOMATOES, chopped, 1 small cucumber, unpeeled and sliced, ¼ teaspoon cayenne pepper, 2 tablespoons extra-virgin olive oil, 3 tablespoons lemon juice, ½ cup ice water in the workbowl of a food processor or in a blender. Process until cucumber is blended in. Refrigerate for 1 hour before serving.

CHUNKY GAZPACHO FOR FOUR: Combine 1 cup diced TOMATOES, ½ cup seeded and diced RED BELL PEPPER, ½ cup seeded and diced YELLOW BELL PEPPER, ¼ cup finely chopped onion, ¼ cup chopped celery, 1 cup blanched diced TURNIPS, 1 clove garlic, minced, 3 cups tomato juice, ¼ teaspoon hot pepper sauce, ½ teaspoon dried basil leaves, ½ teaspoon dried thyme leaves, 2½ teaspoons red wine vinegar, 3 teaspoons mild, light-flavored olive oil, and ¼ teaspoon black pepper in a large glass bowl. Refrigerate for 1 hour before serving.

COLD VEGETABLE BISQUE: Heat 3 tablespoons mild, light-flavored olive oil in a heavy soup pot over medium heat. Add 2 cups chopped onion, 1 clove garlic, minced, and 2 tablespoons chopped celery. Cook until the onion is soft. Stir in 1½ cups low-salt chicken broth, 1¾ cups cubed peeled EGGPLANT, 1⅔ cups chopped zucchini, 1 cup chopped yellow crookneck squash, and ⅛ teaspoon white pepper. Bring to a boil, reduce heat, cover, and simmer for 5 minutes. Remove from heat and transfer contents to the workbowl of a food processor or to a blender. Purée. Return purée to soup pot and add ⅓ cup water, 2½ cups low-salt chicken broth, ¾ cup diced unpeeled yellow squash, and ¾ cup diced unpeeled zucchini. Bring to a boil. Lower heat and simmer for 6 minutes. Remove from heat and stir in 1 TOMATO, chopped. Chill before serving. (6 servings)

CURRIED FRUIT AND VEGETABLE SOUP: Heat 2 tablespoons mild, light-flavored olive oil in a heavy soup pot. Sauté 1 onion, chopped, until very soft. Add 1 teaspoon curry powder and cook for 1 minute. Add 6 cups low-salt chicken broth, 1 cup thinly sliced potato, 2 cups sliced celery, 1 APPLE, peeled and diced, and 1 medium BANANA, peeled and sliced. Bring to a boil, reduce heat, cover, and simmer for 30 minutes. Remove from stove and stir in 1 cup nonfat or low-fat plain yogurt. Transfer to the workbowl of a food processor or to a blender and blend until smooth. Chill. (6 servings)

FRUIT SALAD SOUP: Place 3 cups pineapple juice, 1 BANANA, peeled and cut into 1-inch slices, 1 APPLE, peeled, cored, and chopped, juice of 1 lemon, 1 cup chopped CANTALOUPE, 2 tablespoons honey, 1 cup nonfat or low-fat plain yogurt, and ½ teaspoon dried fresh mint in the workbowl of a food processor or in a blender and blend until smooth. Chill before serving. (4 servings)

VERY BERRY SOUP: Combine 1 pint BLUEBERRIES, 1 pint STRAWBER-RIES, hulled and chopped, 1 cup RASPBERRIES, 2 NECTARINES, chopped, 4 cups cranberry juice, ⅓ cup dry white wine or nonalcoholic white wine, 1 teaspoon ground cinnamon, and ¼ teaspoon ground nutmeg in a large soup pot. Bring to a boil, cover, reduce heat, and simmer for 10–15 minutes. Check to be sure fruit is tender. Let cool and chill until ready to serve. Garnish with strawberry slices. (4–6 servings)

SPICY MELON SOUP: Place 2 cups cubed CANTALOUPE, 3 cups cubed HONEYDEW, 2 cups orange juice, 2 tablespoons lemon juice, 2 tablespoons lime juice, 3 tablespoons honey, ¼ teaspoon ground cloves, ¼ teaspoon ground cinnamon, ¼ teaspoon ground allspice in a large saucepan and simmer for 15 minutes. Purée the soup in the workbowl of a food processor or in a blender. Pour the soup into a large bowl. Stir in 1 cup nonfat or low-fat buttermilk and chill for at least 4 hours. (4 servings)

AT YOUR LEISURE: HOT SOUPS

BASIC VEGETABLE STOCK BASE

This salt-free stock can be served with its vegetables or used as a base for other soups. Strained vegetable stock can be refrigerated for 3 to 4 days or frozen for up to 1 month. Try freezing stock in ice cube trays when you anticipate needing small quantities of it.

YIELD: *8 cups*
PREPARATION TIME: *25 minutes*
COOKING TIME: *1 hour*

2 tablespoons mild, light-flavored olive oil
1 onion, diced
1 carrot, scrubbed and cut into chunks
1 stalk celery, cut into chunks
1 potato, scrubbed and cut into chunks
1 tomato, quartered
1 turnip, peeled and cut into chunks
2 cloves garlic, chopped
2 quarts water
1 bay leaf
½ cup chopped fresh parsley
½ teaspoon black pepper

1. Heat olive oil in a heavy soup pot. Add onion, carrot, celery, potato, tomato, turnip, and garlic. Cook for 10 minutes.
2. Add water, bay leaf, parsley, and black pepper. Cover, bring to a boil, reduce heat, and simmer for 1 hour. If not serving the soup with the vegetables, strain stock and discard vegetables, bay leaf, and parsley.

VARIATION
▪ Substitute or add vegetables, such as chopped yellow squash, zucchini, parsnips, or red and green bell peppers. Avoid strongly flavored vegetables such as broccoli, cabbage, and cauliflower.

BASIC CHICKEN BROTH

This simple salt-free chicken broth can either be served with its chicken and vegetables or used as a base for many of the other soups that follow. Try freezing chicken broth in divided ice cube trays for a ready source of chicken flavoring for a wide variety of dishes.

YIELD: *6 cups*
PREPARATION TIME: *20 minutes*
COOKING TIME: *1 hour and 25 minutes + refrigeration
       time to remove fat from broth*

1 2-pound chicken, cut into quarters and skinned
1 stalk celery, cut into 1-inch chunks
3 carrots, cut into 1-inch chunks
2 onions, cut in half
2 turnips, peeled and cut in half
1 teaspoon dried dillweed
6 cups water
½ teaspoon black pepper
2 cloves garlic, minced

1. Place chicken in a heavy soup pot and add the celery, carrots, onions, turnips, dill, water, black pepper, and garlic. Cover and cook over high heat for 10 minutes or until the soup begins boiling.
2. Reduce heat and simmer for 1 hour and 15 minutes.
3. Remove from heat, cover, and cool.
4. Strain the soup, reserving the chicken and vegetables, and place the strained broth in the refrigerator in a bowl. Cover.
5. Pull the chicken off the bones in bite-sized pieces.
6. Remove the fat that congeals on top of the refrigerated broth.
7. If serving the soup with the vegetables and chicken, return them with the broth to the pot and heat through. If not serving together, store the chicken and vegetables in the refrigerator. Refrigerate or freeze the broth until ready to use.

EGGPLANT SOUP

Eggplant is sautéed in olive oil and simmered with tomatoes, onion, garlic, rice, and basil.

YIELD: *6 servings*
PREPARATION TIME: *20 minutes*
COOKING TIME: *40 minutes*

¼ cup mild, light-flavored olive oil
1 eggplant, about 1 pound, peeled and cut into 1-inch
    cubes
1½ cups chopped onion
1 tablespoon minced garlic
¼ teaspoon black pepper
1 bay leaf
½ teaspoon dried basil leaves
3 cups coarsely chopped fresh or canned tomatoes
¼ cup raw brown rice
5 cups low-salt chicken broth

1. Heat the olive oil in a heavy soup pot over medium heat. Sauté eggplant until lightly browned. Remove eggplant with a slotted spoon and drain on paper towels.
2. Place onion and garlic in the pot, adding additional oil if needed. Sauté onions and garlic for 5 minutes.
3. Return eggplant to the pot and add pepper, bay leaf, and basil. Stir and add tomatoes, rice, and broth. Bring to a boil, stirring. Simmer, uncovered, for 30 minutes. Remove bay leaf.
4. Purée the soup in batches in the workbowl of a food processor or in a blender. Return to soup pot and heat through.

BRUSSELS SPROUTS SOUP

Brussels sprouts, mushrooms, carrots, and onion are combined in this unusual soup.

YIELD: *4 servings*
PREPARATION TIME: *15 minutes*
COOKING TIME: *30 minutes*

¼ cup mild, light-flavored olive oil
¾ cup fresh mushrooms, rinsed and sliced
2 medium carrots, scrubbed and julienned
1 pint Brussels sprouts, trimmed and halved
1 medium onion, chopped
3 cups low-salt chicken broth
1½ tablespoons unbleached all-purpose flour
1 cup skim or low-fat milk
⅛ teaspoon ground nutmeg
¼ teaspoon black pepper

1. Heat 1 tablespoon of the olive oil in a heavy soup pot over medium heat. Sauté mushrooms and carrots for 5 minutes. Remove mushrooms and carrots from skillet and set aside.
2. Add the remaining olive oil to skillet with Brussels sprouts and onion. Sauté for 3 minutes.
3. Add chicken broth, raise heat, and bring to a boil. Reduce heat and simmer for 10 minutes. Remove half of the Brussels sprouts and add to the reserved mushrooms and carrots.
4. Purée the chicken broth-Brussels sprouts mixture in the workbowl of a food processor or in a blender in batches. Return to soup pot.
5. Add flour and milk to soup pot, stirring over low heat until blended.
6. Return reserved mushrooms, carrots, and Brussels sprouts to soup. Add nutmeg and pepper.
7. Bring soup to a boil, reduce heat, and simmer for 10 minutes.

BROCCOLI-POTATO SOUP

Serve this combination of broccoli, potato, mushrooms, onion, and celery with a loaf of herb-cheese bread.

YIELD: *6 servings*
PREPARATION TIME: *20 minutes*
COOKING TIME: *35 minutes*

3 tablespoons mild, light-flavored olive oil
6 cups broccoli stems and florets, chopped
1 large potato, chopped
½ cup chopped fresh mushrooms
½ medium onion, chopped
1 clove garlic, minced
1 stalk celery, chopped
4 cups low-salt chicken broth or vegetable broth
2 teaspoons curry powder
¼ teaspoon black pepper
¾ cup skim or low-fat milk

1. Heat the olive oil in a heavy soup pot over medium heat. Add broccoli, potato, mushrooms, onion, garlic, and celery. Cook 10 minutes or until vegetables are tender.
2. Add broth, curry powder, and pepper. Bring to a boil, reduce heat, and simmer, covered, for 20 minutes.
3. Transfer soup in batches to the workbowl of a food processor or to a blender and purée.
4. Return purée to soup pot. Stir in milk. Heat through for approximately 5 minutes.

RED PEPPER AND PEAR SOUP

This unique blend of red bell peppers, pears, potato, carrots, and onions can be garnished with nonfat or low-fat plain yogurt or sour cream.

> **YIELD:** *4 servings*
> **PREPARATION TIME:** *25 minutes*
> **COOKING TIME:** *35 minutes*
>
> 4 tablespoons mild, light-flavored olive oil
> 3 large onions, chopped
> 1 clove garlic, minced
> 2 carrots, scrubbed and chopped
> 1 medium potato, peeled and thinly sliced
> 2 large red bell peppers, seeded and chopped
> 2 ripe pears, peeled, cored, and chopped
> 3 cups low-salt chicken broth
> 1 tablespoon chopped fresh parsley
> ¼ teaspoon black pepper
> 1 medium green bell pepper, seeded and cut into
>   julienne strips

1. Heat the olive oil in a heavy soup pot over medium heat. Add onions, garlic, carrots, potato slices, and chopped red peppers. Cook for 10 minutes.

2. Add chopped pears, chicken broth, parsley, and black pepper. Simmer for 25 minutes or until vegetables are tender.

3. Transfer the soup in batches to the container of a blender or to the workbowl of a food processor. Purée and return to soup pot. Reheat over low heat.

4. Serve garnished with the green bell pepper strips.

CORN CHOWDER

Made with fresh, frozen, or canned corn, this recipe for classic chowder is accompanied by variations, including one for succotash-fish corn chowder, shrimp corn chowder, and mustard greens corn chowder.

YIELD: *6 servings*
PREPARATION TIME: *20 minutes*
COOKING TIME: *20 minutes*

3 tablespoons mild, light-flavored olive oil
½ cup sliced onion
1 stalk celery, diced
2½ cups water
2 potatoes, peeled and diced
3 whole cloves
1 stick cinnamon
¼ teaspoon ground nutmeg
¼ teaspoon ground allspice
1 teaspoon brown sugar
¼ teaspoon black pepper
3 cups fresh, frozen, or canned corn kernels
2½ cups skim or low-fat milk

1. Heat the olive oil in a heavy soup pot over medium heat. Sauté the onion and celery for 5 minutes. Add water, potatoes, cloves, cinnamon, nutmeg, allspice, brown sugar, and pepper. Reduce heat and simmer for 10 minutes.
2. Add the corn and milk and simmer for 5 minutes or until corn and potatoes are cooked. Remove cinnamon stick and whole cloves.

VARIATIONS
- For a thicker soup, purée 1 cup of the soup in the workbowl of a food processor or in a blender. Return to pot and heat through before serving.
- Replace the 2½ cups water with 2½ cups low-salt chicken broth. Substitute ¾ teaspoon dried thyme leaves for the cloves, cinnamon, nutmeg, and allspice. Add 1 red bell pepper, seeded and diced, and 1 cup fresh or frozen lima beans. When vegetables are tender, add ½ pound haddock or scrod fillet, cut into 1-inch chunks, and cook for 5 more minutes.
- Replace the 2½ cups water with 2½ cups low-salt chicken broth and 1 cup chopped tomatoes. Substitute 1 teaspoon chili powder and ½ teaspoon dried oregano leaves for the cloves, cinnamon, nutmeg, and allspice. Add 1 cup chopped mustard greens with the vegetables.

- Substitute ¼ teaspoon dry mustard, 1 clove garlic, minced, and ½ cup chopped fresh parsley for the cloves, cinnamon, nutmeg, and allspice.
- Substitute 1 hot chili pepper, diced, for the cloves, cinnamon, nutmeg, and allspice. Add 1 small zucchini, finely diced, and 5 ripe plum tomatoes, cut into ¾-inch cubes.
- Delete the cloves, cinnamon, nutmeg, and allspice. Add 1 red bell pepper, seeded and diced, with the other vegetables. When vegetables are tender, add ½ pound cooked shrimp and heat through.
- Substitute ¼ teaspoon ground cumin, 1 teaspoon ground coriander, and 1 teaspoon curry powder for the cloves, cinnamon, nutmeg, and allspice.

SCALLOP-VEGETABLE BISQUE

Scallops are added to a red pepper, apple, corn, and carrot bisque.

YIELD: *6 servings*
PREPARATION TIME: *25 minutes*
COOKING TIME: *35 minutes*

1 tablespoon mild, light-flavored olive oil
4 red bell peppers, seeded and chopped
1 small onion, chopped
1 small apple, peeled and chopped
1 carrot, scrubbed and chopped
4¼ cups low-salt chicken broth
½ cup fresh, frozen, or canned corn kernels
2 tablespoons lime juice
2 tablespoons chopped fresh parsley
¼ teaspoon white pepper
½ cup bay scallops, halved

1. Heat the olive oil in a heavy soup pot over medium heat. Add the red peppers, onion, apple, and carrot. Sauté for 5 minutes.
2. Add the chicken broth and bring to a boil. Reduce heat to a simmer and partially cover soup. Cook for 25 minutes.
3. Place the soup in batches in the workbowl of a food processor or in a blender and purée.
4. Return soup to pot and add corn, lime juice, parsley, and white pepper. Bring to a boil. Reduce heat and simmer for 5 minutes. Bring to a boil once again and add scallops. Turn off heat and cover the pot. Let soup sit for 5 minutes before serving.

VEGETABLE CRAB SOUP

Sweet crab meat and a collection of summer vegetables are united in this Maryland classic. Serve with Strawberry Fruit Salad (page 147).

YIELD: *6 servings*
PREPARATION TIME: *20 minutes*
COOKING TIME: *55 minutes*

2 tablespoons mild, light-flavored olive oil
2 onions, diced
2 cups fresh or canned plum tomatoes
1/4 teaspoon black pepper
1 teaspoon seafood seasoning or 1/4 teaspoon crushed
    red pepper
1 1/2 cups low-salt chicken broth
4 stalks celery, chopped
2 green bell peppers, seeded and diced
1 cup fresh, frozen, or canned corn kernels
1 cup fresh or frozen lima beans
1 cup fresh or frozen peas
1 cup fresh or frozen green beans, cut into 1-inch pieces
2 cups diced potatoes
1 pound fresh or canned crab meat, picked over
1/2 cup chopped fresh parsley

1. Heat the olive oil in a heavy soup pot. Sauté onions for 10 minutes or until slightly brown.
2. Add tomatoes, black pepper, seafood seasoning or crushed red pepper, and chicken broth. Cover and simmer for 10 minutes.
3. Add celery, bell peppers, corn, lima beans, peas, green beans, and potatoes. Cover and simmer for 30 minutes or until vegetables are tender.
4. Stir in crab meat and heat through. Sprinkle with parsley and serve.

VARIATIONS
- Replace part or all of the crab meat with flaked bluefish.
- Replace the crab meat with 1 pound raw medium shrimp, peeled, deveined, and cut in 1/2-inch pieces.
- Remove tomatoes entirely. Increase chicken broth to 3 cups. After adding crab meat, remove soup from heat and stir in 1 cup low-fat buttermilk. Let stand for 5 minutes. Serve warm or chilled.

AT YOUR LEISURE: COLD SOUPS

COLD CREAM OF PEPPER SOUP

This refreshing soup can be made in advance, then chilled until serving time.

YIELD: *4 servings*
PREPARATION TIME: *30 minutes + 4 hours chilling time*
COOKING TIME: *30 minutes*

2 tablespoons mild, light-flavored olive oil
1 large onion, thinly sliced
1 leek, washed and thinly sliced
2 medium carrots, scrubbed and chopped
1 medium potato, peeled and quartered
1 large yellow bell pepper, seeded and chopped
2 large green bell peppers, seeded and chopped
1/4 teaspoon black pepper
4 cups low-salt chicken broth
Dash ground cayenne pepper
Dash ground nutmeg
Dash ground cloves
1 cup skim or low-fat milk
1/2 cup chopped fresh parsley

1. Heat the olive oil in a heavy soup pot. Add onion, leek, and carrots. Sauté for 10 minutes or until tender.
2. Add potato, yellow pepper, green peppers, black pepper, and chicken broth to pot. Bring to a boil and simmer for 20 minutes or until potato and peppers are tender.
3. Remove from heat and stir in cayenne, nutmeg, and cloves.
4. Transfer the mixture in batches to the workbowl of a food processor or to a blender. Process until smooth. Transfer to a large bowl. Chill for at least 4 hours.
5. Immediately before serving, stir in the milk and garnish with the parsley.

FRUIT GAZPACHO

Instead of the traditional combination of vegetables, this gazpacho features a variety of fruits in a tomato-pineapple juice base.

YIELD: *6 servings*
PREPARATION TIME: *20 minutes + 8 hours chilling time*

1½ cups tomato juice
1 cup pineapple juice
2 teaspoons grated lime peel
2 cups cantaloupe, seeded, peeled, and cubed
2 cups honeydew melon, seeded, peeled, and cubed
1 small papaya, seeded, peeled, and cubed
1 large apple, cored and cubed
½ cup hulled sliced fresh strawberries
½ cup blueberries

1. Blend the tomato juice, pineapple juice, lime peel, 1 cup each of the cantaloupe and honeydew, and the papaya in the workbowl of a food processor or in a blender until smooth.
2. Transfer to a serving bowl and add the remaining 1 cup of cantaloupe and honeydew, the apple, the strawberries, and blueberries.
3. Chill covered for at least 8 hours.

FRUIT FANTASY SOUP

This easy chilled soup has a heavenly taste.

YIELD: *4 servings*
PREPARATION TIME: *20 minutes + 2 hours chilling time*

1 large seedless orange, peeled, and separated into
    sections
2 tangerines, peeled, seeded, and separated into
    sections
1 large banana, peeled and sliced
1 cup unsweetened juice-packed or water-packed
    canned peaches
1 cup unsweetened juice-packed or water-packed
    canned pineapple
1 tablespoon honey
$\frac{1}{4}$ cup chopped walnuts
$\frac{1}{2}$ teaspoon ground nutmeg

1. Place the orange and tangerine sections in the workbowl of a food processor or in a blender and purée. Transfer the purée to a large mixing bowl.
2. Place the banana slices, peaches, and pineapple in the workbowl of a food processor or in a blender and purée. Add the purée to the orange-tangerine mixture. Stir in the honey until dissolved.
3. Chill, covered, for 2 hours or more.
4. Sprinkle with chopped walnuts and nutmeg before serving.

Salads, Dressings, and Vinegars

EASY ACCESS: THE BASICS
Marinated Vegetable Salad   Main Dish Vegetable and/or Fruit Salad
Basic Green Salad with Fruit   Main Course Green Salad

Green Salad Combinations

QUICK TAKES
Mixed Vegetables Green Salad   Green Salad with Chick-Peas
Romaine-Orange Salad   Tuna Vegetable Salad   Asparagus Chef Salad
Green Salad with Beef and Fruit   Chicken Chili Salad

Fruit Salads

QUICK TAKES
Apple-Raisin Salad   Apple-Cabbage Salad   Avocado-Apple Salad
Banana-Raspberry Salad   Cantaloupe Salad
Grapefruit and Celery Salad   Kiwi Salad   Orange and Radish Salad
Orange and Avocado Salad   Papaya-Citrus Salad
Pear-Avocado Salad   Pear and Grape Salad
Pineapple and Apple Salad   Pineapple-Carrot Salad
Raspberry and Apricot Salad   Strawberry Romaine Salad
Strawberry Fruit Salad   Tangerine Salad   Apples and Mixed Fruit Salad
Fruit Compote   Raspberry-Blueberry Slaw   Grapefruit Tropicana Salad
Spinach Fruit Salad   Fruitful Slaw   Fall Salad   Summer Salad
Tropical Salad   Lemon-Honey Fruit Salad

Vegetable Salads

QUICK TAKES

Asparagus with Tomato and Dill   Asparagus and Carrot Salad
Spanish Asparagus Salad   Broccoli and Cheese Salad
Cabbage, Tangerine, and Bell Pepper Slaw   Pineapple Slaw
Green and Red Cabbage   Red Cabbage Salad   Carrot Slaw
Cauliflower Salad   Corn and Pepper Salad
Green Bean and Potato Salad   Green Beans with Yellow Pepper
Green Pea, Bean, and Vegetable Salad   Bell Pepper and Tomato Salad
Apple Spinach Salad   Berry Spinach Bowl
Sweet Potato and Broccoli Salad   Sweet Potato–Bell Pepper Salad
Tomato Gazpacho Salad   Tomato, Melon, and Cucumber Salad
Turnip Fruit Salad   Mixed Vegetable Medley   Greek Picnic Salad
November Salad   Parmesan–Raw Vegetable Salad   Summer Peppers
Vegetable Toss   Vibrant Salad

AT YOUR LEISURE

Chilled Quick Ratatouille with Fruit   Sweet Potato–Apple Salad
Cauliflower Salad   Rainbow Slaw   Mango Slaw   Fruit Surprise Slaw
Potato Vegetable Salad au Gratin

Dressings

Banana Dressing   Cranberry Dressing   Mango Dressing
Nectarine Dressing   Papaya Dressing   Raspberry Dressing
Strawberry Dressing   Tomato Vinaigrette   Tomato-Yogurt Dressing
Basil-Honey Dressing   Cumin Dressing   Dill Dressing   Garlic Vinaigrette
Ginger Dressing   Lemon-Lime Vinaigrette   Lemon-Parmesan Dressing
Mustard Vinaigrette   Oregano Vinaigrette   Oriental Dressing
Parsley-Lime Dressing   Poppy Seed Fruit Salad Dressing
Sesame Dressing   Strawberry Vinegar   Nectarine Vinegar

EASY ACCESS: THE BASICS

MARINATED VEGETABLE SALAD
(6 servings)

INGREDIENTS
1½ cups white wine vinegar
½ cup mild, light-flavored olive oil
1 tablespoon sugar
1 teaspoon dried oregano leaves
¼ teaspoon black pepper
1 onion, chopped
4 cups chopped vegetables (see possibilities below)
1 small jalapeño chili pepper, seeded and chopped
    (optional)
½ cup pitted ripe olives

1. Combine vinegar, olive oil, sugar, oregano leaves, and black pepper in a large saucepan and bring to a boil.
2. Add onion, vegetables, chili, and olives. Lower heat, cover, and simmer for 3–4 minutes.
3. Transfer vegetables and poaching liquid to a large bowl.
4. Cover and refrigerate for 4 hours.
5. Drain and serve as a side dish or toss with cooked rice or pasta.

VEGETABLE POSSIBILITIES
Cauliflower; carrots; celery; green bell pepper
Zucchini; green beans; corn; red bell pepper
Yellow crookneck squash; mushrooms; broccoli; red cabbage
Peas; Brussels sprouts; carrots; yellow bell pepper

MAIN DISH VEGETABLE AND/OR FRUIT SALAD

(6–8 servings)

INGREDIENTS

10 cups blanched or raw vegetables and/or fruit, cut
    into bite-sized pieces (see possibilities below)
2 cups meat, poultry, or seafood, cut into thin strips (see
    possibilities below)
2 cups cheese, cut into thin strips (see possibilities below)
1 medium onion, sliced
½ cup sliced stuffed olives
1 cup chopped fresh parsley
¼ cup red wine vinegar
¼ teaspoon black pepper
1 teaspoon Dijon mustard
½ cup extra-virgin olive oil

1. Place vegetables and/or fruit in a large bowl.
2. Add strips of meat, poultry, or seafood.
3. Add strips of cheese.
4. Add onion, olives, and parsley.
5. Combine wine vinegar, pepper, mustard, and olive oil.
6. Toss with salad and serve.

VEGETABLE AND/OR FRUIT POSSIBILITIES

Green bell pepper; red bell pepper; chick-peas; corn; cauliflower
Carrots; green bell pepper; turnips; cucumber; apples
Peas; mushrooms; broccoli; yellow crookneck squash; pears
Asparagus; red cabbage; corn; green beans; tomatoes
Asparagus; celery; red bell pepper; walnuts; parsley

MEAT OR SEAFOOD POSSIBILITIES

Cooked beef, pork, chicken, or turkey
Cooked shrimp, scallops, or flaked fish fillets
Flaked tuna or salmon

CHEESE POSSIBILITIES

Nonfat or low-fat Swiss cheese
Nonfat or low-fat cheddar cheese
Nonfat or low-fat Monterey Jack cheese
Part-skim mozzarella

GREEN SALADS: THE BASICS

When preparing green salads, tear lettuce leaves by hand. Wash salad greens well under cold running water. Drain and dry them in a salad spinner or on toweling. Store in an airtight container in the refrigerator or roll in a towel and refrigerate if greens will be used shortly.

Create green salads using Bibb, Boston, red leaf, and romaine lettuce; cabbage, endive, escarole, parsley, spinach, watercress, and fresh coriander (cilantro); alfalfa and bean sprouts, asparagus, beets, broccoli florets, carrots, cauliflower florets, celery, cucumbers, green peppers, raw or steamed green beans, jicama root, leeks, mushrooms, onions, pea pods, peas, cooked new potatoes, radishes, scallions, summer squash, red bell peppers, tomatoes, water chestnuts, and zucchini; walnuts, pecans, and unsalted peanuts; pumpkin, sunflower, and sesame seeds; apples; orange sections; grapes; raisins; and strawberries.

Garnish salads with grated Parmesan cheese; grated Cheddar cheese and chopped fresh parsley; blanched pea pods; halved grapes; red bell pepper strips; fresh parsley sprigs; fresh watercress leaves; sautéed pine nuts; green bell pepper rings; orange slices; pineapple slices; mandarin orange segments; raisins; sliced almonds; lemon wedges; asparagus tips; sautéed mushrooms sprinkled with paprika; broccoli florets.

Dress green salads just before serving. Add only enough dressing to coat ingredients lightly.

GREENS FOR SALAD

Boston, Bibb, or butter lettuce: 1 medium head yields 5 cups
Chicory: 1 head yields 6 cups
Curly endive: 1 head yields 6 cups
Escarole: 1 head yields 6 cups
Red leaf lettuce: 1 medium head yields 6 cups
Romaine lettuce: 1 medium head yields 5 cups
Spinach: ¾ pound yields 3 cups leaves
Watercress: 1 bunch yields 1½ cups

FRUITS FOR GREEN SALADS

Shredded tart apple	Pineapple
Avocado	Orange
Mango	Grapefruit
Papaya	Apricots

BASIC GREEN SALAD WITH FRUIT

(4 servings)

INGREDIENTS
4 cups salad greens (see above)
4 cups fruit (see above)
1 teaspoon light soy sauce
$\frac{1}{2}$ teaspoon honey
1 teaspoon dry mustard
$\frac{1}{2}$ teaspoon black pepper
2 tablespoons lemon juice
$\frac{1}{2}$ cup extra-virgin olive oil

1. Toss salad greens with fruit.
2. Combine soy sauce, honey, dry mustard, black pepper, lemon juice, and olive oil in a small bowl.
3. Toss with salad before serving.

MAIN COURSE GREEN SALAD

(6–8 servings)

INGREDIENTS
8 cups romaine lettuce or lettuce of your choice, torn in
    bite-sized pieces
2 cups spinach, watercress, or other greens
2 cups raw vegetables (see possibilities below)
4 cups Main Dish Salad Add-ons (see possibilities below)
1 cup mild, light-flavored olive oil
$\frac{2}{3}$ cup lemon juice
$\frac{1}{2}$ teaspoon minced garlic
$1\frac{1}{2}$ teaspoons Dijon mustard
$\frac{1}{2}$ teaspoon black pepper

1. Toss lettuce, spinach, raw vegetables, and add-ons together in a large salad bowl.
2. Combine olive oil, lemon juice, garlic, mustard, and black pepper in a small bowl with a wire whisk.
3. Toss dressing with salad.

RAW VEGETABLE POSSIBILITIES

Tomato slices
Cucumber slices
Shredded carrots
Minced celery
Cubed avocado
Shredded cabbage
Sliced onions
Raw sliced mushrooms
Diced red, yellow, or green bell peppers

MAIN DISH SALAD ADD-ONS

Steamed asparagus; broccoli; carrots; cauliflower; corn; peas; snow peas; green beans; yellow crookneck squash; or zucchini
Roasted, sautéed, or steamed potatoes
Cooked pasta, rice, or couscous
Cooked chicken, beef, turkey, or pork
Cooked fish, shrimp, scallops, or crab
Croutons
Corn chips
Olives
Sautéed mushrooms
Sesame or sunflower seeds

QUICK TAKES: GREEN SALAD COMBINATIONS

MIXED VEGETABLES GREEN SALAD: Toss 8 cups mixed greens, including CHICORY, Boston lettuce, ROMAINE lettuce, escarole, and watercress, 1 stalk celery sliced, 2 scallions, sliced, 1 CARROT, shredded, 4 radishes, sliced, 1 cucumber, sliced, and 6 cherry TOMATOES. Combine ⅓ cup extra-virgin olive oil, 2 tablespoons red wine vinegar, and ¼ teaspoon black pepper. Toss with salad.

GREEN SALAD WITH CHICK-PEAS: Layer 4 cups bite-sized pieces of ROMAINE and CHICORY with 1 can chick-peas, drained, 1 cucumber, sliced, 2 TOMATOES, sliced, and ¼ cup sliced scallions. Combine 3 tablespoons grated Parmesan cheese, 3 tablespoons red wine vinegar, ½ teaspoon dry mustard, and 6 tablespoons extra-virgin olive oil. Toss with salad. Top with toasted whole-grain croutons.

ROMAINE-ORANGE SALAD: Toss 8 cups torn ROMAINE, 2 cups torn CHICORY, 4 scallions, sliced, 2 navel ORANGES, peeled and sliced into rounds, and ⅓ cup chopped toasted walnuts. Combine 2 tablespoons white wine vinegar, 1 teaspoon lemon juice, 2 teaspoons Dijon mustard, ⅛ teaspoon white pepper, ½ cup extra-virgin olive oil. Toss with salad.

TUNA VEGETABLE SALAD: Toss 4 cups torn ROMAINE, 4 cups torn leaf lettuce, ½ cup chopped TOMATO, ½ cup sliced ripe olives, 1 cup steamed BROCCOLI florets, 1 cup steamed CAULIFLOWER florets, 1 cup SNOW PEAS, blanched and halved, 1 cup GREEN PEAS, blanched, 1 cup diced steamed yellow crookneck squash, 1 cup flaked white albacore tuna, and 1 cup nonfat or low-fat shredded cheddar cheese. Combine 5 tablespoons extra-virgin olive oil, 2½ tablespoons lemon juice, 2 tablespoons reduced-calorie mayonnaise, and ½ teaspoon Dijon mustard. Toss with salad.

ASPARAGUS CHEF SALAD: Toss 16 steamed ASPARAGUS spears, cut into 2-inch pieces, 1 cup cooked GREEN PEAS, 2 cups nonfat or low-fat Swiss cheese strips, 1 cup turkey breast strips, ¾ cup sliced radishes, ¼ teaspoon black pepper, and 1 clove garlic, minced. Tear 6 cups ROMAINE lettuce leaves. Fill 6 small individual salad bowls with the torn romaine and top with salad. Combine 1 cup extra-virgin olive oil, ⅔ cup red wine vinegar, 1 teaspoon honey, and ½ teaspoon dried thyme leaves. Pass the dressing with salad.

GREEN SALAD WITH BEEF AND FRUIT: Combine 4 cups torn ROMAINE leaves, 3 cups torn SPINACH, 1½ cups sliced NECTARINES, 1 AVOCADO, sliced, 12 cherry tomatoes, halved, 2 cups lean roast beef strips, ½ cup extra-virgin olive oil, 3 tablespoons red wine vinegar, and 1 tablespoon chopped fresh horseradish.

CHICKEN CHILI SALAD: Combine 2 cups cooked chicken breast strips, 6 cups torn ROMAINE lettuce, 1 cup shredded CARROT, 1 cup chopped celery, 2 medium TOMATOES, chopped, and 3 tablespoons chopped scallions in a salad bowl. Place 2 cups shredded nonfat or low-fat cheddar cheese and ⅔ cup nonfat or low-fat milk in a saucepan over medium heat. Stir until cheese has melted and mixture is smooth. Add 3 tablespoons chopped mild chili peppers and 3 tablespoons chopped ripe olives. Pour over salad and toss.

QUICK TAKES: FRUIT SALADS

APPLE-RAISIN SALAD: Toss 2 APPLES, cored and diced, 1 tablespoon lemon juice, ½ cup seedless raisins, ½ cup chopped walnuts, and ⅓ cup reduced-calorie mayonnaise.

APPLE-CABBAGE SALAD: Combine 3 APPLES, grated, ½ head RED CABBAGE, grated, 2 cups chopped celery, ¼ cup seedless raisins, 1 tablespoon honey, 1 tablespoon lemon juice, and 2 tablespoons mild, light-flavored olive oil. Serve on a bed of ROMAINE lettuce leaves.

AVOCADO-APPLE SALAD: Slice 2 AVOCADOS and 4 APPLES. Place in a bowl, cover with ½ cup grapefruit juice, and let stand for 30 minutes. Drain and serve on ROMAINE lettuce-lined plates. Sprinkle with lemon juice and honey.

BANANA-RASPBERRY SALAD: Combine 1 cup nonfat or low-fat plain yogurt with 2 tablespoons honey. Stir in 1 BANANA, sliced, and ½ cup fresh RASPBERRIES. Top with 1 tablespoon honey and 1 teaspoon toasted sesame seeds.

CANTALOUPE SALAD: Combine 2 cups torn ROMAINE lettuce leaves and 2 small CANTALOUPES, seeded and scooped into balls with a melon-baller. Toss with ⅓ cup nonfat or low-fat plain yogurt, 2 tablespoons lemon juice, 2 tablespoons reduced-calorie mayonnaise, and ¼ teaspoon black pepper.

GRAPEFRUIT AND CELERY SALAD: Peel and separate into sections 2 large GRAPEFRUITS. Chop the grapefruit sections. Toss with 2 stalks celery, chopped, ½ teaspoon dried mint leaves, and 2 tablespoons seedless raisins. Combine ⅔ cup nonfat or low-fat plain yogurt, 1 tablespoon extra-virgin olive oil, 1 tablespoon orange juice, and ¼ teaspoon black pepper. Toss dressing with grapefruit-celery mixture. Chill for 30 minutes.

KIWI SALAD: Toss 2 cups juice-packed canned chunk PINEAPPLE or fresh pineapple chunks, 3 BANANAS, sliced, 2 navel ORANGES, sectioned, 1 cup seedless red grapes, 6 KIWIS, peeled and sliced, and 1 cup chopped walnuts. Combine 1½ tablespoons grated lemon peel, 1 teaspoon grated fresh gingerroot, ¾ cup reduced-calorie mayonnaise, ¾ cup nonfat or low-fat plain yogurt, 2 tablespoons honey, and 1 tablespoon lemon juice. Serve the salad with dressing.

ORANGE AND RADISH SALAD: Toss 4 navel ORANGES, peeled and separated into sections, ¼ cup lemon juice, ½ teaspoon sugar, ⅛ teaspoon ground cinnamon, ½ cup sliced radishes, and ¼ cup pitted ripe olives, rinsed and sliced. Marinate in the refrigerator until ready to serve.

ORANGE AND AVOCADO SALAD: Combine 1 AVOCADO, pitted and cubed, 2 navel ORANGES, peeled and sliced, 1 large red onion, sliced, and salad greens. Toss with olive oil and vinegar.

PAPAYA-CITRUS SALAD: Toss 3 cups PAPAYA cubes, 1 cup GRAPEFRUIT sections, 1 cup navel ORANGE sections, ½ GREEN BELL PEPPER, shredded, 1 small onion, sliced, 2 stalks celery, sliced, ½ cup grated CARROTS, and 2 tablespoons chopped fresh parsley. Arrange on lettuce leaves. Blend together ¼ cup cider vinegar, ¼ cup lemon juice, 1 teaspoon sugar, and 1 cup mild, light-flavored olive oil. Serve dressing with salad.

PEAR-AVOCADO SALAD: Arrange 2 cups canned PEARS, drained, reserving 1 tablespoon of the liquid, and 1 medium AVOCADO, sliced, on ROMAINE lettuce leaves on 4 plates. Top with a dressing made from 1 TOMATO, peeled and chopped, 1 tablespoon chopped green chiles, 1 tablespoon chopped scallions, the reserved 1 tablespoon pear liquid, 1 tablespoon mild, light-flavored olive oil, 1 tablespoon lime juice, and ½ teaspoon ground oregano leaves.

PEAR AND GRAPE SALAD: Toss 5 PEARS, peeled and sliced, 1 tablespoon lemon juice, 2 cups seedless red grapes, ½ cup thinly sliced celery, and ½ cup toasted slivered almonds. Combine ½ cup reduced-calorie mayonnaise, ⅓ cup nonfat or low-fat plain yogurt, ½ teaspoon ground ginger, and ⅛ teaspoon dry mustard. Toss with the pear salad.

PINEAPPLE AND APPLE SALAD: Combine 1½ cups fresh or unsweetened canned PINEAPPLE chunks, 2 cups APPLE chunks, and 2 tablespoons lemon juice. Sprinkle with 4 tablespoons nonalcoholic wine or dry sherry, 1 teaspoon sugar, and 2 tablespoons almonds.

PINEAPPLE-CARROT SALAD: Toss 1 cup chopped PINEAPPLE, 2 cups shredded CARROT, and ½ cup seedless raisins. Blend with ½ cup reduced-calorie mayonnaise and 1 teaspoon lemon juice.

RASPBERRY AND APRICOT SALAD: Toss 1 head green leaf lettuce, rinsed, dried, and torn into bite-sized pieces, 1 cup fresh RASPBERRIES, ½ cup dried apricots, ¾ cup mild, light-flavored olive oil, ¼ cup lemon juice, and ¼ teaspoon ground white pepper.

STRAWBERRY ROMAINE SALAD: Toss 4½ cups torn ROMAINE lettuce, 1½ cups sliced STRAWBERRIES, ½ cup sliced celery, 1 tablespoon toasted almonds, ¼ cup apple cider vinegar, 1½ teaspoons mild, light-flavored olive oil, ¼ teaspoon sugar, and ¼ teaspoon black pepper.

STRAWBERRY FRUIT SALAD: Place 1 pint fresh STRAWBERRIES, hulled and halved, in the workbowl of a food processor or in a blender and purée. Combine with ½ teaspoon dried mint leaves, ½ teaspoon honey, and ½ cup reduced-calorie sour cream. Arrange red leaf lettuce on 4 plates. Top with 1 cup fresh BLUEBERRIES and 1 cup each of sliced navel ORANGES and strawberry slices. Top with puréed strawberry dressing.

TANGERINE SALAD: Combine 4 cups torn ROMAINE lettuce leaves, 1 cup seeded TANGERINE segments, and 6 tablespoons sliced almonds. Combine ⅓ cup extra-virgin olive oil, ¼ cup honey, 3 tablespoons white wine vinegar, 1 tablespoon minced scallion, 1½ teaspoons Dijon mustard, and 1½ teaspoons poppy seeds. Toss with salad.

APPLES AND MIXED FRUIT SALAD: Toss 2 medium APPLES, cored and cut into wedges; 1 navel ORANGE, peeled and sliced, 1 GRAPEFRUIT, peeled, sliced, and the slices halved, 2 KIWIS, peeled and sliced, ¼ cup lime juice, 2 tablespoons honey, 2 tablespoons mild, light-flavored olive oil, and ¼ teaspoon cayenne pepper.

FRUIT COMPOTE: Combine ½ cup honey, 2 tablespoons lemon juice, ½ teaspoon ground ginger, and 1 teaspoon grated orange peel. Pour over the sections of 4 navel ORANGES, peeled, 1½ cups BLUEBERRIES, 2 cups cubed HONEYDEW melon, and 1½ cups halved STRAWBERRIES. Refrigerate for 2 hours.

RASPBERRY-BLUEBERRY SLAW: Combine 2 cups BLUEBERRIES, 2 cups RASPBERRIES or BLACKBERRIES, 3 seedless ORANGES, separated into sections and cut into bite-sized pieces, 1 cup chopped almonds, and 2 cups grated cabbage, chilled. Combine 1½ cups nonfat or low-fat plain yogurt, ¾ cup reduced-calorie mayonnaise, ⅓ cup apple cider vinegar, 1 tablespoon lemon juice, 2 teaspoons sugar, ½ teaspoon white pepper, ⅓ cup orange juice, and 1 tablespoon honey in the workbowl of a food processor or in a blender until smooth. Fold dressing into fruit, almond, and cabbage mixture.

GRAPEFRUIT TROPICANA SALAD: Combine 2 GRAPEFRUIT, peeled and separated into sections, 2 cups PAPAYA chunks, 1 BANANA, sliced, and 1 cup fresh PINEAPPLE chunks.

SPINACH FRUIT SALAD: Toss 3 cups torn SPINACH leaves, 3 cups torn ROMAINE lettuce, and 3 cups stemmed watercress in a large salad bowl. Add 1 GRAPEFRUIT, peeled and separated into sections, 2 navel ORANGES, peeled and separated into sections, 3 cups hulled whole STRAWBERRIES, ½ cup chopped celery, ½ cup chopped GREEN BELL PEPPER, and ¼ cup toasted almonds. Toss with STRAWBERRY DRESSING (page 159).

FRUITFUL SLAW: Combine 8 cups shredded green CABBAGE, 1 cup halved seedless red grapes, 1 TANGERINE, peeled, seeded, separated into sections, and chopped, and 1 cup juice-packed canned crushed PINEAPPLE. Combine ½ cup reduced-calorie mayonnaise and ½ cup nonfat or low-fat plain yogurt, ½ teaspoon ground ginger, 1 teaspoon grated lemon peel, and 1 tablespoon lemon juice. Toss dressing with slaw and chill for 1 hour.

FALL SALAD: Toss 3 APPLES, sliced, 1 BANANA, sliced, 2 teaspoons lemon juice, ½ cup seedless raisins, 1 cup seedless red grapes, ½ cup chopped walnuts, the juice of 1 orange, and ½ cup reduced-calorie mayonnaise.

SUMMER SALAD: Combine 1 ripe PINEAPPLE, cut into 1-inch chunks, 1 cup sliced STRAWBERRIES, 12 ripe plums, quartered, 2 navel ORANGES, peeled and separated into sections, 2 PEARS, cubed, and 2 NECTARINES, sliced. Served topped with honey and nonfat or low-fat plain yogurt.

TROPICAL SALAD: Combine 2 AVOCADOS, sliced, 1 MANGO, cubed, 3 BANANAS, sliced, 1 GRAPEFRUIT, peeled and separated into sections, 1 cup PINEAPPLE chunks, 1 cup seeded WATERMELON balls, and 1 cup HONEYDEW melon balls. Serve in a salad bowl lined with ROMAINE lettuce leaves.

LEMON-HONEY FRUIT SALAD: Combine 1 AVOCADO, cubed, 2 cups torn ROMAINE leaves, ½ cup trimmed steamed GREEN BEANS, ½ cup chopped celery, ½ cup GRAPEFRUIT chunks, and ½ cup steamed GREEN PEAS. Combine ⅔ cup lemon juice, ⅓ cup extra-virgin olive oil, and 3 tablespoons honey. Toss dressing with salad.

QUICK TAKES: VEGETABLE SALADS

ASPARAGUS WITH TOMATO AND DILL: Marinate trimmed steamed ASPARAGUS spears in ⅔ cup extra-virgin olive oil, ⅓ cup red wine vinegar, juice of ½ lemon, 3 tablespoons Dijon mustard, 1 clove garlic, minced, ½ teaspoon dried dill leaves, ¼ teaspoon dried basil leaves, and ¼ teaspoon black pepper for 1 hour. Toss marinated asparagus with 3 TOMATOES, diced, and ½ teaspoon dried dillweed. Serve on ROMAINE lettuce leaves and garnish with pine nuts.

ASPARAGUS AND CARROT SALAD: Combine 1½ pounds steamed ASPARAGUS, cut into 1½-inch pieces, 1½ pounds steamed CARROTS, sliced, ½ cup mild, light-flavored olive oil, ¼ cup lemon juice, 2 cloves garlic, minced, 1 teaspoon dried basil leaves, ¼ teaspoon dried thyme leaves, and ⅛ teaspoon black pepper. Chill for 3 hours before serving.

SPANISH ASPARAGUS SALAD: Place 18 trimmed ASPARAGUS spears in a skillet with a small amount of boiling water. Cover and cook for 8 minutes or until crisp-tender. Drain and cool. Combine ⅓ cup extra-virgin olive oil, ⅓ cup red wine vinegar, and 2 tablespoons sliced scallions. Line salad plates with lettuce leaves. Top with asparagus, 3 TOMATOES, cut into wedges, 12 green olives, sliced, and 1 small RED BELL PEPPER, seeded and cut into strips. Pour the dressing over salads just before serving.

BROCCOLI AND CHEESE SALAD: Toss ¾ pound steamed BROCCOLI stems and florets, 4 ounces nonfat or low-fat cheddar cheese, cut into julienne strips, and ¼ pound mushrooms, thinly sliced. Combine ¼ cup extra-virgin olive oil, 3 tablespoons lemon juice, 2 tablespoons chopped scallions, ¼ teaspoon dry mustard, and ⅛ teaspoon white pepper. Toss with salad. Top with toasted pine nuts.

CABBAGE, TANGERINE AND BELL PEPPER SLAW: Heat ¼ cup mild, light-flavored olive oil, 1 tablespoon sesame oil, 3 tablespoons apple cider vinegar, ½ teaspoon sugar, and ¼ teaspoon pepper in a small saucepan. Pour over ½ head RED CABBAGE, shredded, 1 cup julienned GREEN BELL PEPPER, 1 cup seeded TANGERINE slices, ½ cup sliced scallions, and 3 tablespoons toasted sesame seeds.

PINEAPPLE SLAW: Combine 1 chopped GREEN BELL PEPPER, 3 cups chopped CABBAGE, 1 cup fresh or juice-packed canned PINEAPPLE chunks, ½ cup seedless raisins, ½ cup reduced-calorie mayonnaise, and ½ cup reduced-calorie sour cream.

GREEN AND RED CABBAGE: Steam 3½ cups shredded RED CABBAGE, 3½ cups shredded GREEN CABBAGE, and 2 large CARROTS, grated. Toss with 1 red onion, thinly sliced, 2 tablespoons minced fresh gingerroot, and 1 cup cider vinegar. Marinate in the refrigerator for 4 hours. Drain the marinade into a saucepan and bring to a boil. Remove from heat and stir in ⅓ cup seedless raisins. Let cool. Add 3 tablespoons honey, 2 tablespoons mild, light-flavored olive oil, and 3 sliced scallions. Toss dressing with vegetables.

RED CABBAGE SALAD: Combine ½ small RED CABBAGE, shredded, ¼ cup white vinegar, 2 tablespoons mild, light-flavored oil, 1 teaspoon sugar, and ¼ teaspoon sesame oil.

CARROT SLAW: Combine 6 cups grated CARROTS, 1 cup seedless raisins, ⅓ cup reduced-calorie mayonnaise, ⅓ cup nonfat or low-fat plain yogurt, 1 tablespoon white wine vinegar, 1 teaspoon sugar, and ¼ teaspoon black pepper. Garnish with toasted sesame seeds.

CAULIFLOWER SALAD: Place 2 tablespoons white wine vinegar, 6 tablespoons mild, light-flavored olive oil, 1 tablespoon chopped fresh parsley, and 1 tablespoon finely chopped onion in the workbowl of a food processor or in a blender. Pour the dressing over 3 cups steamed CAULIFLOWER florets, still warm.

CORN AND PEPPER SALAD: Cook 8 ears of shucked CORN in boiling water for 1 minute. Cool by running under cold water. Scrape corn kernels off cobs. Mix corn with 2 cups finely chopped GREEN BELL PEPPERS, ½ cup minced red onion, ½ cup white wine vinegar, 1 teaspoon sugar, 2 teaspoons ground cumin, and ¼ teaspoon black pepper. Chill for 2 hours. Serve garnished with TOMATO wedges and ½ cup grated Parmesan cheese.

GREEN BEAN AND POTATO SALAD: Toss 2 medium potatoes, diced and cooked, 2 large CARROTS, diced and steamed, ½ pound GREEN BEANS, diced and steamed, ½ cup reduced-calorie mayonnaise, and 2 tablespoons chopped onion. Chill for 2 hours.

GREEN BEANS WITH YELLOW PEPPER: Steam 1 pound trimmed GREEN BEANS for 8 minutes. Toss with 1 YELLOW BELL PEPPER, seeded and cut into strips ½ inch thick, 6 tablespoons extra-virgin olive oil, 2 tablespoons white wine vinegar, 1 tablespoon chopped scallions, and 1 tablespoon chopped fresh parsley. Marinate overnight.

GREEN PEA, BEAN, AND VEGETABLE SALAD: Toss 1 cup drained canned kidney beans, ¾ cup steamed GREEN PEAS, ¾ cup steamed frozen lima beans, 1 GREEN BELL PEPPER, seeded and chopped, 1 RED BELL PEPPER, seeded and chopped, 6 scallions, chopped, and 2 tablespoons chopped fresh parsley. Combine 3 tablespoons mild, light-flavored olive oil, 1 tablespoon lemon juice, 1 tablespoon white wine vinegar, 1 teaspoon Dijon mustard, and ¼ teaspoon black pepper. Toss with salad. Chill for 2 hours.

BELL PEPPER AND TOMATO SALAD: Place 3 TOMATOES, sliced, in a bowl with 1 RED BELL PEPPER, seeded and cut into thin strips. Drizzle with 4 tablespoons extra-virgin olive oil, 2 tablespoons red wine vinegar, 1 clove garlic, minced, and 1 teaspoon dried basil leaves. Let stand for 1 hour and serve on a bed of ROMAINE lettuce.

APPLE SPINACH SALAD: Toss 8 cups torn fresh SPINACH, 2 medium

APPLES, sliced, 1 cucumber, sliced, ½ cup sliced radishes, and 2 tablespoons sunflower seeds. Combine ½ cup extra-virgin olive oil, ¼ cup lemon juice, 1 tablespoon sliced scallions, ½ teaspoon dried mint leaves, and ¼ teaspoon black pepper. Toss with salad.

BERRY SPINACH BOWL: Combine 2 tablespoons mild, light-flavored olive oil, 1 tablespoon red wine vinegar, 2 teaspoons honey, and ¼ teaspoon black pepper. Toss 3 cups torn fresh SPINACH, 1 cup STRAWBERRIES, cut in half, 1 cup green grapes, cut in half, and ¼ cup slivered almonds. Toss dressing with salad and serve.

SWEET POTATO AND BROCCOLI SALAD: Combine 4 cooked SWEET POTA-TOES, chopped, ¾ cup blanched BROCCOLI florets, 1½ cups chopped celery, ½ red onion, chopped, ½ cup raisins, ½ cup reduced-calorie mayonnaise, ½ cup reduced-calorie sour cream, ½ cup HARVEST CHUTNEY (page 286), 1½ tablespoons curry powder, ¼ cup minced fresh parsley, 1 teaspoon ground cumin, ⅛ teaspoon black pepper, and ⅛ teaspoon cayenne pepper. Chill before serving.

SWEET POTATO–BELL PEPPER SALAD: Cut 2 medium SWEET POTATOES into julienne strips. Steam for 1½ minutes. Combine 1 slice fresh gingerroot, minced, ½ jalapeño pepper, seeded and minced, 2 table-spoons mild, light-flavored olive oil, 3 tablespoons lemon juice, 1 tablespoon orange juice, and 1 teaspoon honey. Toss with sweet pota-toes and refrigerate for 1 hour. Toss with 1 RED BELL PEPPER, seeded and chopped, and 3 scallions, chopped.

TOMATO GAZPACHO SALAD: Toss 2 TOMATOES, sliced, 2 cucumbers, peeled and sliced, and 1 large onion, chopped. Combine ¼ cup extra-virgin olive oil, ¼ cup cider vinegar, 1 clove garlic, minced, and ¾ teaspoon dried thyme leaves. Toss with vegetables. Let stand at room temperature for 1 hour.

TOMATO, MELON, AND CUCUMBER SALAD: Combine ½ cup extra-virgin olive oil, ¼ cup lime juice, 2 teaspoons sugar, ¼ teaspoon black pepper, 1 tablespoon chopped fresh parsley, and ¼ teaspoon dried mint leaves. Toss with 1 CANTALOUPE, peeled and cut into thin wedges, 1 cucumber, peeled and sliced, and 4 TOMATOES, peeled and cubed. Let stand at room temperature for 45 minutes.

TURNIP FRUIT SALAD: Combine 2 teaspoons cider vinegar, 3 table-spoons light soy sauce, and 1½ teaspoons extra-virgin olive oil. Toss with 3 cups sliced peeled TURNIPS. Stir in 1 tablespoon honey, 2 tablespoons chopped scallions, 1 cup sliced PEARS, 1 cup sliced APPLES, and ½ cup chopped RED BELL PEPPER.

MIXED VEGETABLE MEDLEY: Combine 1 cup blanched BROCCOLI florets, 1 cup blanched ASPARAGUS tips, 1 cup blanched SNOW PEAS, 2 cups thin strips of nonfat or low-fat Swiss cheese, 2 GREEN BELL PEPPERS, seeded and cut into thin strips, 1 onion, sliced, and 24 cherry TOMATOES. Arrange on torn ROMAINE lettuce. Top with a dressing of 1½ cups nonfat or low-fat plain yogurt, ½ cup reduced-calorie sour cream, 1 tablespoon lemon juice, 1 teaspoon minced scallion, and ¼ teaspoon black pepper.

GREEK PICNIC SALAD: Combine 6 ripe TOMATOES, chopped, 2 GREEN BELL PEPPERS, seeded and diced, 1 red onion, diced, 1 cucumber, seeded and diced, ½ cup chopped fresh parsley, ½ cup sliced ripe olives, ¼ pound feta cheese, crumbled. Place 1 cup extra-virgin olive oil, ¼ cup lemon juice, ¼ cup wine vinegar, 1 tablespoon Dijon mustard, ¼ teaspoon black pepper, and 2 cloves garlic, minced, in the workbowl of a food processor or in a blender. Process until well blended and toss with salad ingredients. Marinate for 30 minutes.

NOVEMBER SALAD: Toss 3 medium potatoes, peeled and cubed, ½ pound trimmed GREEN BEANS, steamed, 3 tablespoons red wine vinegar, ¼ teaspoon black pepper, ½ cup extra-virgin olive oil, 1 cup drained canned kidney beans, 1 cup drained canned chick-peas, 2 TOMATOES, sliced, 4 scallions, sliced, and 1 tablespoon chopped fresh parsley.

PARMESAN–RAW VEGETABLE SALAD: Combine 1 pound BROCCOLI stems and florets, chopped, 1 pound CAULIFLOWER florets, 2 large CARROTS, sliced, 1 small zucchini, sliced, ¼ pound mushrooms, thinly sliced, and 1 RED BELL PEPPER, seeded and cut into julienne strips. Combine ¾ cup extra-virgin olive oil, 6 tablespoons lemon juice, 2 cloves garlic, minced, and ¾ teaspoon black pepper. Toss dressing with salad. Top with ¾ cup grated Parmesan cheese.

SUMMER PEPPERS: Cut the tops off 5 large RED BELL PEPPERS. Seed and remove ribs. Cut the kernels from 4 ears of CORN. Toss with 2 AVOCADOS, chopped, ½ GREEN BELL PEPPER, seeded and chopped, 2 stalks celery, chopped, 1 TOMATO, chopped, and the juice of 1 lemon. Stuff corn mixture into raw pepper shells and serve on a bed of ROMAINE lettuce.

VEGETABLE TOSS: Combine ½ cup trimmed GREEN BEANS, steamed, ½ cup cooked lima beans, ½ cup cucumber slices, ½ cup chopped BROCCOLI, 1 cup sliced radishes, ½ cup sliced mushrooms, 1 cup grated CARROTS; and 3 cups torn ROMAINE leaves. Combine ⅔ cup lemon juice, ⅓ cup extra-virgin olive oil, 1 clove garlic, minced, and 3 tablespoons honey. Toss dressing with salad.

VIBRANT SALAD: Toss 1 cup shredded CABBAGE, 1 cup chopped GREEN BELL PEPPER, 1 cup grated CARROTS, 1 cup chopped RO-

MAINE lettuce, 1 cup sliced celery, 1 cup TOMATO chunks, 1 cup cooked GREEN PEAS, ½ cup chopped cucumber, ½ cup diced onion, 1 cup nonfat or low-fat cheddar cheese, ½ cup cider vinegar, and ⅛ teaspoon black pepper. Chill before serving.

AT YOUR LEISURE

CHILLED QUICK RATATOUILLE WITH FRUIT

Nectarines are added to the ingredients list in this refreshingly different version of the classic dish.

YIELD: *6 servings*
PREPARATION TIME: *15 minutes + overnight chilling time*
COOKING TIME: *12 minutes*

1 cup pear nectar or apple juice
1 onion, cut into chunks
2 cloves garlic, minced
2 teaspoons dried basil leaves
1 teaspoon dried thyme leaves
¼ teaspoon black pepper
1 pound eggplant, cut into chunks
¼ cup white wine vinegar
2 cups sliced zucchini
2 tomatoes, chopped
½ cup chopped green bell pepper
2 cups sliced fresh nectarines or peaches
Romaine lettuce leaves

1. Combine pear nectar, onion, garlic, basil, thyme, and pepper in a large saucepan. Simmer for 5 minutes.
2. Add eggplant and vinegar. Simmer for 5 minutes more.
3. Add zucchini, tomatoes, green pepper, and nectarines. Simmer for 2 minutes.
4. Chill overnight. Serve on a bed of romaine leaves.

SWEET POTATO–APPLE SALAD

Shredded sweet potato and apples are accented with vinaigrette dressing and served on a bed of spinach leaves.

YIELD: *6 servings*
PREPARATION TIME: *20 minutes + 1 hour marinating time*
COOKING TIME: *45 seconds*

3½ cups shredded peeled sweet potatoes
¼ cup white wine vinegar
2 tablespoons mild, light-flavored olive oil
2 teaspoons lemon juice
½ teaspoon sugar
½ teaspoon pepper
1 clove garlic, minced
2 apples, cored and shredded
4 cups fresh spinach leaves, washed and trimmed

1. Cook the sweet potatoes in boiling water for 45 seconds. Drain and pat dry on paper towels.
2. Combine wine vinegar, olive oil, lemon juice, sugar, pepper, and garlic in a small bowl.
3. Pour dressing over sweet potatoes, cover, and let stand for 1 hour.
4. Drain sweet potatoes, reserving dressing.
5. Toss shredded apples with half of the reserved dressing.
6. Arrange spinach leaves on 4 salad plates. Divide sweet potatoes and apples on each of the plates. Drizzle with remaining dressing.

CAULIFLOWER SALAD

This simple, elegant cauliflower salad is marinated in an olive oil dressing and served with a topping of walnuts and seedless grapes.

> **YIELD:** *4 servings*
> **PREPARATION TIME:** *15 minutes + 30 minutes marinating time*
> **COOKING TIME:** *8 minutes*

1 medium head cauliflower, cut into florets with stems removed
½ cup olive oil
3 tablespoons white wine vinegar
¼ teaspoon black pepper
1½ cups seedless red grapes
8 whole walnuts
2 tablespoons chopped fresh parsley

1. Bring ¾ inch of water to boil in the bottom of a steamer. Steam cauliflower about 8 minutes. Transfer to a glass bowl.
2. In a small bowl combine the olive oil, vinegar, and black pepper with a wire whisk. Drizzle over cauliflower.
3. Marinate the cauliflower in the olive oil dressing for 30 minutes, turning the florets several times to coat all sides.
4. Lift the cauliflower from the marinade with a slotted spoon and arrange it in a serving bowl. Top with the grapes and walnuts. Sprinkle with parsley and serve.

RAINBOW SLAW

Cabbage, carrots, radishes, cucumber, red onion, apple, and red bell pepper unite to make a zesty slaw.

YIELD: *6 servings*
PREPARATION TIME: *20 minutes*

1 cup reduced-calorie mayonnaise
1/3 cup apple cider vinegar
1 tablespoon lemon juice
2 teaspoons sugar
1/2 teaspoon white pepper
1 medium green cabbage, shredded
2 medium carrots, scrubbed and shredded
8 radishes, shredded
1 small cucumber, peeled and shredded
1 small red bell pepper, seeded and shredded
1 apple, peeled, cored, and shredded
1/4 cup chopped fresh parsley
1/2 teaspoon dried dillweed
1/4 cup finely chopped red onion

1. Combine mayonnaise, vinegar, lemon juice, sugar, and white pepper in a small glass bowl.
2. Combine cabbage, carrots, radishes, cucumber, red pepper, apple, parsley, dill, and red onion in a large bowl. Toss with the dressing.

MANGO SLAW

Mango is the unexpected ingredient in this ginger-accented red cabbage dish.

YIELD: *4 servings*
PREPARATION TIME: *15 minutes*
COOKING TIME: *8 minutes*

2 tablespoons mild, light-flavored olive oil
1 tablespoon grated fresh gingerroot
1 small red cabbage, thinly sliced

3 tablespoons apple cider vinegar
3 tablespoons water
1/2 teaspoon sugar
1 tablespoon soy sauce
1 ripe mango, pitted and cut into 1/2-inch chunks
1 tablespoon lime juice

1. Heat the olive oil in a skillet over medium heat. Add the ginger and cabbage and stir to coat with the oil.
2. Add vinegar and water to the skillet and cook and stir cabbage for 7 minutes.
3. Transfer cabbage mixture to a serving bowl and toss with the sugar and soy sauce. Refrigerate for 3 hours.
4. Sprinkle the mango chunks with the lime juice. Toss with the cabbage salad.

FRUIT SURPRISE SLAW

You can make slaw a special part of supper instead of a humdrum side dish when you serve this cabbage and fruit combination.

YIELD: *4 servings*
PREPARATION TIME: *15 minutes*

3 cups shredded cabbage
1 cup chopped fresh nectarines
1 cup chopped papaya
1/2 cup raisins
1/2 cup mild, light-flavored olive oil
1/3 cup cider vinegar
1/2 cup finely chopped almonds

1. Toss the cabbage, nectarines, papaya, and raisins together in a large salad bowl.
2. Combine the olive oil, vinegar, and almonds in a jar and shake well.
3. Pour the dressing over the salad and toss.

VARIATIONS:
- Substitute peaches, mangoes, or plums for the nectarines.

POTATO VEGETABLE SALAD AU GRATIN

New potatoes and crisp vegetables are served with a melted cheese and tomato topping.

YIELD: *4 servings*
PREPARATION TIME: *15 minutes*
COOKING TIME: *15 minutes*

12 new potatoes, scrubbed and cut into thick slices
1 cup sliced fresh or frozen green beans
2 tablespoons mild, light-flavored olive oil
2 tablespoons white wine vinegar
1 tablespoon chopped fresh parsley
1 clove garlic, minced
½ teaspoon black pepper
¼ teaspoon dry mustard
1 carrot, scrubbed and shredded
½ green bell pepper, seeded and chopped
1 scallion, chopped
¾ cup nonfat or low-fat cheddar cheese
½ cup sliced cherry tomatoes

1. Fill a large pot with water and bring to a boil. Add the potato slices and simmer until tender, about 10 minutes. Drain.
2. Place 1 inch of water in the bottom of a steamer and bring to a boil. Place green beans in a colander or steamer over the boiling water. Cover and steam for 3–4 minutes. Remove with a slotted spoon and set aside.
3. Preheat oven broiler.
4. Combine the olive oil, vinegar, parsley, garlic, black pepper, and dry mustard with a wire whisk.
5. Toss the potatoes in a large ovenproof bowl with the green beans, the carrot, green pepper, scallion, and dressing.
6. Sprinkle the salad with the grated cheddar cheese and place under broiler until cheese melts.
7. Arrange the cherry tomatoes on top and serve.

Dressing and Vinegar Sampler

FRUIT- AND VEGETABLE-BASED DRESSINGS

BANANA DRESSING: Place 1 large BANANA, sliced, the freshly squeezed juice of 1 lemon, ½ teaspoon grated lemon peel, and 1 tablespoon honey in the workbowl of a food processor or in a blender and blend until smooth.

CRANBERRY DRESSING: Simmer ¾ cup raw CRANBERRIES with ⅓ cup orange juice until berries are tender. Purée in a blender. Stir in 2 teaspoons grated lemon peel, 1 tablespoon honey, ¼ cup mild, light-flavored olive oil, ½ teaspoon ground cinnamon, and 1 tablespoon red wine vinegar.

MANGO DRESSING: Combine 1 ripe MANGO, peeled and pitted, 2 tablespoons lime juice, 2 tablespoons lemon juice, 1 teaspoon dried mint, 1 teaspoon lime zest, 1 clove garlic, and ⅛ teaspoon cayenne pepper in the workbowl of a food processor or in a blender. Blend until smooth. Continue blending and add ½ cup mild, light-flavored olive oil. If not serving immediately, keep refrigerated.

NECTARINE DRESSING: Purée 1 NECTARINE, peeled and seeded, 2 tablespoons lemon juice, ¼ cup mild, light-flavored olive oil, 2 tablespoons white wine vinegar, and ⅛ teaspoon black pepper in the workbowl of a food processor or in a blender. Serve with green salads or fruit.

PAPAYA DRESSING: Combine ½ cup mild, light-flavored olive oil, ¼ cup white wine vinegar, ¼ cup chopped fresh PAPAYA, 1 teaspoon sugar, ¼ teaspoon ground ginger, ¼ teaspoon black pepper, and ⅛ teaspoon curry powder in the workbowl of a food processor or in a blender. Blend until thick and creamy. (Great with avocados or tomatoes.)

RASPBERRY DRESSING: Place ¾ cup RASPBERRIES in a bowl. Stir in 2 tablespoons honey and mash berries with a fork. Add ½ cup mayonnaise and chill for 1 hour. Stir in ½ cup walnuts before using.

STRAWBERRY DRESSING: Purée ½ cup hulled sliced STRAWBERRIES, 2 tablespoons orange juice, 2 tablespoons red wine vinegar, and 1 teaspoon honey in the workbowl of a food processor or in a blender. (Use with green salads or fruit.)

TOMATO VINAIGRETTE: Combine 1 ripe TOMATO, 1 cup extra-virgin olive oil, ¼ cup red wine vinegar, ¼ cup lemon juice, 1 tablespoon Dijon mustard, ½ teaspoon dried basil leaves, 2 cloves garlic, minced, ¼ teaspoon black pepper in the workbowl of a food processor or in a blender.

TOMATO-YOGURT DRESSING: Combine 2 TOMATOES, seeded and puréed, ½ teaspoon black pepper, ½ teaspoon sugar, and ¼ cup nonfat or low-fat plain yogurt in a blender and process until well blended. Refrigerate until ready to serve. Add ¼ cup sliced olives, and 1 tablespoon chopped fresh parsley.

FLAVORED VINAIGRETTES

BASIL-HONEY DRESSING: Combine 1 cup extra-virgin olive oil, ⅓ cup lemon juice, ⅓ cup red wine vinegar, 1 teaspoon honey, and 1 teaspoon dried basil leaves.

CUMIN DRESSING: Combine 1 tablespoon red wine vinegar, 1 teaspoon lemon juice, ¼ teaspoon ground cumin, ⅛ teaspoon paprika, ⅛ teaspoon dried oregano, and ¼ cup extra-virgin olive oil.

DILL DRESSING: Combine 2 tablespoons red wine vinegar, 1 teaspoon Dijon mustard, 1 clove garlic, minced, ¼ teaspoon dried dillweed, ⅛ teaspoon black pepper, and 6 tablespoons extra-virgin olive oil.

GARLIC VINAIGRETTE: Combine 2 tablespoons red wine vinegar, ½ tablespoon lemon juice, 2 teaspoons Dijon mustard, 1 clove garlic, minced, ¼ teaspoon black pepper, ½ cup extra-virgin olive oil, and 1 tablespoon chopped fresh parsley.

GINGER DRESSING: Combine 3 tablespoons reduced-calorie mayonnaise, 2 tablespoons mild, light-flavored olive oil, 2 teaspoons rice vinegar, 1 teaspoon lemon juice, 1 teaspoon minced fresh gingerroot, ½ teaspoon light soy sauce, and ½ teaspoon sesame oil in the workbowl of a food processor or in a blender. Process until smooth. Transfer to a jar and refrigerate for 1 hour. Toss with chopped fresh vegetables and seafood.

LEMON-LIME VINAIGRETTE: Combine ¼ cup fresh lemon or lime juice with ¼ teaspoon each of salt and black pepper. Pour ⅔ cup extra-virgin olive oil into the juice in a steady stream, whisking until well blended. Can refrigerate for 1 week. Return to room temperature before serving.

LEMON-PARMESAN DRESSING: Combine 2 tablespoons lemon juice, 1 tablespoon grated Parmesan cheese, 1 clove garlic, minced, ½ teaspoon grated lemon rind, ¼ teaspoon white pepper, and ⅓ cup extra-virgin olive oil.

MUSTARD VINAIGRETTE: Combine ¼ cup red wine vinegar with ¼ teaspoon salt, ¼ teaspoon black pepper, and 1 teaspoon Dijon mustard. Pour ⅔ cup extra-virgin olive oil into the vinegar in a steady stream, whisking until well blended. Can refrigerate for 1 week. Return to room temperature before serving.

OREGANO VINAIGRETTE: Combine 1 tablespoon red wine vinegar, 2 teaspoons lemon juice, 1 clove garlic, minced, ½ teaspoon dried oregano, ⅛ teaspoon black pepper, and ¼ cup extra-virgin olive oil.

ORIENTAL DRESSING: Combine ½ cup rice vinegar; 3 tablespoons light soy sauce, 3 tablespoons mild, light-flavored olive oil, 1 teaspoon minced garlic, ½ teaspoon sugar, and 2 tablespoons minced scallions. Can refrigerate for 3 days.

PARSLEY-LIME DRESSING: Combine ¼ cup plus 2 tablespoons extra-virgin olive oil, ½ cup lime juice, 1 tablespoon minced parsley, ¼ teaspoon dried oregano, ⅛ teaspoon cayenne pepper, and ¼ teaspoon black pepper in a 12-ounce jar and shake. Serve at once or refrigerate until ready to use. Serve with mixed greens, avocado, or orange, tangerine, or grapefruit sections.

POPPY SEED FRUIT SALAD DRESSING: Combine ⅔ cup honey, 1 teaspoon paprika, 1 teaspoon dry mustard, ⅓ cup lemon juice, 1 cup extra-virgin olive oil, and 2 teaspoons poppy seeds.

SESAME DRESSING: Combine ¼ cup extra-virgin olive oil, ¼ cup rice vinegar, 1 tablespoon lime juice, 1 teaspoon sesame seeds, ½ teaspoon light soy sauce, ¼ teaspoon sesame oil, and ⅛ teaspoon black pepper with a wire whisk. Toss with mixed greens; papaya or mango; scallions; and sliced poultry.

FRUIT VINEGARS

STRAWBERRY VINEGAR: Place 2 cups halved STRAWBERRIES, 1 slice fresh gingerroot, and 1 bay leaf in a glass jar. Heat 2½ cups white wine vinegar but don't allow to boil. Pour over berries, cover jar, and leave unrefrigerated overnight. Drain vinegar, discard solids, and store vinegar in the refrigerator.

NECTARINE VINEGAR: Combine 3 ripe NECTARINES, coarsely chopped, 1 cinnamon stick, broken into several pieces, and 12 ounces white wine vinegar. Cover and let stand at room temperature for 24 hours, stirring and mashing fruit occasionally. Strain mixture through several layers of cheesecloth into a saucepan. Discard solids. Bring to a boil. Remove from heat and let cool. Pour vinegar into jars and seal with airtight lids.

Poultry

Chicken Cutlets
(Boneless Breasts)

EASY ACCESS: THE BASICS
Stir-Fried Chicken Cutlets with Vegetables and/or Fruit
Chicken Cutlets and Vegetables in Tomato Sauce

QUICK TAKES
Chicken Broccoli Kung Pao   Chicken with Cantaloupe
Chicken with Spinach   Chicken with Red Peppers

AT YOUR LEISURE
Mexicali Chicken, Corn, and Nectarine Skillet
Algerian Chicken Couscous   Grilled Chicken Fajitas with Mango

Chicken Parts
(Bone-in Breasts or Other Parts of Choice)

EASY ACCESS: THE BASICS
Baked Chicken Breasts with Fruit

QUICK TAKE
Chicken with Cabbage and Apples

AT YOUR LEISURE
Grilled Chicken with Spinach and Raspberries   Chicken Caribe

Turkey Cutlets

EASY ACCESS: THE BASICS
Curried Fruit and Turkey Cutlets

QUICK TAKES
Basil-Tomato Turkey Cutlets

AT YOUR LEISURE
Turkey Vegetable Cutlets

Whole Chickens

QUICK TAKES
Roast Chicken with Corn Stuffing   Roast Chicken with Cranberry Stuffing
Roast Chicken with Apple Raisin Stuffing

Cooked Diced Chicken or Turkey

QUICK TAKES
Skillet Poultry and Vegetable Ratatouille   Broccoli Poultry Salad
Grapefruit Poultry Salad   Spinach and Fruit Chicken Salad
Green Bean, Poultry, and Potato Salad   Tangerine Poultry Salad

In addition to the recipes below, remember that you can create an elegant meal with baked, sautéed, grilled, or broiled chicken cutlets or turkey cutlets, or baked, sautéed, grilled, or broiled chicken parts with the addition of one of the Low-Fat sauces (page 269).

The following sauces work particularly well with chicken and turkey:

Tomato Salsa (page 272)
Basic Vegetable Sauce (page 271)
Honey-Blueberry Sauce (page 275)
Avocado Salsa (page 275)
Strawberry Relish (page 276)
Raspberry-Cranberry Relish (page 276)
Raw Cranberry–Pineapple Relish (page 277)
Instant Cranberry-Orange Relish (page 277)
Refrigerated Corn Relish (page 277)
Apple-Blueberry Sauce (page 278)
Melon Sauce (page 282)
Asparagus Sauce (page 283)
Spinach Sauce (page 284)
Cauliflower Sauce (page 284)
Tomato-Jalapeño Sauce (page 285)
Pepper-Apple Relish (page 286)
Carrot Chutney (page 287)

Chicken Cutlets
(Boneless Breasts)

EASY ACCESS: THE BASICS

STIR-FRIED CHICKEN CUTLETS WITH VEGETABLES AND/OR FRUIT

(4 servings)

INGREDIENTS
2 slices fresh gingerroot, minced
1 scallion, minced, and/or 1 clove garlic, minced
1 teaspoon cornstarch
1 tablespoon sherry (optional)
2 tablespoons water
1 whole chicken breast, halved, skinned, boned, and thinly
    sliced, diced, or cut into strips
3 tablespoons mild, light-flavored olive oil or canola oil
3–4 cups chopped, sliced or diced vegetables and/or fruit
    (see possibilities below)
1 tablespoon light soy sauce
½ cup low-salt chicken broth

1. Combine gingerroot, scallion or garlic, cornstarch, sherry, and water.
2. Toss chicken in ginger-scallion mixture. Let stand for 15 minutes, stirring several times.
3. Heat 1½ tablespoons of the oil in a heavy skillet or wok. Add chicken and stir-fry for 3 minutes. Remove from pan.
4. Heat remaining oil. Add vegetables and stir-fry to coat with oil. Sprinkle with soy sauce.
5. Stir in chicken broth, raise heat, and simmer until vegetables are done.
6. Add chicken, stir for 30 seconds, and serve.

VEGETABLE AND/OR FRUIT COMBINATION POSSIBILITIES

Tomatoes; onions
Peas; cucumber; bamboo shoots
Asparagus; bean sprouts; bamboo shoots
Green or red bell peppers; celery; water chestnuts; onions
Blanched eggplant; tomatoes; zucchini
Green bell pepper; pineapple chunks; water chestnuts
Snow peas; apple; bamboo shoots
Green peas; mushrooms; celery; onion
Blanched broccoli; celery; mushrooms; water chestnuts
Green bell pepper; cabbage; tomato; celery; bamboo shoots
Blanched broccoli; blanched cauliflower; blanched carrots
Yellow summer squash; nectarines; blanched green beans

CHICKEN CUTLETS AND VEGETABLES IN TOMATO SAUCE

(4 servings)

INGREDIENTS
2 tablespoons mild, light-flavored olive oil
1 leek, rinsed and chopped
2 cloves garlic, minced
2 whole chicken breasts, halved, skinned, boned, and cut
    into strips
1 teaspoon dried basil leaves
1 teaspoon dried oregano leaves
2 tablespoons chopped fresh parsley
3–4 cups sliced or chopped vegetables (see possibilities
    below)
1 cup chopped fresh or canned tomatoes
1¼ cups low-salt chicken broth
¼ cup dry white wine or nonalcoholic white wine (or an
    additional ¼ cup chicken broth)
4 tablespoons tomato paste
¼ teaspoon black pepper

1. Heat olive oil in a large skillet over medium heat. Add leek and garlic and cook until tender, about 8 minutes. Add chicken and stir-fry for 4 minutes. Stir in basil, oregano, and parsley. Remove chicken mixture with a slotted spoon and set aside.

2. Add vegetables to skillet and stir-fry for 5 minutes. Remove vegetables with the slotted spoon. Pour any remaining oil out of pan. Return chicken and vegetables to pan. Add tomatoes, chicken broth, wine, tomato paste, and black pepper. Stir, cover, reduce heat, and simmer for 15–20 minutes or until vegetables are tender.

VEGETABLE POSSIBILITIES

Eggplant; zucchini; green bell pepper
Red bell pepper; mushrooms; broccoli
Cauliflower; carrots; celery
Brussels sprouts; corn; green beans
Spinach; mushrooms; carrots
Peas; turnips; yellow summer squash
Pumpkin; corn; green bell pepper

QUICK TAKES

CHICKEN BROCCOLI KUNG PAO: Toss 2 whole chicken breasts, halved, skinned, boned, and diced, with 1 tablespoon cornstarch. Heat 2 tablespoons mild, light-flavored olive oil in a wok or heavy skillet. Add ¼ teaspoon dried crushed red pepper and stir-fry for 2 minutes. Add chicken and stir-fry for 2 minutes. Remove with slotted spoon and set aside. Add 2 tablespoons olive oil to wok. Add 4 scallions, chopped, 2 cloves garlic, minced, and 1 teaspoon minced fresh gingerroot. Stir-fry for 1 minute. Add 3 cups BROCCOLI florets and stir-fry for 2 minutes. Combine 3 tablespoons water, 2 tablespoons light soy sauce, 1 tablespoon sherry (optional), and ½ teaspoon sugar. Pour soy sauce mixture over broccoli and cover wok or skillet. Cook for 3 minutes. Add chicken and ½ cup chopped peanuts. Toss to heat through and serve over rice. (4 servings)
CHICKEN WITH CANTALOUPE: Sprinkle 2 whole chicken breasts, halved, skinned, and boned with ⅛ teaspoon black pepper. Heat 2 tablespoons mild, light-flavored olive oil in a skillet over medium heat. Sauté chicken for 8 minutes until golden brown. Spoon 2 tablespoons honey over chicken. Continue to cook over low heat for another 8 minutes. Baste chicken and turn several times. Remove chicken from skillet with a slotted spoon and set aside. Add 2 tablespoons sherry or nonalcoholic white wine and 2 tablespoons cider vinegar to the

skillet over low heat, scraping up any brown bits. Add 1 cup low-salt chicken broth and 1 tablespoon minced fresh gingerroot. Bring sauce to a boil and cook until reduced to ½ cup. Add ¾ cup CANTALOUPE balls, ¾ cup HONEYDEW balls, and 2 KIWIS, peeled and sliced. Heat until warmed through. Return chicken to pan and reheat briefly. (4 servings)

CHICKEN WITH SPINACH: Heat 2 tablespoons mild, light-flavored olive oil in a skillet over medium heat. Add 2 whole chicken breasts, halved, skinned, and boned. Cook 3–4 minutes on each side. Add ½ cup low-salt chicken broth. Cook for 2 minutes. Remove chicken to serving plate and keep warm. Add 4 teaspoons lemon juice to pan juices. Stir and pour over chicken. Add 1 tablespoon olive oil to skillet. Stir in 10–12 ounces fresh SPINACH and 12 cherry TOMATOES, halved, and cook until spinach wilts. Arrange around chicken and serve. (4 servings)

CHICKEN WITH RED PEPPERS: Heat 2 tablespoons mild, light-flavored olive oil in a skillet over medium heat. Add 2 whole chicken breasts, halved, skinned, and boned. Cook 2 minutes on each side. Add 1 clove garlic, minced, ½ cup chopped onion, and 2 medium RED BELL PEPPERS, seeded and diced. Cook, stirring for 2–3 minutes. Add 2 tablespoons red wine vinegar, ¼ cup low-salt chicken broth, 3 cups chopped fresh or canned TOMATOES, ¼ cup chopped olives, and 1 teaspoon dried thyme leaves. Cover, lower heat, and simmer for 20 minutes. (4 servings)

MEXICALI CHICKEN, CORN, AND NECTARINE SKILLET

Corn, chiles, chicken, tomatoes, and nectarines are simmered in fruit juices and spices.

YIELD: *4 servings*
PREPARATION TIME: *20 minutes*
COOKING TIME: *30 minutes*

2 tablespoons mild, light-flavored olive oil
2 whole chicken breasts, skinned, boned, and cut into
    1-inch chunks
¾ cup pear or apple juice
1 cup onion chunks
1 clove garlic, minced
1 teaspoon dried oregano leaves
½ teaspoon ground cumin
2 cups fresh or canned chopped tomatoes
1 4-ounce can green chiles, cut into chunks
1½ cups fresh, frozen, or canned corn kernels
1½ cups nectarine or peach halves
¼ cup chopped fresh parsley

1. Heat olive oil in a skillet over medium heat and sauté chicken chunks for 10 minutes or until lightly browned. Remove chicken from skillet and set aside.
2. Place pear juice, onion, garlic, oregano, and cumin in a heavy soup pot and simmer for 5 minutes.
3. Add chicken, tomatoes, chiles, corn, and nectarine halves. Simmer for 15 minutes.
4. Stir in parsley and serve.

ALGERIAN CHICKEN COUSCOUS

This traditional sweet and spicy North African stew is served with couscous, a wheat product made from high-protein semolina. Look for couscous in the rice section on your grocer's shelf.

YIELD: *4 servings*
PREPARATION TIME: *25 minutes*
COOKING TIME: *30 minutes*

2 tablespoons mild, light-flavored olive oil
1 medium onion, sliced and separated into rings
2 cloves garlic, minced
1 tablespoon ground cumin
½ teaspoon ground cinnamon
¼ teaspoon cayenne pepper
2 cups chopped fresh or canned tomatoes, drained
2 carrots, cut into 1-inch pieces
2 stalks celery, cut into 1-inch pieces
1 cup cauliflower florets
1 red bell pepper, seeded, cut into 1-inch pieces
1 medium turnip, peeled and cubed
¾ cup low-salt chicken broth
1 pound boneless skinless chicken breasts, cut into 1-inch
    strips
1 medium zucchini, cut into ½-inch pieces
½ cup seedless raisins
1 cup water
1 cup quick-cooking whole-wheat couscous
3 tablespoons chopped fresh parsley
1 apple, peeled, cored, and chopped

1. Heat the olive oil in a heavy soup pot over medium heat. Sauté onion and garlic for 5 minutes or until tender.
2. Stir in cumin, cinnamon, and cayenne. Mix well.
3. Add tomatoes, carrots, celery, cauliflower, red bell pepper, turnip, and broth. Bring to a boil, reduce heat, and simmer for 15 minutes.
4. Add chicken and cook for 5 minutes.
5. Add zucchini and raisins. Cook for 5 more minutes.
6. Heat the water in a saucepan to cook the couscous. When it comes to a boil, add the couscous and simmer for 5 minutes. Fluff with a fork.

7. Immediately before serving, stir apple and parsley into chicken stew. Divide couscous among 4 serving bowls and top with the stew.

VARIATIONS
- Substitute 1½ cups drained cooked chick-peas for the chicken
- Substitute diced sweet potato, diced butternut squash, or chopped cabbage for the turnip
- Substitute 2 bay leaves, ½ teaspoon ground coriander, 6 inches stick cinnamon, or 1½ teaspoons chili powder for any of the spices.

GRILLED CHICKEN FAJITAS WITH MANGO

Fajitas are tacos made with flour tortillas. These chicken fajitas are served with mango slices and a selection of accompaniments.

YIELD: *4 servings*
PREPARATION TIME: *30 minutes + 1 hour marinating time*
COOKING TIME: *25 minutes*

MARINADE
⅓ cup mild, light-flavored olive oil
⅓ cup vinegar
1 teaspoon lime juice
½ teaspoon ground cumin
½ teaspoon Dijon mustard
1 clove garlic, minced
2 whole skinless boneless chicken breasts, halved

SALSA
2 cups chopped fresh or canned tomatoes
½ fresh jalapeño pepper, seeded and minced
1 clove garlic, minced
2 scallions, finely chopped
1 avocado, peeled and sliced
½ cup nonfat or low-fat plain yogurt
1 large tomato, chopped
1 green bell pepper, seeded and diced
1 small head green leaf lettuce, shredded
1 red onion, thinly sliced
8 7-inch flour tortillas
1 large mango, pitted and sliced

1. To make the marinade, combine the olive oil, vinegar, lime juice, cumin leaves, mustard, and garlic in a glass bowl. Add chicken and marinate it for 1 hour.

2. Preheat a prepared charcoal or top-of-stove grill or broiler. Also preheat oven to 325 degrees.

3. To make the salsa, combine tomatoes, jalapeño pepper, garlic, and scallions in a medium glass bowl. Set salsa aside.

4. Arrange avocado, yogurt, tomatoes, green bell pepper, lettuce, and red onion in individual serving bowls.

5. Wrap tortillas in foil and place in oven for 15 minutes.

6. Grill chicken 4 inches from hot coals for 5 minutes on each side. Cool slightly and thinly slice.

7. Divide chicken evenly among tortillas. Top with salsa and a few slices of mango on each. Serve with bowls of accompaniments in the center of the table.

Chicken Parts
(Bone-in Breasts or Other Parts of Choice)

EASY ACCESS: THE BASICS

BAKED CHICKEN BREASTS WITH FRUIT

(4 servings)

INGREDIENTS
2 whole chicken breasts, skinned and halved
¼ teaspoon paprika
¾ cup orange juice
1 tablespoon mild, light-flavored olive oil
1 teaspoon grated lemon peel
½ teaspoon dried basil leaves
4 cups fresh or juice-packed fruit (see possibilities below)

1. Preheat oven to 350 degrees.

2. Place chicken breasts in a large baking dish. Sprinkle with paprika.

3. Combine ½ cup orange juice, olive oil, lemon peel, and basil leaves. Pour over chicken.

4. Bake for 20 minutes. Add fruit and remaining orange juice.

5. Bake for 25 minutes or until chicken is done, basting several times.

FRUIT POSSIBILITIES

Pear halves
Apple wedges
Apricot halves
Nectarine wedges
Pineapple spears
Seeded orange and grapefruit sections

QUICK TAKE

CHICKEN WITH CABBAGE AND APPLES: Heat ¼ cup mild, light-flavored olive oil in a heavy soup pot or Dutch oven. Sauté 2 whole chicken breasts, skinned and halved, until browned. Remove from pot and set aside. Add 2 APPLES, cut into wedges, to the pot and sauté for 5 minutes. Remove from pot and set aside. Add 1 large head CABBAGE, coarsely sliced, 1 medium onion, sliced, 1 medium GREEN BELL PEPPER, seeded and cut into strips, and stir-fry until tender. Add 1 tablespoon brown sugar, 1 tablespoon cider vinegar, and ¼ teaspoon caraway seeds. Return apples and chicken to pot. Reduce heat to low, cover, and simmer for 35 minutes until chicken is tender. (4 servings)

GRILLED CHICKEN WITH SPINACH AND RASPBERRIES

Grilled chicken is served on a bed of spinach tossed with raspberry dressing.

YIELD: *4 servings*
PREPARATION TIME: *15 minutes*
COOKING TIME: *10 minutes*

2 whole chicken breasts, skinned, boned, and halved
1 pint fresh raspberries
$\frac{1}{2}$ cup red wine vinegar
2 teaspoons Dijon mustard
1 teaspoon dried basil leaves
$\frac{1}{2}$ cup chopped fresh parsley
1 tablespoon lemon juice
$\frac{1}{4}$ teaspoon black pepper
5 cups fresh spinach leaves, well washed and trimmed
2 seedless oranges, separated into sections
$\frac{1}{4}$ cup chopped walnuts

1. Preheat a prepared charcoal or top-of-stove grill or broiler.
2. Grill chicken 4 inches from heat for 5 minutes on each side. Cool slightly and thinly slice.
3. Combine raspberries, vinegar, mustard, basil, parsley, lemon juice, and pepper in the workbowl of a food processor or in a blender. Process briefly, but do not purée completely.
4. Toss spinach with the raspberry mixture. Divide among 4 plates. Arrange grilled chicken slices over spinach. Top with orange slices and toasted walnuts.

CHICKEN CARIBE

This irresistible Caribbean chicken dish is a combination of lime-marinated chicken, tomatoes, onions, raisins, chili pepper, and pineapple.

YIELD: *4 servings*
PREPARATION TIME: *20 minutes + 30 minutes*
      marinating time
COOKING TIME: *55 minutes*

Juice of 1 lime
Grated peel of 1 lime
¼ teaspoon black pepper
2 whole chicken breasts, skinned and halved
⅓ cup mild, light-flavored olive oil
1½ cups chopped onions
2 cups chopped fresh or canned tomatoes
3 tablespoons seedless raisins
½ red serrano chili pepper, seeded and chopped
1 clove garlic, minced
cup pineapple juice, reserved from pineapple (see below)
¾ cup low-salt chicken broth
1 fresh pineapple, peeled, cored, sliced, and cut into chunks
    or 1 16-ounce can juice-packed pineapple chunks

1. Combine lime juice, lime peel, and black pepper. Place chicken in a glass bowl. Pour lime marinade over chicken and marinate at room temperature for 30 minutes. Turn the pieces every 10 minutes. Drain chicken.
2. Heat olive oil in a skillet over medium heat. Add chicken and brown until lightly golden. Stir in onions, tomatoes, raisins, chili pepper, and garlic.
3. Combine the pineapple juice and the chicken broth. Pour into skillet. Cover and cook over medium heat for 45 minutes or until chicken is tender. Turn chicken several times.
4. Remove chicken with a slotted spoon and place on a serving dish. Keep warm.
5. Add pineapple to skillet. Raise heat and boil to reduce the sauce. When sauce has thickened slightly and pineapple is heated through, spoon it over the chicken.

Turkey Cutlets

EASY ACCESS: THE BASICS

CURRIED FRUIT AND TURKEY CUTLETS

(4 servings)

INGREDIENTS
4 cups chopped fruit (see possibilities below)
2 teaspoons curry powder
4 tablespoons water
4 ½-inch-thick turkey breast cutlets

1. Combine fruit with curry powder and water in a saucepan. Stir and simmer over low heat until fruit is tender.
2. Place each turkey cutlet in the center of a square of aluminum foil and top with 1 cup of fruit.
3. Seal foil packets with double folds.
4. Place in oven and bake at 350 degrees for 20 minutes.

FRUIT POSSIBILITIES

Apples; pears; oranges; bananas
Mango; papaya; pears; pineapple
Apricots; cantaloupe; kiwi; pears
Seeded grapefruit; seeded tangerines; bananas

QUICK TAKE

BASIL-TOMATO TURKEY CUTLETS: Place a ½-inch-thick turkey cutlet in the center of a piece of aluminum foil and top with 1 slice of To-MATO, 1 tablespoon of 1% cottage cheese, and ¼ teaspoon dried basil leaves. Seal foil and bake at 350 degrees for 20 minutes. (1 serving)

TURKEY VEGETABLE CUTLETS

Breaded turkey cutlet strips are served with corn, peppers, scallions, tomatoes, and spinach.

> **YIELD:** *4 servings*
> **PREPARATION TIME:** *25 minutes*
> **COOKING TIME:** *15 minutes*
>
> 1/3 cup plus 2 tablespoons mild, light-flavored olive oil
> 1/4 cup red wine vinegar
> 1/4 teaspoon black pepper
> 3 cups fresh, frozen, or canned corn kernels
> 1 1/2 cups chopped red bell pepper
> 1 1/2 cups chopped green bell pepper
> 1/2 cup chopped scallions
> 1 tomato, diced
> 1/2 cup whole-wheat bread crumbs
> 1/4 teaspoon dried oregano leaves
> 1/4 teaspoon dried basil leaves
> 4 turkey cutlets, 1/4 pound each
> 5 cups fresh spinach leaves, well washed and trimmed

1. Place the 1/3 cup olive oil, red wine vinegar, black pepper, corn, red pepper, and green pepper in a large saucepan. Bring to a boil and reduce heat to medium. Cook for 5 minutes.

2. Remove vegetables from heat and stir in scallions and tomato.

3. Combine bread crumbs with oregano and basil.

4. Dredge turkey cutlets in herbed bread crumbs.

5. Heat the 2 tablespoons olive oil in a skillet over medium heat and sauté turkey cutlets until lightly browned on both sides.

6. Cut turkey cutlets into thin strips.

7. Toss turkey cutlets with vegetable mixture. Serve on a bed of spinach leaves.

Whole Chickens

QUICK TAKES

ROAST CHICKEN WITH CORN STUFFING: Stuff a 4-pound roasting chicken with corn stuffing. To make, sauté ½ onion, chopped, ½ RED BELL PEPPER, seeded and chopped, 1 clove garlic, minced, and 1 cup fresh, frozen and thawed, or canned CORN kernels in 1 tablespoon mild, light-flavored olive oil for 5 minutes. Combine with bread crumbs, made from 5 slices whole-grain bread, ½ teaspoon dried thyme leaves, ½ teaspoon black pepper, ¼ cup tomato juice, and 1 beaten egg white. (You can also bake this stuffing for 30 minutes and serve as a side dish.) (6 servings)

ROAST CHICKEN WITH CRANBERRY STUFFING: Stuff a 4-pound roasting chicken with cranberry nut stuffing. Combine 1½ cups chopped CRANBERRIES, ¾ cup raisins, 1 teaspoon grated orange peel, ¼ teaspoon ground cinnamon, ⅓ cup chopped walnuts, and 2 cups soft whole-grain bread crumbs. Toss with 2 tablespoons melted diet or reduced-calorie margarine and ½ cup low-salt chicken broth. (6 servings)

ROAST CHICKEN WITH APPLE RAISIN STUFFING: Stuff a 4-pound roasting chicken with a mixture of 2 cups chopped APPLES, 2 cups soft whole-grain bread crumbs, ½ cup seedless raisins, 2 tablespoons mild, light-flavored olive oil, 1 tablespoon lemon juice, 1 teaspoon grated lemon peel, ½ teaspoon ground cinnamon, and ¼ cup apple juice. Baste the chicken frequently as it roasts with apple juice. (6 servings)

Cooked Diced Chicken or Turkey

QUICK TAKES

SKILLET POULTRY AND VEGETABLE RATATOUILLE: Steam 1 large EGG-PLANT, diced, 3 medium RED BELL PEPPERS, seeded and diced, and 1 red onion, diced, for 8 minutes. Place in a large bowl with 1 small zucchini, thinly sliced, 1 small yellow squash, thinly sliced, and 4 cups diced cooked chicken or turkey cutlet. Heat 3 tablespoons mild, light-flavored olive oil in a large skillet over medium heat. Sauté 1 clove garlic, minced. Stir in ¼ cup tomato paste and 1 teaspoon red wine vinegar. Add vegetables and chicken. Cook until heated through. Stir in ½ teaspoon dried basil leaves and ¼ teaspoon black pepper. Serve. (4 servings)

BROCCOLI POULTRY SALAD: Mix 2 cups cubed cooked chicken or turkey with 2 cups BROCCOLI florets; 2 TOMATOES, sliced, 1 cup chopped cucumber, 1 cup trimmed SNOW PEAS, and ⅓ cup diced red onion. Toss with ½ cup nonfat or low-fat plain yogurt and 1 tablespoon dried dill leaves. (3–4 servings)

GRAPEFRUIT POULTRY SALAD: Mix 2 cups diced cooked chicken or turkey with 2 GRAPEFRUIT, peeled, seeded, and cut into bite-sized pieces, ¼ cup chopped celery, 1 scallion, minced, ¼ cup reduced-calorie mayonnaise, ¼ cup nonfat or low-fat plain yogurt, and ¼ cup minced fresh parsley. Serve on a bed of salad greens. (3–4 servings)

SPINACH AND FRUIT CHICKEN SALAD: Toss ½ cup mild, light-flavored olive oil, ⅓ cup white wine vinegar, ¼ teaspoon sugar, 1 teaspoon Dijon mustard, ¼ teaspoon dried mint leaves, 1 bunch fresh SPINACH, washed, trimmed, and torn, 1 cup hulled sliced fresh STRAWBERRIES, 1 seedless ORANGE, peeled and separated into sections, 1 AVOCADO, peeled, pitted, and diced, and 1 cup diced cooked chicken. (4 servings)

GREEN BEAN, POULTRY AND POTATO SALAD: Toss 2½ pounds new potatoes, steamed, 1 pound GREEN BEANS, steamed, 1 pound diced cooked turkey breast, ½ teaspoon dried basil leaves, and 1 TOMATO, diced, with 6 tablespoons extra-virgin olive oil, 2 tablespoons red wine vinegar, and ¼ teaspoon black pepper. (4 servings)

TANGERINE POULTRY SALAD: Mix 2 cups diced cooked turkey with 1½ cups TANGERINE sections, seeded and cut into bite-sized pieces, ¼ cup reduced-calorie mayonnaise, ¼ cup nonfat or low-fat plain yogurt, 1 cup diced CANTALOUPE, ½ cup diced celery, and ½ cup chopped walnuts. Serve on a bed of salad greens. (4 servings.)

Seafood

EASY ACCESS: THE BASICS
Broiled Fish Fillets with Fruit Sauce
Baked Fish Fillets with Vegetables and/or Fruit in Foil Packets

QUICK TAKES
Broiled Fish with Vegetable Relish   Mahimahi with Pears

AT YOUR LEISURE
Haddock Eggplant Bake   Chilled Sea Bass with Cantaloupe and Snow Peas

Fish Steaks

QUICK TAKES
Broiled Fish Steaks with Pineapple Salsa   Salmon with Spinach

AT YOUR LEISURE
Sautéed Salmon with Cranberry Relish   Apple and Codfish Curry
Grilled Tuna with Fruit and Vegetable Relish

Scallops and Shrimp

EASY ACCESS: THE BASICS
Stir-fried Shrimp or Scallops and Vegetables and/or Fruit
Shrimp or Scallop Fruit and/or Vegetable Salad

QUICK TAKES
Scallop Asparagus Bake   Shrimp with Citrus   Shrimp with Spinach

AT YOUR LEISURE
Scallop Stew

Canned or Shredded Fish or Crab

QUICK TAKES
Vegetable Crab Toss   Papaya Crab Salad   Tuna Garden Macaroni
Eggplant Tuna Salad   Salmon Berry Salad   Broccoli Crab Pasta Salad

AT YOUR LEISURE
Salmon Vegetable Bake   Tuna Salad Niçoise with Fruit

n addition to the recipes below, you can also enhance baked, sau-téed, grilled, or broiled fish fillets, fish steaks, or whole fish with one of the Low-Fat sauces (page 269).

The following sauces work particularly well with fish:

Tomato Salsa (page 272)
Basic Vegetable Sauce (page 271)
Vegetable Relish (page 273)
Sweet and Pungent Vegetable Sauce (page 274)
Lemon, Mango, Papaya Sauce (page 275)
Tropical Salsa (page 275)
Raspberry Salsa (page 276)
Mango Salsa (page 276)
Strawberry Relish (page 276)
Raspberry-Cranberry Relish (page 276)
Crunchy Vegetable Topping (page 277)
Apple-Blueberry Sauce (page 278)
Pineapple Sauce (page 279)
Melon Sauce (page 282)
Eggplant Sauce (page 282)
Spinach Sauce (page 284)
Pepper-Apple Relish (page 286)
Harvest Chutney (page 286)

Fish Fillets

EASY ACCESS: THE BASICS

BROILED FISH FILLETS WITH FRUIT SAUCE

(4 servings)

INGREDIENTS
1 pound flounder fillets or other fish fillets
1 tablespoon mild, light-flavored olive oil
2 cups chopped fruit (see possibilities below)
¾ cup orange juice

1. Preheat broiler.
2. Place fish fillets in oiled broiler pan. Brush fillets with olive oil. Broil for 5 minutes per inch of thickness, turning once.
3. Place half the fruit in the workbowl of a food processor or in a blender and purée.
4. Pour orange juice into a medium saucepan and bring to a boil. Stir in fruit purée and remaining whole or sliced fruit.
5. Spoon fruit sauce over flounder before serving.

FRUIT POSSIBILITIES
Apricots
Blueberries
Mango and kiwi
Nectarines
Strawberries
Papaya
Cantaloupe
Raspberries
Seeded tangerines

BAKED FISH FILLETS WITH VEGETABLES
AND/OR FRUIT IN FOIL PACKETS

(4 servings)

INGREDIENTS
1 pound white-fleshed fish fillet, such as turbot, cut into
    4 portions
¼ teaspoon black pepper
¼ teaspoon ground ginger
4 cups chopped vegetables and/or fruit (see possibilities
    below)

1. Preheat oven to 400 degrees.
2. Sprinkle fillets with pepper and ginger.
3. Cut 4 12-inch squares of aluminum foil.
4. Place a portion of fish on each piece of foil.
5. Combine vegetables and/or fruit.
6. Divide vegetable and/or fruit mixture among the 4 fish packets.
7. Seal the foil packets with a double fold. Place packages in a baking pan and bake for 30 minutes or until the fish flakes when tested with a fork.

VEGETABLE AND FRUIT POSSIBILITIES

Pineapple; green bell pepper; tomato
Navel oranges; red bell pepper; carrots
Red grapefruit; green beans; celery
Cauliflower; yellow summer squash; nectarines
Broccoli; corn; tomatoes

QUICK TAKES

BROILED FISH WITH VEGETABLE RELISH: Brush 4 1-inch-thick fish fillets with 2 tablespoons mild, light-flavored olive oil and sprinkle with black pepper. Broil for about 6 minutes or until fish is just opaque. Heat 2 tablespoons mild, light-flavored olive oil in a skillet over medium heat. Sauté 1 GREEN BELL PEPPER, seeded and cut into thin strips, 1 RED BELL PEPPER, seeded and cut into thin strips, 1 YELLOW BELL PEPPER, seeded and cut into thin strips, 1 jalapeño pepper, seeded and chopped, 1 cup sliced fresh mushrooms, and 1 teaspoon dried basil leaves for 4 minutes. Serve broiled fish fillets topped with sautéed vegetables. (4 servings)

MAHIMAHI WITH PEARS: Preheat oven to 500 degrees. Place 4 ¼-pound pieces of mahimahi or swordfish on 4 squares of aluminum foil. Combine 1 onion, thinly sliced, 1 pound PEARS, cored and cut into thin strips, 1 teaspoon minced fresh gingerroot, the juice of 2 limes, and ½ teaspoon ground allspice. Top the fish with this mixture. Fold foil to seal packets tightly. Place packets in the oven and bake for 15 minutes or until mahimahi flakes when tested with a fork. (4 servings)

AT YOUR LEISURE

HADDOCK EGGPLANT BAKE

This simple combination of haddock and eggplant is baked in a tomato sauce with a bread-crumb topping.

> **YIELD:** *4 servings*
> **PREPARATION TIME:** *20 minutes*
> **COOKING TIME:** *30 minutes*
>
> 5 tablespoons mild, light-flavored olive oil
> 1½ cups chopped onions
> 1 pound eggplant, peeled and cut into 1-inch cubes
> 1 clove garlic, minced
> ⅛ teaspoon cayenne pepper
> 1 bay leaf
> 4 cups chopped fresh or canned tomatoes
> 2 tablespoons tomato paste
> 1 pound haddock fillets, cut into 2-inch chunks
> ¼ cup chopped fresh parsley
> 1 cup whole-grain bread crumbs

1. Heat 2 tablespoons of the olive oil in a skillet over medium heat. Sauté onions for 3 minutes.
2. Add 2 more tablespoons of olive oil to the skillet. Add eggplant. Sauté for 5 minutes.
3. Preheat oven to 425 degrees.
4. Stir in garlic, cayenne, bay leaf, tomatoes, and tomato paste. Cook, covered, for 5 minutes. Uncover and cook for 5 minutes more.
5. Stir the fish and parsley into the vegetable mixture. Spoon the mixture into a lightly oiled baking dish.

6. Heat remaining 1 tablespoon olive oil in the skillet and sauté the bread crumbs.

7. Sprinkle bread crumbs over vegetable-fish mixture in baking dish. Bake for 15 minutes.

CHILLED SEA BASS WITH CANTALOUPE AND SNOW PEAS

Chunks of sea bass are simmered in a marinade, chilled, and tossed with melon and snow peas.

> **YIELD:** *4 servings*
> **PREPARATION TIME:** *20 minutes + 1 hour marinating time*
> **COOKING TIME:** *7 minutes*
>
> 1 tablespoon grated lemon peel
> 6 tablespoons lemon juice
> 3 tablespoons light soy sauce
> 1¾ cups water
> 1 pound sea bass fillets, cut into 1-inch cubes
> ½ pound snow peas, trimmed and cut into 1-inch pieces
> 2 tablespoons mild, light-flavored olive oil
> 1 tablespoon minced scallion
> ¼ teaspoon dried thyme leaves
> 2 cups cantaloupe chunks
> 1 tablespoon chopped fresh parsley

1. Combine lemon peel, 4 tablespoons of the lemon juice, 1 tablespoon of the soy sauce, and the water in a large skillet. Heat until simmering. Add fish cubes and simmer for 4 minutes.

2. Drain fish. Place in a covered bowl and refrigerate for 1 hour.

3. Ten minutes before serving time, bring a small saucepan of water to a boil. Add snow peas and cook for 2 minutes. Plunge into cold water and drain.

4. Toss snow peas with the remaining 2 tablespoons lemon juice, the remaining 2 tablespoons soy sauce, olive oil, scallion, thyme, cantaloupe, and parsley.

5. Add fish and toss again.

Fish Steaks

QUICK TAKES

BROILED FISH STEAKS WITH PINEAPPLE SALSA: Preheat broiler. Combine 1 small fresh PINEAPPLE, peeled, cored, and cut into small cubes, 1 red onion, diced, 1 RED BELL PEPPER, seeded and diced, 1 YELLOW BELL PEPPER, seeded and diced, 1 teaspoon ground cumin, 2 tablespoons lime juice, 1 large clove garlic, minced, in a medium bowl. Set salsa aside. Brush both sides of 2 medium fish steaks (1 pound of swordfish, halibut, or other fish of choice) with ¼ cup mild, light-flavored olive oil. Season with ¼ teaspoon black pepper. Broil for 5 minutes on each side or until fish is no longer translucent and flakes easily when tested with a fork. Serve fish topped with salsa. (4 servings)

SALMON WITH SPINACH: Preheat broiler. Broil 1 pound salmon steaks 4 inches from heat for 5 minutes. Turn salmon and season with ¼ teaspoon black pepper and 1 teaspoon dried dillweed. Broil for 5 minutes more or until fish flakes when tested with a fork. While salmon is broiling, place 1 tablespoon mild, light-flavored olive oil in a skillet and heat over medium heat. Add 1 onion, chopped, and 1 clove garlic, minced, and sauté for 5 minutes. Stir in 2 pounds SPINACH, washed and leaves cut into 1-inch strips. Cover pan and cook over high heat for 3 minutes. Transfer spinach mixture to a serving dish and top with broiled salmon. (4 servings)

AT YOUR LEISURE

SAUTÉED SALMON WITH CRANBERRY RELISH

Sautéed salmon is topped with a zesty combination of cranberries, orange bits, scallions, and celery.

YIELD: *4 servings*
PREPARATION TIME: *20 minutes*
COOKING TIME: *20 minutes*

1 cup fresh cranberries, chopped
¾ cup orange juice
1 teaspoon sugar
¼ cup chopped celery
2 large seedless oranges, peeled, separated into
    sections, and chopped
2 tablespoons chopped scallions
1 teaspoon red wine vinegar
2 tablespoons mild, light-flavored olive oil
1 pound salmon steaks, each ¾ inch thick.

1. Place cranberries, orange juice, and sugar in a heavy saucepan. Bring to a boil, reduce heat, and simmer for 10 minutes.
2. Add celery, oranges, scallions, and vinegar. Simmer for 2 minutes. Cover and remove from heat.
3. Heat oil in a large skillet over medium heat. Add salmon. Sauté for 5 minutes. Turn and sauté for 4 more minutes. Salmon is done when flesh is opaque and flakes easily when tested with a fork at the thickest part.
4. Place salmon on a serving platter and spoon the cranberry relish over it.

APPLE AND CODFISH CURRY

Serve this quick and easy curry with brown rice.

> **YIELD:** *4 servings*
> **PREPARATION TIME:** *25 minutes*
> **COOKING TIME:** *25 minutes*
>
> 2 tablespoons mild, light-flavored olive oil
> 1 onion, chopped
> 2 cloves garlic, minced
> 2 teaspoons curry powder
> 3 cups fresh or canned crushed tomatoes
> ¼ cup seedless raisins
> 2 medium apples, peeled, cored, and chopped
> 1 pound cod steaks, skin and bones removed, cut into
>   1-inch pieces.

1. Heat olive oil in a skillet over medium heat. Sauté onion and garlic for 5 minutes.

2. Stir in curry powder, tomatoes, raisins, and apples. Cook for 15 minutes.

3. Stir fish pieces into tomato mixture and cook for 10 minutes or until fish is tender.

GRILLED TUNA WITH FRUIT AND VEGETABLE RELISH

Tuna steaks are rubbed with olive oil and pepper, grilled, and served with a pungent fruit and vegetable relish.

YIELD: *4 servings*
PREPARATION TIME: *20 minutes + 1 hour chilling time*
COOKING TIME: *10 minutes*

RELISH
¼ cup mild, light-flavored olive oil
1 red bell pepper, seeded and cut into strips
½ red onion, chopped
1 clove garlic, minced
6 firm nectarines, pitted, peeled, and diced
½ teaspoon dried basil leaves
¼ cup red wine vinegar
¼ cup orange juice

1½ pounds tuna steaks, each 1 inch thick
4 tablespoons mild, light-flavored olive oil
¼ teaspoon white pepper
¼ teaspoon black pepper.

1. To make the relish, heat 1 tablespoon of the olive oil in a skillet over medium heat and sauté red pepper, onion, and garlic for 3 minutes.
2. Combine sautéed vegetables with the remaining olive oil, nectarines, basil, vinegar, and orange juice in a glass bowl and refrigerate for 1 hour.
3. Rub tuna steaks with oil and pepper. Grill over medium heat for 5 minutes. Turn and grill for 5 more minutes.
4. Serve tuna topped with relish.

Scallops and Shrimp

EASY ACCESS: THE BASICS

STIR-FRIED SHRIMP OR SCALLOPS AND VEGETABLES AND/OR FRUIT

(4 servings)

INGREDIENTS
3 tablespoons mild, light-flavored olive oil
1 scallion, minced
2 slices fresh gingerroot, minced
1 clove garlic, minced
1 pound shrimp, shelled and deveined, or 1 pound
    scallops, cut into 1/4-inch slices if large or cut in half
    if small
3 cups sliced or diced vegetables and/or fruit (see
    possibilities below)
1/3 cup low-salt chicken broth
2 tablespoons light soy sauce
1 tablespoon nonalcoholic wine or dry sherry

1. Heat 2 tablespoons olive oil in a wok or skillet over medium heat. Add scallion, gingerroot, and garlic. Stir-fry for 30 seconds.
2. Add shrimp and stir-fry until they turn pink.
3. Remove ingredients from wok and set aside.
4. Add remaining oil. Add vegetables and/or fruit. Stir-fry for 2 minutes.
5. Stir in broth and heat quickly. Cook, covered, over medium heat until vegetables are nearly done.
6. Return shrimp to wok or skillet and stir.
7. Add soy sauce and wine. Stir to blend flavors. Serve.

VEGETABLE AND/OR FRUIT POSSIBILITIES
Green bell peppers; tomatoes; pineapple
Peas; mushrooms; bamboo shoots; nectarines
Green beans; onion; oranges

Green beans; bean sprouts; celery; tomatoes; onion
Broccoli; celery; onion; seeded tangerines
Asparagus; bamboo shoots; water chestnuts; yellow summer squash

SHRIMP OR SCALLOP FRUIT AND/OR VEGETABLE SALAD

(4 servings)

INGREDIENTS
1 pound cooked shelled shrimp or scallops
8 medium mushrooms, sliced
8 cups chopped, sliced, or sectioned fruits and vegetables
    (see possibilities below)
¼ cup mild, light-flavored olive oil
¼ cup orange juice
1 tablespoon lemon juice
¼ teaspoon black pepper

1. Toss shrimp or scallops, mushrooms, fruits and/or vegetables together in a large salad bowl.
2. Combine olive oil, orange juice, lemon juice, and black pepper in a jar with a tight-fitting lid and shake well.
3. Toss salad with dressing.

FRUIT AND/OR VEGETABLE POSSIBILITIES

Steamed green beans; asparagus; chopped tomatoes; oranges; avocado
Green peas; nectarines or peaches; shredded red cabbage; corn; red bell
    peppers
Raw spinach; carrots; blanched cauliflower; blueberries; green bell pepper
Shredded romaine lettuce; blanched broccoli; cantaloupe; cooked lima
    beans; zucchini
Avocado; red apple; yellow or green apple; green bell pepper; cooked
    lima beans
Shredded romaine lettuce; watercress; papaya; mango; kiwi; pineapple

QUICK TAKES

SCALLOP ASPARAGUS BAKE: Sauté 1 onion, thinly sliced, and 1 clove garlic, minced, in 4 tablespoons mild, light-flavored olive oil until the onion is limp. Add 1 pound bay scallops and sauté for 3 minutes. Arrange 1 pound steamed ASPARAGUS on an ovenproof platter. Surround with scallop mixture. Sprinkle with bread crumbs, grated parmesan cheese, and minced parsley. Broil until lightly browned. (4 servings)

SHRIMP WITH CITRUS: Mix 1½ cups cooked shrimp with ½ cup drained unsweetened PINEAPPLE chunks, 1 cup seedless ORANGE sections, cut into bite-sized pieces, 1 cup thinly sliced celery, 1 tablespoon lemon juice, ¼ teaspoon black pepper, and 2 tablespoons mild, light-flavored olive oil. (2–3 servings)

SHRIMP WITH SPINACH: Combine 1 large bunch torn SPINACH, 3 cups CAULIFLOWER florets, 1 cup cooked medium shrimp, 1 AVOCADO, chopped, 4 scallions, chopped. Combine ¼ cup white wine vinegar, 1 tablespoon honey, 1 teaspoon curry powder, ½ teaspoon dry mustard, ¼ teaspoon white pepper, and ⅔ cup extra-virgin olive oil. Toss dressing with salad. (4 servings)

AT YOUR LEISURE

SCALLOP STEW

Bay scallops are added to a spicy stew.

> **YIELD:** *4 servings*
> **PREPARATION TIME:** *20 minutes*
> **COOKING TIME:** *34 minutes*
>
> 2 tablespoons mild, light-flavored olive oil
> 1 onion, chopped
> 1 clove garlic, minced
> ¼ teaspoon ground cumin
> ¼ teaspoon cayenne pepper
> 3½ cups chopped fresh or canned plum tomatoes with
>   their juice
> 1¼ cups water

½ teaspoon dried oregano leaves
2 cups cauliflower florets
1 cup sliced green beans
1 cup sliced carrots
1 pound bay scallops
¼ teaspoon black pepper
¼ cup chopped fresh parsley

1. Heat olive oil in a heavy soup pot over medium heat. Sauté onion for 5 minutes.
2. Add garlic, cumin, and cayenne. Sauté for 2 minutes.
3. Place tomatoes and juice in the workbowl of food processor or in a blender and purée.
4. Add tomatoes, water, and oregano to soup pot. Cook for 10 minutes.
5. Add cauliflower, green beans, and carrots. Cook for 15 minutes.
6. Add scallops and cook for 2 minutes or until they are opaque.

Canned or Shredded Fish and Crab

QUICK TAKES

VEGETABLE CRAB TOSS: Heat 3 tablespoons mild, light-flavored olive oil in a skillet over medium heat. Sauté 1 cup sliced celery, 1 cup sliced CARROTS, 1 cup sliced mushrooms, 1 chopped GREEN BELL PEPPER, and 1 clove garlic, minced, for 5 minutes. Stir in 6 ounces fresh or canned shredded crab meat, ½ cup cooked fresh or frozen GREEN PEAS, ⅓ cup water, ¼ teaspoon dried dillweed, and ¼ teaspoon black pepper. Simmer for 4 minutes. Toss with cooked drained rotini or rice. (4 servings)
PAPAYA CRAB SALAD: Combine 3 whole PAPAYAS, cut into 1-inch chunks, 12 ounces fresh or canned crab meat, ½ cup chopped scallions, 3 tablespoons seedless raisins, ¾ cup nonfat or low-fat plain yogurt, 1½ teaspoons curry powder, and 1 tablespoon lime juice. Chill and serve on a bed of lettuce leaves. (4 servings)
TUNA GARDEN MACARONI: Mix 1 7½-ounce can of white albacore tuna, packed in water and drained, 2 cups cooked macaroni, 1 cup grated

CARROTS, 1 cup seeded ORANGE sections, cut into bite-sized pieces, 1 cup diced celery, 1 scallion, minced, 1 tablespoon lemon juice, and ½ cup reduced-calorie mayonnaise. Chill for 2 hours and serve on salad greens. (4 servings)

EGGPLANT TUNA SALAD: Toss 1 medium EGGPLANT, diced and steamed, 1 large RED BELL PEPPER, seeded and chopped, ½ cup mild, light-flavored olive oil, ⅓ cup red wine vinegar, 1 teaspoon dried oregano leaves, 1 large TOMATO, chopped, ½ cup pitted olives, and 1 7½-ounce can water-packed white albacore tuna, drained and flaked. Cover and refrigerate for 1 hour. Drain marinade, reserving 1 tablespoon. Toss eggplant tuna mixture with the 1 tablespoon marinade. Sprinkle, if desired, with crumbled feta cheese. (4 servings)

SALMON BERRY SALAD: Toss 2 cups flaked canned salmon, bones removed, ½ cup hulled sliced fresh STRAWBERRIES, ½ cup whole BLUE-BERRIES, 1 cup HONEYDEW melon chunks, and ½ cup seedless red grapes in a large bowl. Combine 2 tablespoons nonfat or low-fat plain yogurt, 2 tablespoons reduced-calorie mayonnaise, 1 teaspoon lemon juice, and 1 tablespoon chopped chives or scallions. Toss dressing with salmon fruit mixture. Serve over 2 cups shredded ROMAINE lettuce or RED CABBAGE. (4 servings)

BROCCOLI CRAB PASTA SALAD: Bring 1 inch of water to a boil in a steamer. Place 1 cup BROCCOLI florets in the steamer basket and set over the boiling water. Cover and steam until tender, about 8 minutes. Toss broccoli with ½ pound pasta shells, cooked, ½ cup sliced radishes, 12 ounces fresh or canned crab meat, 1 YELLOW BELL PEPPER, seeded and cut into thin strips, 2 AVOCADOS, peeled, pitted, and diced, ¼ cup chopped scallions, ¼ cup chopped fresh parsley, ½ cup mild, light-flavored olive oil, 1 tablespoon honey, 1 tablespoon lemon juice, ⅛ teaspoon black pepper, 2 tablespoons Dijon mustard, and 1 clove garlic, minced. (4 servings)

AT YOUR LEISURE

SALMON VEGETABLE BAKE

Vitamin- and fiber-rich broccoli and cauliflower are combined with the heart-helping Omega 3 oils in salmon.

YIELD: *4 servings*
PREPARATION TIME: *20 minutes*
COOKING TIME: *45 minutes*

1½ cups cauliflower florets
1½ cups broccoli florets and chopped stems
1½ tablespoons mild, light-flavored olive oil
2 scallions, minced
2 tablespoons unbleached all-purpose flour
1½ cups skim or low-fat milk
¾ cup grated nonfat or low-fat cheese
½ cup chopped mushrooms
1 tablespoon chopped fresh parsley
½ teaspoon dried dill leaves
1 7¾-ounce can salmon, drained and cut into chunks
     with skin and bones removed
¼ cup grated Parmesan cheese

1. Preheat oven to 350 degrees. Lightly oil a 2-quart casserole.
2. Steam the cauliflower and broccoli until just tender.
3. Heat the olive oil in a large saucepan. Sauté scallions until soft. Remove scallions with a slotted spoon and set aside.
4. Stir the flour into the oil in the saucepan and cook until mixture bubbles. Add milk and stir constantly to keep lumps from forming.
5. Add cheese, mushrooms, parsley, and dill. Stir until cheese has melted.
6. Add salmon, steamed cauliflower and broccoli, and sautéed scallions to cheese mixture. Transfer to casserole. Sprinkle with Parmesan cheese.
7. Bake, uncovered, for 35 minutes or until the cheese has formed a light brown crust.

TUNA SALAD NIÇOISE WITH FRUIT

This classic salad makes a splendid meal that's packed with albacore tuna, crisp green beans, red potato slices, radishes, green pepper, apple, and pear.

YIELD: *6 servings*
PREPARATION TIME: *25 minutes*
COOKING TIME: *12 minutes + egg cooking time*

1 pound small fresh green beans, trimmed
2 cups sliced unpeeled red potatoes
1 12½-ounce can white albacore tuna, packed in water, drained
¾ pound cherry tomatoes, halved
¾ cup diced apple, cored but not peeled, tossed with lemon juice
¾ cup diced pear, cored but not peeled, tossed with lemon juice
1 medium green bell pepper, seeded and cut into thin strips
½ cup chopped red onion
6 large radishes, sliced
¼ cup black olives, rinsed
3 hard-cooked egg whites, quartered
2 tablespoons chopped fresh parsley
¼ cup extra-virgin olive oil
⅓ cup lemon juice
1 clove garlic, minced
¼ teaspoon black pepper
1 large head leaf lettuce, torn

1. Cook green beans in a small amount of boiling water for 5 minutes or until crisp-tender. Drain and plunge into ice water. Drain and set aside.

2. Cook potatoes in boiling water for 7 minutes. Drain and plunge into ice water. Drain and let cool.

3. Toss beans, potatoes, tuna, tomatoes, apple, pear, pepper strips, onion, radishes, olives, and egg whites together in a large bowl.

4. Combine parsley, olive oil, lemon juice, garlic, and black pepper in a jar with a tight-fitting lid. Shake well and pour over tuna mixture.

5. Line a large serving platter with the lettuce. Spoon tuna salad over the leaves.

Meat

Pork

EASY ACCESS: THE BASICS
Stir-Fried Pork and Vegetables and/or Fruit   Pork and Fruit Salad

QUICK TAKES
Pork, Spinach, and Fruit Toss   Orange Pork Salad

AT YOUR LEISURE
Dijon Rosemary Pork with Apple Tomato Sauce
Simmered Fruit and Vegetable Pork   Pork Stew with Eggplant
Pork Chops with Cranberries

Beef

EASY ACCESS: THE BASICS
Stir-fried Beef and Vegetables   Vegetable and Ground Beef Chili

QUICK TAKES
Roast Beef and Vegetable Hash   Roast Beef Salad   Ground Beef Stew

AT YOUR LEISURE
Beef Vegetable Stew   Grapefruit and Beef Stew   Pumpkin and Beef Stew

Veal

QUICK TAKES
Veal Cutlet with TriColor Peppers   Veal Scallops and Pears

AT YOUR LEISURE
Veal Chops with Apricots
Paprika Veal and Carrots and Turnips with Applesauce

Lamb

QUICK TAKES
Ground Lamb and Red Pepper Bake   Garden Lamb

AT YOUR LEISURE
Spiced Lamb and Vegetables

In addition to the recipes below, you can prepare baked, sautéed, grilled, or broiled pork chops, veal chops, lamp chops, roast beef slices, or hamburgers with the addition of one of the Low-Fat sauces (page 269).

The following sauces work particularly well with meat.

Tomato Salsa (page 272)
Basic Vegetable Sauce (page 271)
Vegetable Relish (page 273)
Sweet and Pungent Vegetable Sauce (page 274)
Raspberry-Cranberry Relish (page 276)
Spicy Paradise Chutney (page 277)
Eggplant Sauce (page 282)
Asparagus Sauce (page 283)
Spinach Sauce (page 284)
Tomato Jalapeño Sauce (page 285)
Pepper-Apple Relish (page 286)
Harvest Chutney (page 286)

Pork

EASY ACCESS: THE BASICS

STIR-FRIED PORK AND VEGETABLES AND/OR FRUIT

(4 servings)

INGREDIENTS
¾ pound lean boneless pork
2 tablespoons light soy sauce
1½ cups water
3 tablespoons dry sherry or nonalcoholic wine
4 tablespoons mild, light-flavored olive oil
1 onion, thinly sliced
1 clove garlic, minced
1½ cups water
3 cups chopped, sliced, or diced vegetables and/or fruit
    (see possibilities below)

1. Slice pork into narrow strips, 1½ inches long x ¼ inch thick.
2. Combine 1 tablespoon of the soy sauce, 1 tablespoon of the water, and 1 tablespoon of the sherry in a small bowl. Pour over pork and marinate for 20 minutes.
3. Heat olive oil in a wok or large skillet. Add pork and stir-fry until brown on all sides. Add onion and garlic and stir-fry for 1 minute more.
4. Add remaining water, soy sauce, and sherry. Stir in vegetables and/or fruit. Cover and cook for 5 minutes.

VEGETABLE POSSIBILITIES

Blanched cauliflower; snow peas; water chestnuts; bamboo shoots
Cabbage; tomatoes
Blanched green beans; tomatoes; onions
Blanched carrots; peas; celery; almonds
Green bell peppers; tomatoes; mushrooms; onions
Pineapple; green bell pepper; water chestnuts
Spinach; blanched carrots

Green bell pepper; zucchini; orange segments
Blanched green beans; carrots; pears

PORK AND FRUIT SALAD

(4 servings)

INGREDIENTS
6 cups torn romaine lettuce
1 pound thinly sliced cooked pork strips
2½ cups chopped fruit (see possibilities below)
1½ cups toasted chopped walnuts
¼ cup light soy sauce
2 tablespoons honey
1 tablespoon red wine vinegar
2 tablespoons lemon juice
1 teaspoon minced fresh gingerroot
1 clove garlic, minced
¼ cup mild, light-flavored olive oil

1. Place romaine in a salad bowl. Top with pork, fruit, and walnuts.
2. Combine soy sauce, honey, vinegar, lemon juice, ginger, garlic, and oil. Toss with salad.

FRUIT POSSIBILITIES

Apricots; bananas; strawberries
Nectarines; blueberries; pineapple
Pears; seeded tangerines; kiwi
Cantaloupe; watermelon; apricots

QUICK TAKES

PORK, SPINACH, AND FRUIT TOSS: Heat 2 tablespoons mild, light-flavored olive oil in a skillet over medium heat. Sauté 1 pound lean boneless pork loin, cut into thin strips, for 5 minutes or until cooked through. Set aside. Combine 1 pound fresh SPINACH, rinsed and stemmed, 1 cup chopped celery, 1 cup seedless red grapes, ½ cup chopped scallions, 1 can water chestnuts, drained and sliced, and 1 APPLE, cored and chopped, in a large salad bowl. Heat ½ cup olive oil, 2 tablespoons white wine vinegar, 2 tablespoons Dijon mustard, and 1 teaspoon brown sugar in a saucepan until the sugar is dissolved. Add pork to saucepan and stir to coat with dressing. Add 2 tablespoons toasted sesame seeds to dressing. Pour warm dressing over spinach mixture and toss. (4 servings)

ORANGE PORK SALAD: Heat 2 tablespoons mild, light-flavored olive oil in a skillet over medium heat. Sauté 1 clove garlic, minced, until golden brown. Add ½ pound lean boneless pork, trimmed and cut into 1-inch-long thin strips, and sauté until lightly browned. Add 2 tablespoons crushed unsalted roasted peanuts and sauté for 2 minutes. Add 2 tablespoons light soy sauce, 2 tablespoons water, ⅛ teaspoon paprika, and ⅛ teaspoon black pepper. Stir-fry for 4 minutes. Remove from heat. Tear 1 small head red leaf lettuce, separated into leaves, washed, and dried, and arrange on salad plates with 4 large seedless ORANGES, peeled and separated into sections. Divide pork and sauce among the plates, pouring the sauce over the oranges and lettuce. Sprinkle the salads with 2 tablespoons chopped scallions. Chill until ready to serve. (4 servings)

AT YOUR LEISURE

DIJON ROSEMARY PORK WITH APPLE TOMATO SAUCE

Lean pork is roasted with an array of spices.

> **YIELD:** *4 servings*
> **PREPARATION TIME:** *15 minutes*
> **COOKING TIME:** *40 minutes*
>
> 1 pound lean pork tenderloin
> 2 cloves garlic, minced
> 1½ tablespoons Dijon mustard
> 1 teaspoon dried rosemary leaves
> ¼ teaspoon ground cloves
> 2 tablespoons apple juice
> 3 cups fresh or canned crushed tomatoes
> 3 large apples, peeled, cored, and cut into ½-inch slices

1. Preheat oven to 450 degrees.
2. Place the pork tenderloin in a lightly oiled baking dish.
3. Combine garlic, mustard, rosemary, and cloves. Spread over pork. Bake for 10 minutes.
4. Reduce heat to 400 degrees and sprinkle apple juice over pork. Bake for 10 minutes.
5. Spoon tomatoes and apples over and around the pork. Bake for 20 minutes.

SIMMERED FRUIT AND VEGETABLE PORK

This simmered pork dish should be served with brown rice.

YIELD: *6 servings*
PREPARATION TIME: *20 minutes*
COOKING TIME: *1 hour and 30 minutes*

1½ pounds lean pork shoulder, cut into 2-inch cubes
2 cups water
8 tablespoons mild, light-flavored olive oil
1 clove garlic, minced
1 onion, chopped
3 tablespoons unbleached all-purpose flour
3 cups low-salt chicken broth
1 tablespoon light soy sauce
2½ cups fresh or canned juice-packed pineapple cubes
3 stalks celery, cut into 1-inch pieces
1 green bell pepper, seeded and cut into 1-inch pieces

1. Place pork in a heavy soup pot with the water and simmer until almost tender, about 1¼ hours. Add more water, if needed, and turn pork frequently. Lift pork from pot and set aside. Pour any remaining water out of pot.
2. Heat olive oil in pot over medium heat. Sauté garlic and onion for 5 minutes. Remove pot from heat and stir flour into onion-garlic mixture. Return to moderate heat and add broth, stirring, until the sauce comes to a boil and thickens.
3. Add soy sauce, pork, and pineapple. Reduce heat and simmer for 15 minutes or until meat is tender. Add celery and green pepper and cook for 2 minutes more.

PORK STEW WITH EGGPLANT

Lean pork is simmered with onion and paired with eggplant for a soul-warming stew.

YIELD: *4 servings*
PREPARATION TIME: *15 minutes*
COOKING TIME: *1 hour and 50 minutes*

1 pound lean boneless pork chunks
3 tablespoons unbleached all-purpose flour
4 tablespoons mild, light-flavored olive oil
6 tablespoons chopped onion
1/2 teaspoon dried thyme leaves
1/4 teaspoon ground sage
1/4 teaspoon ground allspice
1/4 teaspoon black pepper
1 cup water
2 cups 1-inch eggplant cubes

1. Dredge the pork in the flour.
2. Heat the olive oil in a heavy soup pot and add the onion. Sauté for 5 minutes. Add the pork and sauté until it is lightly browned on all sides.
3. Add the thyme, sage, allspice, pepper, and water. Cover and cook over low heat until the pork is tender, about 1½ hours.
4. Add the eggplant, cover, and cook for 15 minutes more or until the eggplant is tender.

PORK CHOPS WITH CRANBERRIES

Pork chops are baked with cranberries and honey in this easy-to-fix recipe. Prepare it in ten minutes, pop it in the oven, and relax!

YIELD: *4 servings*
PREPARATION TIME: *10 minutes*
COOKING TIME: *1 hour*

4 lean pork chops
2 tablespoons mild, light-flavored olive oil
¼ teaspoon black pepper
½ pound raw cranberries
½ cup honey
2 tablespoons water

1. Preheat oven to 350 degrees. Sauté pork chops in the olive oil until browned on both sides.
2. Place chops in a casserole and sprinkle with black pepper.
3. Crush the cranberries and combine them with the honey and water in a small bowl. Pour over the pork chops in the casserole.
4. Cover the casserole and bake for 1 hour.

Beef

EASY ACCESS: THE BASICS

STIR-FRIED BEEF AND VEGETABLES

(4 servings)

INGREDIENTS

1 tablespoon cornstarch
1 tablespoon light soy sauce
1 tablespoon sherry or nonalcoholic white wine
½ teaspoon sugar
3 tablespoons mild, light-flavored olive oil
¾ pound lean beef, sliced thin across the grain
2 slices fresh gingerroot, minced
1 clove garlic, minced
1 scallion, minced
3 cups chopped, sliced, or diced vegetables (see
    possibilities below)
½ cup low-salt chicken broth

1. Combine cornstarch, soy sauce, sherry, and sugar. Add to beef and toss to coat. Let stand 15 minutes, stirring several times.
2. Heat 1½ tablespoons of the olive oil in a wok or heavy skillet. Add the beef and stir-fry about 2 minutes or until it is no longer pink. Remove from wok with a slotted spoon and set aside.
3. Add remaining oil to wok. Add gingerroot, garlic, and scallion and stir-fry for 30 seconds.
4. Add chopped vegetables and stir-fry to heat and coat with oil.
5. Add broth and cook, covered, until vegetables are nearly tender.
6. Return beef to wok and stir-fry for 2 minutes more. Serve over rice.

VEGETABLE POSSIBILITIES

Cabbage; celery; onion
Green bell pepper; blanched carrots; celery; bean sprouts
Green peas; mushrooms

Blanched cauliflower; green peas; red bell peppers
Snow peas; water chestnuts; celery
Asparagus; mushrooms; blanched carrots
Blanched broccoli; red bell peppers; bamboo shoot

VEGETABLE AND GROUND BEEF CHILI

(6 servings)

INGREDIENTS

1½ pounds lean ground beef
3 tablespoons mild, light-flavored olive oil
1 large onion, chopped
4 cups chopped vegetables (see possibilities below)
1 28-ounce can Italian plum tomatoes with juice
¾ cup water
1 6-ounce can tomato paste
2 tablespoons chili powder
2 cloves garlic, minced
1 teaspoon dried oregano leaves
1 teaspoon dried basil leaves
¼ teaspoon ground cumin
1 15-ounce can red kidney beans or pinto beans, drained

1. Cook ground beef in a heavy soup pot over high heat, crumbling with fork, for 8 minutes or until browned. Pour off accumulated fat.
2. Heat olive oil in a heavy skillet over medium heat. Add onion and chopped vegetables and cook, stirring frequently, for 10 minutes.
3. Add to ground beef with canned tomatoes and their juices, water, tomato paste, chili powder, garlic, oregano, basil, and cumin.
4. Bring to a boil, reduce heat, cover, and simmer for 45 minutes, stirring occasionally.
5. Stir in kidney beans and simmer for 15 more minutes.

VEGETABLE POSSIBILITIES

Green bell pepper; zucchini; carrots
Red bell pepper; yellow summer squash; broccoli
Green beans; yellow bell pepper; cauliflower
Corn; diced sweet potato; peas
Pumpkin; Brussels sprouts; mushrooms

QUICK TAKES

ROAST BEEF AND VEGETABLE HASH: Heat 2 tablespoons mild, light-flavored olive oil in a skillet over medium heat. Add 1 onion, chopped, and sauté until light brown. Add 2 cups cooked TURNIPS, CARROTS, and potatoes (or 2 cups of any other combination of vegetables you have on hand) and stir-fry for 2 minutes. Add 2 cups leftover chopped roast beef, 1 tablespoon light soy sauce, and 1 teaspoon dried thyme leaves and stir-fry until heated through, about 2 minutes. (4 servings)

ROAST BEEF SALAD: Combine ½ head shredded CABBAGE, 4 cups shredded SPINACH, 2 large CARROTS, shredded, and 1 pound lean cooked roast beef, cut into julienne strips. Serve with a dressing of 1 cup nonfat or low-fat plain yogurt, 2 teaspoons grated horseradish, and 1 teaspoon Dijon mustard (4 servings)

GROUND BEEF STEW: Cook 1½ pounds lean ground beef in a heavy soup pot until browned. Remove meat with a slotted spoon and pour off accumulated fat. Set meat aside. Heat 3 tablespoons mild, light-flavored olive oil in the pot and stir-fry 3 medium CARROTS, scrubbed and cut into 1½-inch chunks, and 2 medium potatoes, cut into 1½-inch chunks for 10 minutes until browned on all sides. Remove from pot and set aside. Adding olive oil if needed, sauté ½ pound mushrooms, sliced, 1 medium ZUCCHINI, sliced, and 1 EGGPLANT, cut into 1½-inch chunks. Stir-fry for 5 minutes. Stir in 4 cups fresh or canned chopped TOMATOES, ¾ cup water, ¼ teaspoon black pepper, and ¼ teaspoon dried thyme leaves. Return meat and carrots and potatoes to pot. Bring to a boil, reduce heat, cover, and simmer for 25 minutes. (4 servings)

AT YOUR LEISURE

BEEF VEGETABLE STEW

Make this classic beef stew, which features extra-lean beef and seven vegetables, on a lazy day at home. Pack the leftovers in a thermos for a hearty lunch or save for an evening when there's no time to cook.

YIELD: *6 servings*
PREPARATION TIME: *20 minutes*
COOKING TIME: *2½ hours*

¾ pound extra-lean round steak, diced
10 cups water
¼ cup raw barley
1 onion, diced
2 carrots, scrubbed and sliced
1 stalk celery, sliced
1 turnip, diced
1 potato, diced
½ cup fresh or frozen green lima beans
¼ teaspoon dried marjoram leaves
½ teaspoon ground sage
1 cup chopped kale leaves
1 tablespoon chopped fresh parsley
½ teaspoon black pepper

1. Sear steak in a large soup pot over medium heat. Reduce heat to low and add the water.
2. Stir in barley, onion, carrots, celery, turnip, potato, lima beans, marjoram, and sage. Simmer, covered, for 1½ to 2 hours, until meat and vegetables are tender.
3. Add kale, parsley, and pepper and simmer for 30 more minutes.

GRAPEFRUIT AND BEEF STEW

Grapefruit and carrots are stewed with lean round steak in a flavorful herb sauce.

YIELD: *4 servings*
PREPARATION TIME: *20 minutes*
COOKING TIME: *1¼ hours*

2 tablespoons mild, light-flavored olive oil
1 onion, sliced
1 pound lean round steak, trimmed of all fat
¼ cup all-purpose flour
1 cup nonalcoholic red wine or white wine
¼ teaspoon dried rosemary leaves
¼ teaspoon dried thyme leaves
¼ teaspoon dried basil leaves
1 cup water
1 large grapefruit, peeled, separated into sections, and
    seeded
3 large carrots, scrubbed and cut into quarters
2 teaspoons brown sugar
¼ teaspoon black pepper

1. Heat olive oil in a heavy soup pot over medium heat. Sauté onion for 5 minutes. Remove onion from pot with a slotted spoon and set aside.
2. Dredge round steak in flour and pound flour into steak. Cut meat into large chunks.
3. Sauté meat in olive oil remaining in soup pot. Brown well on both sides.
4. Reduce the heat to low and slowly stir in wine, rosemary, thyme, and basil. Add water.
5. Stir in onion, grapefruit, carrots, sugar, and black pepper. Cover and simmer for at least 1¼ hours. Check to see if meat is tender. Season with additional brown sugar if too tart for your taste.

PUMPKIN AND BEEF STEW

This South American dish is loaded with onions, garlic, two kinds of potatoes, chunks of pumpkin, green pepper, carrots, tomatoes, zucchini, corn, pears, and dried apricots.

YIELD: *6 servings*
PREPARATION TIME: *25 minutes*
COOKING TIME: *1 hour and 20 minutes*

3 tablespoons mild, light-flavored olive oil
1 cup chopped onions
1 tablespoon chopped garlic
1½ pounds boneless lean beef chuck, trimmed and cut
   into 1½-inch chunks
1 cup sliced carrots
½ cup chopped green bell pepper
4 cups low-salt beef broth
1 teaspoon honey
2 cups chopped fresh or canned tomatoes
½ teaspoon dried oregano leaves
¼ teaspoon dried marjoram leaves
¼ cup chopped fresh parsley
½ teaspoon black pepper
2 medium white potatoes, peeled and diced
2 medium sweet potatoes, peeled and diced
12-pound pumpkin, seeded, peeled, and cut into ½-inch
   cubes
1 medium zucchini, cut into 1-inch slices
1 8-ounce can unsweetened canned pears, drained and
   cut into quarters
1½ cups fresh, frozen, or canned corn kernels
½ cup chopped dried apricots

1. Heat the olive oil in a large soup pot. Add the onions and sauté for 1 minute. Add the garlic and sauté for 4 minutes. Remove onion and garlic with a slotted spoon and set aside.
2. Add the beef to the pot and sauté until browned on all sides.
3. Add the carrots, green pepper, beef broth, honey, tomatoes, oregano, marjoram, parsley, black pepper, and the reserved onions and garlic. Bring to a boil. Reduce heat, cover, and simmer for 15 minutes.

4. Add white potatoes, sweet potatoes, and pumpkin to pot. Cover and cook for 45 minutes.

5. Preheat oven to 350 degrees.

6. Scoop out 1½ cups of the vegetables and ½ cup of liquid and transfer to the workbowl of a food processor or to a blender. Purée and return to pot. Simmer for 10 minutes.

7. Add zucchini, pears, corn and apricots. Simmer for 15 minutes.

8. Transfer to a large ovenproof casserole and bake for 15 minutes.

VARIATION:

- Scoop out a 10- to 12-pound pumpkin and transfer the stew to it after Step 7. Place the pumpkin in a roasting pan and bake in a 350 degree oven for 15 minutes.

Veal

QUICK TAKES

VEAL CUTLETS WITH TRICOLOR PEPPERS: Heat 2 tablespoons mild, light-flavored olive oil in a skillet over medium heat. Sauté 1 clove garlic, minced, until lightly browned. Add 1 onion, sliced, 2 GREEN BELL PEPPERS, seeded and sliced, 1 RED BELL PEPPER, seeded and sliced, and 1 YELLOW BELL PEPPER, seeded and sliced. Stir-fry for 2 minutes. Stir in 2 tablespoons red wine vinegar, 1 teaspoon dried basil leaves, ½ teaspoon oregano leaves, and ¼ teaspoon pepper. Reduce heat, cover, and cook for 10 minutes. Remove vegetables from skillet with slotted spoon. Coat 1 pound of veal cutlets, pounded to ⅛-inch thickness, with flour. Heat 2 tablespoons mild, light-flavored olive oil in the skillet. Cook cutlets until lightly browned on both sides. Serve cutlets covered with peppers. (4 servings)

VEAL SCALLOPS AND PEARS: Place ¼ cup unbleached all-purpose flour and ⅛ teaspoon black pepper in a shallow dish and dredge 1 pound ¼-inch-thick veal scallops, lightly pounded. Heat 1 tablespoon mild, light-flavored olive oil in a skillet over medium heat. Sauté veal for 2 minutes on each side or until lightly browned. Transfer to a serving dish and cover. Place ¼ cup low-salt chicken broth in skillet and add 2 scallions, minced, and 3 PEARS, cored and thinly sliced. Heat pears for 5 minutes or until soft. Spoon pears over veal and cover serving dish. Add 1 cup low-salt chicken broth to skillet and boil until reduced by half. Stir in ½ teaspoon Dijon mustard, ⅛ teaspoon ground nutmeg, and ½ cup chopped fresh parsley. Pour sauce over veal and pears and serve. (4 servings)

AT YOUR LEISURE

VEAL CHOPS WITH APRICOTS

Veal chops are sautéed in olive oil, then simmered in apricot purée.

YIELD: *4 servings*
PREPARATION TIME: *15 minutes*
COOKING TIME: *25 minutes*

16 fresh apricots, peeled, pitted, and halved, or
    32 canned apricot halves, drained
4 tablespoons mild, light-flavored olive oil
4 veal chops, each ¾ inch thick
½ teaspoon dried thyme leaves
¼ teaspoon grated nutmeg
¼ teaspoon white pepper
2 cups low-salt chicken broth
½ teaspoon dry mustard

1. Purée 16 apricot halves in the workbowl of a food processor or in a blender. Set aside.
2. Heat olive oil in a skillet over medium heat. Brown veal chops on both sides. Sprinkle with thyme, nutmeg, and pepper.
3. Add 1½ cups of the chicken broth and simmer for 15 minutes or until chops are tender. Turn chops several times while simmering.
4. Remove chops from pan and set aside. Discard any juices remaining in pan.
5. Combine apricot purée and dry mustard. Add to skillet. Add the remaining ½ cup chicken broth. Cook for 5 minutes.
6. Add remaining apricot halves. Stir into sauce and cook for 2 minutes.
7. Return chops to pan and simmer for 3 minutes.

PAPRIKA VEAL AND CARROTS AND TURNIPS
WITH APPLESAUCE

Delicate veal scallops are combined with carrots, onions, and turnips, spiced with paprika, and topped with fruit sauce.

YIELD: *4 servings*
PREPARATION TIME: *15 minutes*
COOKING TIME: *20 minutes*

1 medium onion, sliced
2 carrots, scrubbed and thinly sliced
1 turnip, scrubbed and diced
1 large apple, peeled, cored, and quartered
1 tablespoon lemon juice
¼ cup low-salt chicken broth
¼ teaspoon black pepper
2 tablespoons mild, light-flavored olive oil
1 pound veal scallops or turkey cutlets
½ teaspoon paprika

1. Bring water to a boil in a steamer and place onion, carrots, and turnip in a steamer basket. Steam, covered, for 12 minutes or until vegetables are tender-crisp.
2. Place apple and lemon juice in the workbowl of a food processor or in a blender and purée. Add purée to a saucepan with chicken broth and black pepper. Heat and keep warm until ready to use.
3. Heat the olive oil in a skillet over medium heat. Cook the veal scallops on each side for approximately 2 minutes or until lightly browned.
4. Place veal on a serving platter and top with steamed vegetables. Pour apple sauce over veal and vegetables. Sprinkle with paprika.

Lamb

QUICK TAKES

GROUND LAMB AND RED PEPPER BAKE: Blanch 6 large RED BELL PEP-
PERS, seeded and cut into quarters. Sauté 1 pound ground lamb, 1
onion, chopped, 1 tablespoon dried mint leaves, and 1 clove garlic,
minced, until lamb is browned. Add 1 cup low-salt chicken broth.
Stir in 2 cups cooked rice, ½ cup raisins, and ½ cup chopped walnuts.
Remove from heat. Oil a 12- by 8-inch baking dish and line with red
pepper quarters. Top with lamb mixture and a layer of TOMATOES,
sliced. Cover dish with foil. Bake for 35 minutes. (4 servings)

GARDEN LAMB: Heat 3 tablespoons mild, light-flavored olive oil in a
heavy soup pot over medium heat. Sauté 1 pound lean boneless lamb,
cut into 1½-inch cubes, stirring until well browned. Add 2 CARROTS,
sliced, and 1 cup low-salt chicken broth. Cover pot, reduce heat, and
simmer for 25 minutes, stirring several times. Add 4 TOMATOES,
sliced, 1 cup GREEN PEAS, 1 onion, chopped, 1 teaspoon red wine
vinegar, and ¾ cup low-salt chicken broth. Cover and cook over low
heat for 30 minutes or until lamb is tender. Stir in 1 tablespoon
chopped fresh parsley and ½ teaspoon dried dillweed before serving.
(4 servings)

AT YOUR LEISURE

SPICED LAMB AND VEGETABLES

YIELD: *4 servings*
PREPARATION TIME: *30 minutes*
COOKING TIME: *1½ hours*

2 tablespoons mild, light-flavored olive oil
1 pound lean boneless lamb shoulder meat, trimmed and
    cut into 1-inch cubes
1 clove garlic, minced
4 tablespoons unbleached all-purpose flour
4 cups low-salt chicken broth
1 onion, minced
2 stalks celery, chopped
1 green bell pepper, seeded and diced
1 turnip, scrubbed and diced
¼ teaspoon dried thyme leaves
¼ teaspoon dried oregano leaves
⅛ teaspoon ground nutmeg
⅛ teaspoon ground ginger
⅛ teaspoon ground cloves
⅛ teaspoon ground cinnamon
½ teaspoon black pepper
2 cups shredded cabbage
1 cup cauliflower florets
2 cups chopped fresh or canned tomatoes
2 cups cooked chick-peas

1. Heat the olive oil in a heavy soup pot over medium heat. Add lamb cubes and brown on all sides.
2. Add garlic and flour. Stir until flour is lightly browned.
3. Gradually add chicken broth, stirring constantly.
4. Add onion, celery, green bell pepper, turnip, thyme, oregano, nutmeg, ginger, cloves, cinnamon, and black pepper. Cover and simmer for 1 hour.
5. Add cabbage, cauliflower, and tomatoes. If broth seems too thick, add water. Simmer 20 minutes. Check to see if lamb is tender.
6. Stir in chick-peas and warm through. Serve with instant couscous.

Side Dishes

EASY ACCESS: THE BASICS
Curried Vegetables with Chutney
Basic Stir-Fried Mixed Vegetables and/or Fruit   Basic Baked Vegetables
Steamed Vegetables with Honey Vinaigrette
Basic Vegetables with Cheese   Sautéed Fruit   Spiced Oven-Baked Fruit

Fruit Dishes

QUICK TAKES
Baked Apples, Carrots, and Cranberries   Sautéed Apples and Snow Peas
Baked Bananas and Oranges   Broiled Grapefruit
Nectarine and Broccoli Toss   Gingered Oranges
Baked Papaya and Pineapple   Zippy Pears and Nectarines
Curried Pineapple, Apricots, Nectarines, and Apples
Winter Berry Compote

Vegetable Dishes

QUICK TAKES
Gingered Steamed Asparagus   Broccoli with Ginger
Broccoli with Lemon   Apple Broccoli Purée
Broccoli with Red Pepper Sauce   Broccoli with Potatoes

Brussels Sprouts with Red Peppers   Brussels Sprouts and Apples
Red Cabbage and Applesauce   Cabbage with Spinach and Peas
Carrots and Oranges   Carrots with Raisins   Cauliflower and Tomatoes
Curried Cauliflower   Corn and Tomatoes   Succotash
Eggplant Casserole   Eggplant with Ginger   Eggplant Oven Fries
Green Beans and Pears   Green Beans and Peanut Sauce
Green Beans with Green Peppers and Tomato   Green Peas and Spinach
Green Peas and Tomatoes   Snow Peas with Peppers   Stewed Peppers
Pumpkin Purée with Green Peppers   Pumpkin Toss   Spinach Parmesan
Spinach with Potatoes   Sweet Potatoes and Bananas
Sweet Potatoes and Apples   Sautéed Sweet Potatoes with Peas
Pineapple and Sweet Potato Stir-Fry   Simple Stewed Tomatoes
Turnips and Apple Cider   Turnips and Zucchini
Acorn Squash with Carrot-Apple Stuffing
Butternut Squash with Cranberries
Roasted Eggplant, Carrots, Yellow Squash, and Green Pepper
Vegetable and Chick-Pea Stew   Fall Harvest Stew
Spring Harvest Vegetables   Summer Stew   Basic Ratatouille

AT YOUR LEISURE
Eggplant Fritters   Mashed Sweet Potatoes and Pears
Mashed Potatoes with Sautéed Apples   Spiced Hot Fruit Salad
Vegetable Curry   Fall Fruit and Vegetable Medley
Vegetables, Vegetables, and More Vegetables
Fruit and Vegetable Ratatouille   Basic Applesauce   Honey Baked Apples

EASY ACCESS: THE BASICS

CURRIED VEGETABLES WITH CHUTNEY
(4 servings)

INGREDIENTS
3 tablespoons mild, light-flavored olive oil
4 cups chopped or diced vegetables (see possibilities
    below)
1 tomato, diced
4 mushrooms, sliced
1 green bell pepper, seeded and diced
1¾ cups Harvest Chutney (page 286) or chutney of your
    choice
1 tablespoon curry powder
½ cup nonfat or low-fat plain yogurt

1. Heat olive oil in a large skillet over medium heat. Add the 4 cups
vegetables, tomato, mushrooms, and green bell pepper. Sauté for 8
minutes.
2. Stir in the chutney and curry powder and bring the mixture to a
simmer.
3. Serve topped with yogurt.

VEGETABLE POSSIBILITIES
Blanched broccoli; blanched cauliflower; eggplant; peas
Green beans; corn; carrots; yellow crookneck squash
Steamed sweet potatoes; broccoli; corn; carrots
Steamed new potatoes; green beans; zucchini; blanched cauliflower

BASIC STIR-FRIED MIXED VEGETABLES AND/OR FRUIT

(4 servings)

INGREDIENTS
3 slices fresh gingerroot, minced
½ cup low-salt chicken broth
1 tablespoon light soy sauce
½ teaspoon sugar
2 tablespoons mild, light-flavored olive oil or canola oil
4 cups chopped, sliced or diced steamed, blanched, or
    raw vegetables and/or fruit (see possibilities below)

1. Combine gingerroot, broth, soy sauce, and sugar.
2. Heat oil in a large skillet or wok. Add the 4 cups vegetables and stir-fry to coat with the oil and heat through.
3. Add broth mixture and bring to a boil. Simmer, covered, over medium heat until vegetables are done crisp tender.

VEGETABLE AND/OR FRUIT COMBINATIONS

Blanched cauliflower; snow peas; water chestnuts; bamboo shoots; apple
Cabbage; tomatoes; onion
Blanched green beans; tomatoes; onions; pineapple
Blanched carrots; peas; celery; almonds; pears
Green bell peppers; tomatoes; mushrooms; onions
Pineapple; green bell pepper; water chestnuts
Spinach; blanched carrots; steamed pumpkin; scallions
Green bell pepper; zucchini; orange segments
Blanched green beans; carrots; pears; turnips
Cabbage; celery; onion; apples
Green bell pepper; blanched carrots; celery; bean sprouts
Green peas; mushrooms; pears; pineapple
Blanched cauliflower; green peas; red bell peppers
Snow peas; bamboo shoots; blanched carrots; eggplant
Green beans; water chestnuts; celery; blanched Brussels sprouts
Asparagus; mushrooms; blanched carrots
Blanched broccoli; red bell peppers; bamboo shoots
Blanched broccoli; green beans; cabbage; mushrooms; onion
Blanched cauliflower; asparagus; peas; celery; cabbage; bamboo shoots;
    mushrooms
Green bell pepper; romaine lettuce; cucumber; zucchini; tomatoes

BASIC BAKED VEGETABLES

(5–6 servings)

INGREDIENTS

7 cups raw, sliced, or chopped vegetables (see possibilities below)
2 cups chopped fresh or canned tomatoes
1 cup thinly sliced onion
1 medium green bell pepper, seeded and cut into strips
2 tablespoons mild, light-flavored olive oil
2 cloves garlic, minced
2 teaspoons dried basil leaves
¼ cup whole-grain bread crumbs

1. Heat oven to 350 degrees. Oil an 11- by-7-inch baking dish.
2. Toss vegetables, tomatoes, onion, green bell pepper, olive oil, garlic, and basil leaves in a large bowl.
3. Transfer vegetable mixture to the baking dish. Bake for 40 minutes.
4. Sprinkle with bread crumbs. Bake for 25 minutes more.

VEGETABLE POSSIBILITIES

Eggplant; yellow squash; zucchini
Broccoli; cauliflower; red bell pepper; zucchini
Asparagus; carrots; cauliflower; green beans
Sweet potatoes; corn; Brussels sprouts
Turnips; carrots; potatoes; green beans

STEAMED VEGETABLES WITH HONEY VINAIGRETTE

(4 servings)

INGREDIENTS

⅓ cup honey
⅓ cup white wine vinegar
3 tablespoons Dijon mustard
¾ cup mild, light-flavored olive oil
¾ cup water
2 tablespoons poppy seeds
7 cups chopped, sliced, or diced steamed vegetables, still
    hot (see possibilities below)

1. Combine honey, vinegar, mustard, olive oil, water, and poppy seeds in a blender.
2. Pour vinaigrette over the hot vegetables.
3. Serve hot or chilled.

VEGETABLE POSSIBILITIES

Broccoli, cauliflower, yellow crookneck squash
Potatoes; green beans; asparagus
Brussels sprouts; corn; carrots
Winter squash; red bell peppers; peas
Pumpkin; green bell peppers, lima beans

BASIC VEGETABLES WITH CHEESE

(4 servings)

INGREDIENTS

¼ cup mild, light-flavored olive oil
½ cup diced onion
2 cloves garlic, minced
½ cup sliced mushrooms
2 cups chopped fresh or canned tomatoes
7 cups fresh chopped, sliced, or diced vegetables (see
    possibilities below)
½ pound nonfat or low-fat cheese, cut into small cubes
2 tablespoons chopped scallion

1. Heat olive oil in a saucepan over medium heat. Sauté onion and garlic for 3 minutes.

2. Add mushrooms and stir-fry for 2 minutes. Preheat oven to 350 degrees.

3. Add tomatoes, cover, and simmer for 10 minutes.

4. Place the vegetables in a large bowl. Pour tomato sauce over them. Stir in half of the cheese cubes and the scallion.

5. Transfer mixture to a lightly oiled 11- by-7-inch baking dish. Top with remaining cheese.

6. Bake for 1 hour.

VEGETABLE POSSIBILITIES

Potatoes; green beans; asparagus
Broccoli; corn; pumpkin
Zucchini; cauliflower; green bell peppers
Red bell peppers; yellow crookneck squash; lima beans; turnips

SAUTÉED FRUIT

(4 servings)

INGREDIENTS

3 tablespoons mild, light-flavored olive oil or reduced-fat
    or diet margarine
1 small onion, chopped
1½ teaspoons minced fresh gingerroot
4 cups sliced or sectioned fruit (see possibilities below)
2 tablespoons lime juice
2 tablespoons brown sugar

1. Heat olive oil or melt margarine in a skillet over medium heat. Add onion and ginger. Stir-fry for 1 minute.

2. Add fruit and cook for 3–5 minutes or until tender.

3. Toss fruit with lime juice and sugar. Serve warm.

FRUIT POSSIBILITIES

Apricots	Mangoes
Apples	Nectarines
Bananas	Papayas
Oranges	Pears
Grapefruit	Pineapple
Seeded tangerines	

SPICED OVEN-BAKED FRUIT

(4 servings)

INGREDIENTS
¼ cup regular stick margarine
1 teaspoon ground ginger
½ teaspoon curry powder
2 tablespoons honey
2 tablespoons lime juice
2 pounds sliced or halved fruit (see possibilities below)

1. Preheat oven to 325 degrees.
2. Combine margarine, ginger, and curry powder in a small saucepan and cook over low heat until bubbly. Stir in honey and lime juice.
3. Place fruit in a baking pan. Brush margarine mixture over fruit.
4. Bake until tender. See suggested cooking times below.

FRUIT POSSIBILITIES
Apples (peeled, cored, and sliced). Bake 20 minutes
Apricots (peeled and left whole). Bake 15 minutes
Bananas (halved and peel left on). Bake 15 minutes
Oranges (peeled and halved). Bake 15–20 minutes
Grapefruit (peeled and halved). Bake 25 minutes
Nectarines (halved and pitted). Bake 25 minutes
Pears (cored and quartered). Bake 20 minutes
Pineapple (cored, peeled, and quartered). Bake 20 minutes

QUICK TAKES: FRUIT DISHES

BAKED APPLE, CARROTS, AND CRANBERRIES: Place 1 APPLE, grated, 1 cup fresh CRANBERRIES, 4 cups grated CARROTS, 1 tablespoon brown sugar, and ½ cup apple cider in a lightly oiled casserole. Dot with 2 tablespoons diet or reduced-calorie margarine. Cover and bake in a 350 degree oven for 40 minutes.
SAUTÉED APPLES AND SNOW PEAS: Sauté 1 tablespoon minced fresh gingerroot in 1 tablespoon mild, light-flavored olive oil. Add 3 cups peeled, cored, thinly sliced APPLES and ¼ pound trimmed fresh SNOW PEAS and stir-fry for 5 minutes. Sprinkle with sesame oil before serving.

BAKED BANANAS AND ORANGES: Peel 6 large BANANAS and cut them in half lengthwise. Place in a lightly oiled casserole. Top with ½ cup ORANGE sections, 1 tablespoon brown sugar, and 2 tablespoons each of orange juice and lemon juice. Bake in a 350 degree oven for 30 minutes.

BROILED GRAPEFRUIT: Cut 2 red or pink GRAPEFRUIT in half and loosen each section with a sharp knife. Cover with brown sugar and cinnamon, or reduced-calorie maple syrup, or all-fruit jam. Place under the broiler and broil until bubbly, about 3–6 minutes.

NECTARINE AND BROCCOLI TOSS: Heat 1 teaspoon mild, light-flavored olive oil in a large skillet over medium heat. Stir-fry 3 cups BROCCOLI florets and 2 small ZUCCHINI, thinly sliced, for 5 minutes. Stir in 1 TOMATO, diced, and 2 NECTARINES, pitted and sliced. Cover and cook for 4 minutes.

GINGERED ORANGES: Serve sliced seedless ORANGES topped with a mixture of 1 cup nonfat or low-fat plain yogurt, 1 teaspoon peeled finely grated fresh gingerroot, 1 teaspoon sugar, ¼ teaspoon black pepper, ½ teaspoon cayenne pepper, and ½ teaspoon ground cumin.

BAKED PAPAYA AND PINEAPPLE: Baked sliced fresh PAPAYA and fresh or canned juice-packed PINEAPPLE chunks, sprinkled with lime juice, light brown sugar, and bits of soft tub or liquid polyunsaturated margarine, in a casserole for 40 minutes.

ZIPPY PEARS AND NECTARINES: Cut 3 ripe PEARS, cored, and 2 NECTARINES, pitted, into ½-inch slices. Sprinkle ½ cup chopped red onion over the fruit. Combine ¼ cup lemon juice, 1 teaspoon brown sugar, ½ teaspoon dried mint leaves, 1 teaspoon minced garlic, and ¼ teaspoon black pepper. Pour dressing over fruit and marinate in the refrigerator for several hours.

CURRIED PINEAPPLE, APRICOTS, NECTARINES, AND APPLES: Melt 3 tablespoons soft tub or liquid polyunsaturated margarine in a medium saucepan over medium heat. Add 2 teaspoons honey, 1 tablespoon curry powder, and ½ teaspoon ground ginger. Cook, stirring, for about 5 minutes. Add 1 8-ounce can juice-packed or water-packed PINEAPPLE chunks, drained with ¼ cup of the juice reserved, 1 large APPLE, cored and cut into chunks, 1 PEAR, cored and cut into chunks, 1 NECTARINE halved, pitted, and cut into chunks, and 6 APRICOTS, halved and pitted. Cover and cook for 5 minutes.

WINTER BERRY COMPOTE: Combine 2 cups frozen RASPBERRIES, 2 cups frozen BLUEBERRIES, 3 cups frozen STRAWBERRIES, ½ cup raisins, 10 ounces all-fruit strawberry jam, ½ teaspoon ground cinnamon, ½ teaspoon ground cloves, 1 teaspoon grated orange zest, ½ cup orange juice, and ½ teaspoon ground ginger in a nonaluminum saucepan. Bring to a boil over medium heat. When jelly has dissolved, lower heat and simmer for 1 hour. Let stand for 20 minutes. Serve warm or cold.

QUICK TAKES: VEGETABLE DISHES

GINGERED STEAMED ASPARAGUS: Combine 1 clove garlic, minced, 1 teaspoon minced fresh gingerroot, 1 teaspoon sugar, 4 tablespoons light soy sauce, 1 teaspoon sesame oil, 2 tablespoons white wine vinegar, ¼ teaspoon black pepper, and 2 tablespoons chopped scallions. Pour over 2 pounds steamed ASPARAGUS.

BROCCOLI WITH GINGER: Steam 1½ pounds BROCCOLI florets and sliced stems. Heat 2 tablespoons mild, light-flavored olive oil, 2 tablespoons orange juice, 1 tablespoon light soy sauce, 2 teaspoons Dijon mustard, ½ teaspoon ground ginger, and ½ teaspoon sugar in a skillet. When the mixture starts to simmer, add the steamed broccoli and cook for 3 minutes or until heated through.

BROCCOLI WITH LEMON: Steam 4 cups BROCCOLI florets for 5 minutes. Drizzle with 1½ tablespoons lemon juice and 1 tablespoon extra-virgin olive oil.

APPLE BROCCOLI PURÉE: Steam 1¾ pounds BROCCOLI florets and stems, cut into ½-inch pieces. Heat 1 tablespoon mild, light-flavored olive oil in a skillet over medium heat. Sauté 1 APPLE, cored and sliced, for 1 minute. Add ¼ cup apple juice and ½ cup low-salt chicken broth. Bring to a boil, reduce heat, and cook for 5 minutes. Stir in the broccoli and heat through. Transfer the contents of the skillet to the workbowl of a food processor or to a blender and purée until smooth. Add additional apple juice if necessary to gain a smooth consistency.

BROCCOLI WITH RED PEPPER SAUCE: Steam 1 pound BROCCOLI florets. Heat 1 tablespoon mild, light-flavored olive oil in a skillet over medium heat. Sauté 1 clove garlic, minced, for 1 minute. Add 2 RED BELL PEPPERS, seeded and chopped. Sauté for 3 minutes. Add ½ cup low-salt chicken broth, ¼ teaspoon white pepper, and 1½ teaspoons white wine vinegar. When pepper sauce reaches a simmer, pour it over steamed broccoli and serve.

BROCCOLI WITH POTATOES: Toss 4 medium cooked potatoes, peeled and diced, with 1 pound steamed BROCCOLI, chopped into 1-inch pieces. Combine ½ cup mild, light-flavored olive oil, ¼ cup cider vinegar, 1 clove garlic, minced, ½ teaspoon dried basil leaves and 2 scallions, sliced, in a saucepan. Bring to a boil over medium heat. Toss with broccoli and potatoes.

BRUSSELS SPROUTS WITH RED PEPPERS: Heat 1 tablespoon mild, light-flavored olive oil in a large skillet over medium heat. Stir-fry 2 RED BELL PEPPERS, seeded and cut into thin strips, for 3 minutes. Stir in 1 teaspoon dried basil leaves and 1 teaspoon Dijon mustard. Add 2 pounds steamed BRUSSELS SPROUTS and heat through.

BRUSSELS SPROUTS AND APPLES: Heat ⅓ cup mild, light-flavored olive oil in a skillet over medium heat. Add 1 onion, chopped, and cook until soft. Combine 1½ pounds trimmed and steamed BRUSSELS SPROUTS with 2 APPLES, chopped, 2 tablespoons seedless raisins, and the onion mixture. Combine 3 tablespoons each of honey and lemon juice. Pour over Brussels sprouts and apples and serve.

RED CABBAGE AND APPLESAUCE: Sauté 1 onion, chopped, in 2 tablespoons mild, light-flavored olive oil for 5 minutes. Add 2 pounds RED CABBAGE, cut into ¼-inch slices, and cook until wilted. Add ¼ teaspoon ground cloves, 3 tablespoons red wine vinegar, 1 tablespoon sugar, and ½ cup natural applesauce. Cook for 15 minutes, stirring often.

CABBAGE WITH SPINACH AND PEAS: Heat 1 tablespoon mild, light-flavored olive oil in a large skillet over medium heat. Stir-fry 4 cups chopped CABBAGE for 3 minutes. Add 1½ cups chopped SPINACH, 1 TOMATO, diced, 1½ cups frozen PEAS, and ½ teaspoon dried basil leaves. Sauté for 2 minutes. Cover and sauté for 2 more minutes.

CARROTS AND ORANGES: Toss cooked CARROTS with 1 teaspoon orange zest, 1 ORANGE, peeled, separated into sections, and cut into bite-sized pieces, 1 tablespoon mild, light-flavored olive oil and 1 tablespoon chopped scallions.

CARROTS WITH RAISINS: Heat 1 tablespoon mild, light-flavored olive oil in a skillet over medium heat. Sauté 1¼ pounds CARROTS, sliced and steamed, for 2 minutes. Sprinkle ½ tablespoon brown sugar over carrots and add ½ cup seedless raisins. Stir-fry for 2 minutes. Combine 1 tablespoon honey, ½ tablespoon lemon juice, 1 tablespoon Dijon mustard, and 1 teaspoon curry powder. Stir into carrot mixture in skillet.

CAULIFLOWER AND TOMATOES: Heat 1 tablespoon mild, light-flavored olive oil in a skillet over medium heat. Add 1 onion, chopped, and 1 clove garlic, minced, and sauté for 3 minutes. Stir in 2 cups chopped fresh or canned TOMATOES. Cover and simmer for 15 minutes. Add 4 cups CAULIFLOWER florets, steamed, 1 GREEN BELL PEPPER, seeded and chopped, and ¼ teaspoon black pepper. Simmer for 5 minutes.

CURRIED CAULIFLOWER: Steam 2 cups CAULIFLOWER florets. Combine 1 cup nonfat or low-fat plain yogurt, 2 tablespoons Harvest Chutney (page 286) and ½ tablespoon curry powder. Spoon over steamed cauliflower and serve.

CORN AND TOMATOES: Heat 2 tablespoons mild, light-flavored olive oil in a skillet over medium heat. Sauté 1 clove garlic, minced, and 1 onion, diced. Add 1 GREEN BELL PEPPER, seeded and diced, and 1 RED BELL PEPPER, seeded and diced. Cook for 5 minutes. Stir in 2 cups fresh, frozen, or canned CORN kernels, 4 TOMATOES, diced, and 2 tablespoons chili powder. Cook for 10 minutes.

SUCCOTASH: Heat 2 tablespoons mild, light-flavored olive oil in a skillet. Sauté 1 onion, chopped, and 2 cloves garlic, minced, until lightly browned. Add 2 cups chopped fresh or canned TOMATOES and ½ teaspoon dry mustard. Cook for 5 minutes. Add 1 cup frozen lima beans, 2 cups fresh, frozen, or canned CORN kernels, and 1 cup GREEN BEANS, cut in 1-inch lengths. Cook for 10 minutes or until beans are tender.

EGGPLANT CASSEROLE: Heat ⅓ cup mild, light-flavored olive oil in a large skillet. Sauté 1 large EGGPLANT, cut into ⅓-inch slices, until tender and golden on both sides, adding oil if needed. Remove from skillet and set aside. Sauté 1 onion, chopped, and 1 GREEN BELL PEPPER, seeded and diced, in the remaining oil. Sprinkle with ½ teaspoon dried basil leaves and ¼ cup chopped fresh parsley. Combine sautéed onion and green pepper with 4 cups cooked brown rice. Place half of the eggplant in the bottom of an ungreased 3-quart casserole. Top with half of the rice mixture. Slice 3 large TOMATOES. Cover rice layer with tomato slices. Sprinkle with ¾ cup grated part-skim mozzarella cheese. Repeat layers, ending with ¾ cup more cheese. Bake for 15 minutes.

EGGPLANT WITH GINGER: Cut 1 medium EGGPLANT, peeled, into ¼-inch slices and marinate for 45 minutes in 2 tablespoons light soy sauce. Place 1 tablespoon mild, light-flavored olive oil in a skillet over medium heat and sauté 1 slice fresh gingerroot, minced, for 30 seconds. Add eggplant and sauté until lightly browned on all sides, adding oil as needed. When eggplant is tender, sprinkle with 2 tablespoons minced fresh parsley, 2 teaspoons lemon juice, and 2 teaspoons sesame seeds.

EGGPLANT OVEN FRIES: Peel 1 medium EGGPLANT and cut into 1- by 4-inch strips. Line a baking sheet with foil. Combine ¾ cup whole-grain bread crumbs, ½ teaspoon dried basil leaves, and ¼ cup grated

Parmesan cheese. Toss eggplant strips in ½ cup mild, light-flavored olive oil. Roll oiled strips in crumb mixture. Place on baking sheet and bake in a 375 degree oven for 20 minutes. Sprinkle with grated Parmesan before serving.

GREEN BEANS AND PEARS: Toss 1 pound trimmed GREEN BEANS, steamed, with 2 PEARS, peeled, cored, and chopped.

GREEN BEANS AND PEANUT SAUCE: Toss 1 pound trimmed GREEN BEANS, steamed, with a peanut sauce made by combining 4 tablespoons smooth natural peanut butter, ½ cup skim or low-fat milk, 3 tablespoons nonfat or low-fat plain yogurt, ½ teaspoon dried oregano leaves, and ½ teaspoon cayenne pepper.

GREEN BEANS WITH GREEN PEPPERS AND TOMATO: Sauté ¼ cup chopped GREEN BELL PEPPER and 1 onion, chopped, in 2 tablespoons mild, light-flavored olive oil for 5 minutes. Add 1 large TOMATO, chopped, and ¼ teaspoon dried oregano leaves and simmer for 10 minutes. Toss with 1 pound steamed, trimmed GREEN BEANS.

GREEN PEAS AND SPINACH: Heat 1 tablespoon mild, light-flavored olive oil in a skillet over medium heat. Sauté ½ cup chopped red onion until tender. Add 1½ cups fresh SPINACH, chopped, and 3½ cups frozen GREEN PEAS. Sauté for 2 minutes. Add ¼ cup diced TOMATO and ½ teaspoon dried rosemary leaves. Sauté until peas are tender.

GREEN PEAS AND TOMATOES: Heat 2 tablespoons mild, light-flavored olive oil in a skillet over medium heat. Add 1 onion, chopped, and 1 clove garlic, minced, and sauté for 5 minutes. Stir in 2 teaspoons paprika and cook for 1 more minute. Add 2 cups chopped fresh or canned TOMATOES with their juice and ¼ teaspoon black pepper. Bring to a boil, lower heat, and simmer for 10 minutes. Pour over 3 cups steamed frozen GREEN PEAS.

SNOW PEAS WITH PEPPERS: Heat 1 tablespoon mild, light-flavored olive oil in a skillet over medium heat. Add 1 RED BELL PEPPER, seeded and cut into strips, 1 GREEN BELL PEPPER, seeded and cut into strips, ¼ pound trimmed SNOW PEAS, and the juice of 1 lemon. Cook for 5 minutes. Sprinkle with ¼ teaspoon black pepper and serve.

STEWED PEPPERS: Heat 2 tablespoons mild, light-flavored olive oil in a medium skillet. Add 1 onion, sliced, and sauté until lightly browned. Add 3 GREEN BELL PEPPERS, seeded and cut into julienne strips, 3 RED BELL PEPPERS, seeded and cut into julienne strips, and 3 cloves garlic, minced. Cook for 10 minutes, stirring several times. Add ½ pound ripe TOMATOES, diced, ½ teaspoon dried oregano leaves, 3 tablespoons chopped fresh parsley, ½ teaspoon sugar, and ¼ teaspoon black pepper. Simmer for 20 minutes.

PUMPKIN PURÉE WITH GREEN PEPPERS: Heat 3 tablespoons mild, light-flavored olive oil in a skillet over medium heat. Sauté 1 GREEN BELL PEPPER, chopped, 1 medium onion, chopped, 1½ teaspoons curry powder, and 1 clove garlic, minced, for 5 minutes. Stir in 4 cups PUMPKIN purée and simmer for 10 minutes, stirring frequently.

PUMPKIN TOSS: Heat 2 tablespoons mild, light-flavored olive oil in a skillet and sauté ¾ cup chopped onion for 5 minutes. Add 1 clove garlic, chopped, 1 cup fresh, frozen, or canned CORN kernels, 2 cups chopped fresh or canned TOMATOES, 1 cup lima beans, 2½ cups PUMPKIN chunks, and ¼ cup water. Cook over low heat for 20 minutes until vegetables are tender.

SPINACH PARMESAN: Heat 2 tablespoons mild, light-flavored olive oil in a skillet over medium heat. Sauté 1 pound SPINACH, well rinsed and shredded, and 2 cloves garlic, minced, for 3 minutes. Sprinkle with grated Parmesan cheese.

SPINACH WITH POTATOES: Cook 1 pound fresh SPINACH, well rinsed, until just wilted, squeeze dry, and chop. Peel and dice ½ pound potatoes. Cover with water in a saucepan and cook for 7 minutes or until potatoes are soft. Drain. Heat 1 tablespoon mild, light-flavored olive oil in a skillet over medium heat. Add potatoes and 1 clove garlic, minced, and sauté for 5 minutes. Add 1 teaspoon paprika and ¼ teaspoon black pepper. Add spinach and cook until it is warmed through. Toss with 1 tablespoon red wine vinegar and serve.

SWEET POTATOES AND BANANAS: Preheat oven to 325 degrees. Place 4 SWEET POTATOES, cooked and sliced, and 3 BANANAS, sliced, in a baking dish. Sprinkle with ½ cup brown sugar, ½ cup pineapple juice, and 2 tablespoons diet or reduced-calorie margarine. Bake for 40 minutes.

SWEET POTATOES AND APPLES: Slice raw SWEET POTATOES and place in a lightly oiled baking dish, alternating with the slices from 2 large APPLES. Sprinkle the layers with ¼ cup raisins and ¼ cup chopped walnuts. Mix 2 tablespoons honey and ⅓ cup orange juice and pour over vegetables. Dust with ground cinnamon and bake in a 350 degree oven for 1 hour.

SPICED SAUTÉED SWEET POTATOES WITH PEAS: Heat 2 tablespoons mild, light-flavored olive oil in a skillet over medium heat. Add 1¼ pounds peeled SWEET POTATOES, cut into ½-inch cubes. Sauté for 10 minutes, stirring frequently. Add 1 onion, chopped, 3 tablespoons cider vinegar, and ⅓ cup water. Cook, stirring, for 5 minutes. Add 2 tablespoons honey, ½ teaspoon chili powder, and ½ teaspoon ground cinnamon. Add ¾ cup frozen GREEN PEAS. Cook, stirring, until peas are tender and heated through. Serve.

PINEAPPLE AND SWEET POTATO STIR-FRY: Heat 1 tablespoon mild, light-flavored olive oil in a skillet over medium heat. Sauté 8 large mushrooms, sliced, 1 large GREEN BELL PEPPER, seeded and chopped, and 1 onion, diced, for 5 minutes. Add 1 peeled SWEET POTATO, steamed for 25 minutes, peeled, and sliced, 1 8-ounce can drained juice-packed PINEAPPLE chunks, ¼ teaspoon dried basil leaves, ¼ teaspoon ground ginger, ½ teaspoon curry powder, and ½ cup chopped drained water chestnuts. Stir-fry for 5 minutes.

SIMPLE STEWED TOMATOES: Heat 1 tablespoon mild, light-flavored olive oil in a saucepan over medium heat. Sauté 1 small onion, chopped, and 1 clove garlic, minced, until tender. Add 10 large fresh TOMATOES, cut into chunks, and 1 teaspoon honey. Simmer for 15 minutes. Season with ¼ teaspoon black pepper. You can also add 1½ teaspoons dried basil leaves, dried thyme leaves, ground cumin, dried marjoram leaves or curry powder, or ½ teaspoon ground cinnamon to the stewed tomatoes. To thicken tomatoes, add ¾ cup whole-grain bread or cracker crumbs with the seasonings. Stewed tomatoes can also be placed in a casserole, sprinkled with grated Parmesan cheese, and broiled until the cheese bubbles.

TURNIPS AND APPLE CIDER: Combine 1 pound TURNIPS, peeled and cut into pieces 2 inches long by 1 inch wide, 1 cup apple cider, 2 tablespoons regular stick margarine, containing no more than 2 grams saturated fat per tablespoon, 1 teaspoon sugar, and ½ teaspoon black pepper in a heavy saucepan. Cook over high heat for 8 minutes or until turnips are tender, adding more cider if needed.

TURNIPS AND ZUCCHINI: Steam 3 large TURNIPS, peeled and cut into julienne strips, ¼ cup sliced radishes, and 1 small ZUCCHINI, cut into julienne strips. Combine 3 tablespoons lime juice, 1 tablespoon white wine vinegar, 1 tablespoon extra-virgin olive oil, ½ teaspoon honey, and ¼ teaspoon black pepper in a small saucepan. Bring to a boil. Pour over steamed turnip mixture.

ACORN SQUASH WITH CARROT-APPLE STUFFING: Combine 1 APPLE, peeled, cored, and chopped, 1 CARROT, grated, 1 small ZUCCHINI, grated, 1 small onion, minced, ¼ cup grated Parmesan cheese, and ¼ teaspoon black pepper in a bowl. Preheat oven to 400 degrees. Cut 2 ACORN SQUASH in half and remove the seeds. Pour enough water in a baking dish to fill it by 1 inch. Stuff squash halves with apple mixture. Set squash halves in the baking dish. Cover dish with foil and bake for 45 minutes.

BUTTERNUT SQUASH WITH CRANBERRIES: Preheat oven to 350 degrees. Cut BUTTERNUT SQUASH in half, place cut side down on baking sheet, and bake for 1 hour. Let cool and cut into 2-inch pieces. Combine 2 cups CRANBERRIES with ¼ cup sugar in a heavy saucepan over medium heat. Cook, stirring frequently, for 4 minutes. Combine 4 APPLES, chopped, with ¼ cup sugar in another heavy saucepan over medium heat. Cook for 12 minutes, stirring frequently. Combine cranberries and apples with cooked squash.

ROASTED EGGPLANT, CARROTS, YELLOW SQUASH, AND GREEN PEPPER: Preheat oven to 500 degrees. Cut 1½ cups CARROTS, 1½ cups EGGPLANT, 1½ cups yellow squash, 1½ cups parboiled potatoes, 1½ cups GREEN BELL PEPPER, and 1½ cups red onion into ½ inch cubes. Toss with ⅓ cup mild, light-flavored olive oil, 2 cloves garlic, minced, 1 teaspoon dried rosemary leaves, and ¼ teaspoon black pepper. Spread vegetables in a single layer on a baking sheet and bake for 20 minutes. Run under broiler until edges of vegetables blacken.

VEGETABLE AND CHICK-PEA STEW: Heat 3 tablespoons mild, light-flavored olive oil in a large skillet over medium heat. Sauté 1 red onion, sliced, for 3 minutes. Add 2 cloves garlic, minced, 1 cup sliced GREEN BEANS, 1 medium diced ZUCCHINI, 1 cup CAULIFLOWER florets, and 1 GREEN BELL PEPPER, seeded and cut into strips. Sauté until lightly browned. Add 2 TOMATOES, sliced, and 2 cups drained cooked chick-peas. Cover, reduce heat, and simmer for 25 minutes. Serve as a side dish or over cooked pasta or rice as a main dish.

FALL HARVEST STEW: Heat 3 tablespoons mild, light-flavored olive oil in a heavy soup pot. Sauté 2 medium onions, chopped, and 2 large CARROTS, sliced, until lightly browned. Add 1 cup shredded green CABBAGE, 1 medium TURNIP, peeled and diced, 1 yellow crookneck squash, diced, 1½ cups diced fresh or canned TOMATOES, 1 teaspoon grated fresh gingerroot, 1 teaspoon ground cinnamon, ½ teaspoon ground cumin, and ½ cup raisins. Cover and cook over low heat, stirring frequently, for 20 minutes. Add water in small amounts as needed while cooking until the vegetables have the consistency of a thick stew. Serve garnished with slivered almonds.

SPRING HARVEST VEGETABLES: Heat ⅓ cup mild, light-flavored olive oil in a saucepan over medium heat. Sauté 2 scallions, sliced, for 2 minutes. Add 2 CARROTS, sliced, and sauté for 2 more minutes. Add 1¼ cups low-salt chicken broth and ¼ teaspoon black pepper. Bring to a boil, lower heat, cover, and simmer for 10 minutes. Add 1½ cups each of frozen lima beans and frozen GREEN PEAS and simmer for 10 minutes. Stir 1 teaspoon cornstarch into 1 tablespoon hot chicken broth to make a paste. Add to the saucepan and stir for 5 minutes. Stir in 6 tablespoons skim or low-fat milk and allow to heat through. Serve at once, sprinkled with parsley.

SUMMER STEW: Heat 1 tablespoon mild, light-flavored olive oil in a heavy soup pot over medium heat. Add ½ pound fresh mushrooms, sliced, 1 yellow crookneck squash, diced, 2 stalks celery, sliced, 1 RED BELL PEPPER, seeded and cut into 1-inch strips, and sauté them for 2 minutes. Remove with a slotted spoon and set aside. Heat 2 more tablespoons olive oil in the pot and sauté 1 small eggplant, cut into 1-inch cubes, until lightly browned. Remove and set aside. Stir-fry 1 clove garlic, minced, for 30 seconds. Return all of the vegetables to the pot with 2 TOMATOES, chopped, and 1 cup low-salt chicken broth. Cook for 5 minutes. Add 1 potato, peeled and grated, ¾ cup fresh, frozen, or canned CORN kernels, ¾ cup trimmed sliced GREEN BEANS, and ¾ cup sliced CARROTS. Simmer, uncovered, for 20 minutes, until vegetables are tender. Add more chicken broth or water if needed. Serve sprinkled with grated Parmesan cheese.

BASIC RATATOUILLE: Heat ½ cup mild, light-flavored olive oil in a heavy soup pot over medium heat. Sauté 1 onion, diced, and 1 clove garlic, minced, for 5 minutes. Add 1 medium EGGPLANT, cut into 1-inch chunks and 1 RED BELL PEPPER, seeded and cut into 1-inch pieces, and cook for 5 minutes, stirring frequently. Stir in 3 medium ZUC-CHINI, cut into 1-inch chunks, ½ cup water, 2 teaspoons dried oregano leaves, and ½ teaspoon dried basil leaves. Reduce heat to medium-low and simmer for 30 minutes, or until eggplant is tender. Stir in 2 TOMATOES, sliced.

AT YOUR LEISURE

EGGPLANT FRITTERS

Mashed cooked eggplant is mixed with a flour batter.

YIELD: *4 servings (2 fritters each)*
PREPARATION TIME: *15 minutes*
COOKING TIME: *50 minutes*

1 medium eggplant
2 tablespoons mild, light-flavored olive oil
1 clove garlic, minced
1 tablespoon minced scallions
1/3 cup plus 4 tablespoons unbleached all-purpose flour
1/2 teaspoon baking powder
1 whole egg and 2 egg whites
1/2 cup low-salt chicken broth
2 tablespoons chopped fresh parsley
1/2 teaspoon black pepper

1. Preheat oven to 350 degrees.
2. Place eggplant on a baking sheet and bake for 30 minutes.
3. Remove eggplant from oven, cut open, scoop out flesh, and mash in a large bowl.
4. Heat 1 tablespoon of the olive oil in a skillet over medium heat. Sauté garlic and scallions for 2 minutes. Add to eggplant.
5. Add flour, baking powder, eggs, chicken broth, parsley, and pepper.
6. Heat the remaining olive oil in a skillet over medium heat. Drop the eggplant mixture in the skillet by tablespoonfuls. Flatten into disks with the back of a spoon and cook until well browned on the bottom, about 3 minutes. Turn and cook on the second side, about 2 minutes. Drain on paper towels. Serve hot.

MASHED SWEET POTATOES AND PEARS

Sweet potatoes and pears are simmered with apple juice and spices, then mashed.

YIELD: *6 servings*
PREPARATION TIME: *15 minutes*
COOKING TIME: *50 minutes*

2 pounds sweet potatoes
2 pears, peeled, cored, and cut into 1-inch cubes
3 tablespoons lemon juice
1 teaspoon curry powder
½ teaspoon ground cinnamon
1 tablespoon mild, light-flavored olive oil
1½ cups chopped onions
1 cup apple juice
¼ teaspoon black pepper

1. Preheat oven to 450 degrees.
2. Prick the sweet potatoes with a fork and bake for 30 minutes. Remove from oven to cool.
3. Combine pears, lemon juice, curry powder, and cinnamon.
4. Peel cooled sweet potatoes and cut into small chunks. Add to pear mixture.
5. Heat olive oil in a skillet over medium heat. Sauté onions for 5 minutes and stir in apple juice, pears and sweet potatoes, and pepper. Simmer for 15 minutes.
6. Mash by hand with a potato masher.

MASHED POTATOES WITH SAUTÉED APPLES

Potatoes are diced, boiled, and mashed with sautéed apples.

YIELD: *4 servings*
PREPARATION TIME: *20 minutes*
COOKING TIME: *25 minutes*

2 pounds potatoes, peeled and diced
1 tablespoon mild, light-flavored olive oil
2 large apples, peeled, cored, and thinly sliced
½ cup grated onion
2 teaspoons caraway seeds
¼ teaspoon black pepper

1. Cook the potatoes in enough water to cover them in a covered pot for 15 minutes.
2. Heat the olive oil in a skillet over medium heat. Sauté apple slices until tender.
3. Toss apple slices, potato cubes, and onion together.
4. Mash by hand with a potato masher.
5. Stir in caraway seeds and pepper.

SPICED HOT FRUIT SALAD

Cloves, cinnamon, and nutmeg provide a special sparkle to this baked fruit dish. Try serving it with your next turkey dinner.

YIELD: *12 servings*
PREPARATION TIME: *15 minutes*
COOKING TIME: *25 minutes*

1-pound can juice-packed or water-packed peach halves
1-pound can juice-packed or water-packed pear halves
1-pound can juice-packed or water-packed apricot
    halves
1-pound can juice-packed or water-packed pineapple
    chunks
1-pound can juice-packed or water-packed pitted sweet
    cherries
2 apples, peeled, cored, and cubed
Freshly squeezed juice of 1 lemon
½ teaspoon ground nutmeg
½ teaspoon ground cinnamon
½ teaspoon ground cloves
⅓ cup brown sugar, firmly packed
3 tablespoons diet or reduced-calorie margarine,
    containing no more than 1 gram of saturated fat per
    tablespoon
2 cups seedless fresh grapes
3 bananas, peeled and cut into chunks.

1. Preheat oven to 350 degrees. Drain the canned peaches, pears, apricots, pineapple, and cherries. Reserve 1½ cups of the combined drained liquids.
2. Place the peaches, pears, apricots, pineapple, cherries, and apples in a covered 2½-quart baking dish. Sprinkle with the lemon juice.
3. Add nutmeg, cinnamon, cloves, and brown sugar to the reserved liquid. Pour over the fruit in the baking dish. Dot with the margarine.
4. Cover baking dish and bake for 20 minutes. Stir in grapes and bananas, cover, and bake for 5 more minutes.

VEGETABLE CURRY

This easy-to-prepare main dish can be made with any combination of vegetables you have on hand. Add more curry powder if you want a spicier version.

YIELD: *4 servings*
PREPARATION TIME: *20 minutes*
COOKING TIME: *35 minutes*

1 tablespoon diet or reduced-calorie margarine,
    containing no more than 1 gram of saturated fat per
    tablespoon
1 tablespoon curry powder
1¼ cups low-salt chicken broth
2 potatoes, peeled and cubed
1 cup green beans, cut into 1-inch lengths
1 tomato, peeled and chopped
½ cup sliced scallions
1 small head cauliflower, divided into florets
½ cup fresh or frozen green peas
⅓ cup cashews, halved

1. Melt margarine in a saucepan. Add curry powder and chicken broth. When broth is simmering, add potatoes, green beans, tomato, and scallions. Cover and simmer for 10 minutes.
2. Add cauliflower and simmer for 10 more minutes.
3. Add peas and simmer for 10 more minutes or until liquid has almost disappeared.
4. Toss with cashews before serving.

FALL FRUIT AND VEGETABLE MEDLEY

This combination of sweet potatoes, carrots, squash, and dried fruit is a perfect addition to an autumn or winter meal.

YIELD: *8 servings*
PREPARATION TIME: *15 minutes*
COOKING TIME: *1½ hours*

3 large sweet potatoes, peeled and thinly sliced
4 large carrots, scrubbed and thinly sliced
1 small butternut squash, peeled, seeded, and thinly sliced
½ cup seedless raisins
¼ cup pitted prunes
¼ cup chopped dates
Grated rind of ½ orange
Juice of 1 orange
1 tablespoon brown sugar
¼ cup honey

1. Preheat oven to 350 degrees. Lightly oil a 9- by 13-inch baking pan.
2. Layer the sweet potatoes, carrots, squash, raisins, prunes, and dates in the baking pan.
3. Sprinkle the vegetables and fruit with orange rind, juice, brown sugar, and honey.
4. Cover the pan with aluminum foil and bake for 1½ hours or until vegetables are tender.

VEGETABLES, VEGETABLES, AND MORE VEGETABLES

Eleven vegetables are baked in a dill-tomato sauce in this hearty casserole.

YIELD: *6 servings*
PREPARATION TIME: *30 minutes*
COOKING TIME: *1 hour and 10 minutes*

3 tablespoons mild, light-flavored olive oil
2 onions, chopped
2 cloves garlic, minced
5 ounces acorn squash, cubed
2 medium carrots, scrubbed and sliced
1½ cups fresh mushrooms, sliced
1 cup sliced zucchini
1 cup cauliflower florets
1 cup eggplant cubes
1 green bell pepper, seeded and chopped
2 stalks celery, chopped
2 potatoes, diced
1 cup fresh, frozen, or canned corn kernels
1 cup sliced string beans
Juice of ½ lemon
1 cup low-salt chicken broth
2 cups chopped fresh or canned tomatoes
½ teaspoon dried dill leaves
½ teaspoon black pepper

1. Preheat oven to 350 degrees. Lightly oil a large casserole.
2. Heat the olive oil in a large skillet or soup pot over medium heat and sauté the onion and garlic for 4 minutes.
3. Add the squash, carrots, mushrooms, zucchini, cauliflower, eggplant, green pepper, celery, potatoes, corn, and beans. Cover tightly and cook for 5 minutes over medium-low heat.
4. Add the lemon juice, chicken broth, tomatoes, dill, and pepper to the vegetables and transfer to the casserole. Bake for 1 hour, stirring several times.

FRUIT AND VEGETABLE RATATOUILLE

Instead of limiting yourself to the familiar vegetables you traditionally use in ratatouille, expand your horizons with the addition of some seasonal fruit.

YIELD: *6 servings*
PREPARATION TIME: *20 minutes*
COOKING TIME: *17 minutes*

2 tablespoons mild, light-flavored olive oil
2 cups thinly sliced zucchini
2½ cups diced eggplant
1 onion, sliced
2 cups tomatoes, diced
2 nectarines, pitted and diced
1 peach, pitted and diced
1 plum, pitted and diced
1 clove garlic, minced
¼ teaspoon black pepper
½ teaspoon dried basil leaves
½ teaspoon dried oregano leaves
1 teaspoon lemon juice

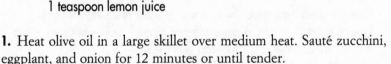

1. Heat olive oil in a large skillet over medium heat. Sauté zucchini, eggplant, and onion for 12 minutes or until tender.
2. Add tomatoes, nectarines, peach, plum, garlic, pepper, basil, and oregano. Cover and cook for 5 minutes.
3. Toss with lemon juice and serve.

BASIC APPLESAUCE

This unsweetened applesauce can be served plain or sprinkled with cinnamon. It is also an ideal addition to quick bread and muffin recipes.

YIELD: *4 servings (approximately 1 cup each)*
PREPARATION TIME: *15 minutes*
COOKING TIME: *30 minutes*

10 medium apples, peeled, cored, and cut into quarters
1½ cups apple juice
1 tablespoon lemon juice
1 teaspoon ground nutmeg

1. Place the apples in a large noncorrosive saucepan with the apple juice.
2. Cover and simmer for 30 minutes or until apples are softened.
3. Mash the apples with the back of a wooden spoon. Stir in lemon juice and nutmeg.
4. Cook for 12 more minutes.

VARIATIONS

- Make hot spiced Apple-Maple Sauce by adding ⅓ cup reduced-calorie maple syrup, 1 teaspoon ground cinnamon, ¼ teaspoon ground nutmeg, ¼ teaspoon ground allspice, ¼ teaspoon ground ginger, and 2 teaspoons grated lemon peel.
- Add 1 tablespoon grated lime rind, 2 tablespoons honey, ½ teaspoon ground ginger, and ½ teaspoon curry powder to 2 cups applesauce.
- Stir fresh berries—whole, cut or mashed—into applesauce.
- Stir in grated orange, lemon or lime rind.
- Stir a spoonful of all-fruit raspberry jelly into the applesauce.
- Create an applesauce whip: Add 2 teaspoons lemon juice to 2 cups applesauce. Beat 3 egg whites with ⅛ teaspoon salt until frothy. Gradually add 6 tablespoons sugar, beating constantly until peaks are formed. Fold beaten egg whites into the applesauce and serve at once.

HONEY BAKED APPLES

Baked apples are one of those wonderful foods we tend to take for granted. This splendid version includes honey, orange juice, and nutmeg. Serve warm from the oven.

YIELD: *6 servings*
PREPARATION TIME: *15 minutes*
COOKING TIME: *50 minutes*

6 large apples
6 tablespoons honey
¼ cup orange juice
2 teaspoons sugar
½ teaspoon ground nutmeg

1. Preheat oven to 400 degrees.
2. Core apples, being careful not to cut all the way through to the bottom. Peel about ⅓ of the way down from the stem end.
3. Combine honey and orange juice. Pour into centers of apples.
4. Pour a little hot water in the bottom of a baking dish and set apples in the dish.
5. Bake for 50 minutes or until apples are tender.
6. Sprinkle tops with sugar and nutmeg. Run under broiler before serving.

Rice and Pasta

Rice

EASY ACCESS: THE BASICS

Rice and Fruit or Vegetable Salad   Basic Fried Rice

QUICK TAKES

Apple-Raisin Rice Salad   Pepper, Chicken, and Rice–Stuffed Peppers
Rainbow Rice Salad

AT YOUR LEISURE

Pear Vegetable Rice   Red and Green Rice   Mixed Vegetable Risotto
Garden Biryani   Melon and Papaya Wild Rice Salad
Wild Rice Vegetable Medley

Pasta

EASY ACCESS: THE BASICS

Multi-Vegetable Pasta   Vegetable Pasta Salad

Warm Pasta Dishes

QUICK TAKES

Apple and Shrimp Pasta Salad   Ziti with Broccoli and Chicken
Cauliflower and Shells   Carrot Zucchini Pasta   Corn and Tomato Pasta
Eggplant and Green Pepper Pasta
Pasta with Snow Peas and Red Pepper
Uncooked Tomato Sauce and Pasta

Cold Pasta Dishes

QUICK TAKES

Asparagus and Scallop Pasta Salad   Carrot and Mushroom Pasta Salad
Bean and Pasta Salad   Pineapple Chicken Pasta Salad
Vegetable and Tuna Pasta Salad

AT YOUR LEISURE

Baked Macaroni and Cheese and Vegetables
Linguine with Orange, Chicken, and Spinach   Pasta Salad Primavera
Pasta Shells with Ground Turkey and Eggplant

Rice Dishes

I've suggested using brown rice in many of the recipes that follow since it includes the healthful bran layer that has been identified as having a variety of nutritional benefits, including cholesterol-lowering properties. Brown rice has three times the dietary fiber of white rice and more vitamins, minerals, and proteins. You can substitute white rice for brown in any of the recipes, but you'll need to modify your rice cooking time according to the package directions. Cooking times given are for conventional brown rice, although some brands of quick-cooking brown rice are now on the market. If you choose one of these, follow package directions to reduce cooking time. Never stir rice while it is cooking or you will end up with a sticky finished product. Cooked rice can be kept for 4 to 5 days in the refrigerator.

EASY ACCESS: THE BASICS

RICE AND FRUIT OR VEGETABLE SALAD

(6 servings)

INGREDIENTS
2 tablespoons sugar
⅛ teaspoon dry mustard
2 tablespoons white wine vinegar
½ cup mild, light-flavored olive oil
1 tablespoon minced scallion
1 cup cooked long-grain white or brown rice, tossed with
    1 tablespoon mild, light-flavored olive oil and cooled
    to room temperature
2 cups chopped fruit or vegetables (see possibilities
    below)
Whole small fruit or fruit slices and pecan halves for
    garnish

1. Combine sugar, mustard, vinegar, and olive oil in a workbowl of a food processor or in a blender and blend until sugar is dissolved and mixture begins to thicken.

2. Add scallion to dressing and pour over rice.

3. Toss with fruit or vegetables and garnish.

FRUIT AND VEGETABLE POSSIBILITIES

Navel orange sections; pineapple chunks; strawberries; poppy seeds

Mango; kiwi; blueberries; bananas

Apricots; blackberries; tangerines

Raw cranberries; pears

Papaya; cantaloupe; raspberries; nectarines

Apple; raisins; carrots; almonds

Pineapple; green bell pepper; red bell pepper; celery; snow peas; cashew
   nuts

Zucchini; radishes; mushrooms; cucumber; spinach leaves

Blanched asparagus tips; zucchini; blanched green beans; spinach leaves;
   blanched peas; celery; tomatoes

Blanched asparagus tips; carrots; spinach leaves; blanched peas

Red, green, and yellow bell peppers; zucchini; yellow summer squash;
   parsley

Steamed sweet potatoes; blanched green beans; blanched peas; tomatoes;
   carrots

Broccoli; corn; carrot; cauliflower

OTHER EASY ACCESS ADD-INS

Flaked tuna

Flaked salmon

Chopped egg white

Olives

Cooked shrimp

Cooked chicken and turkey

BASIC FRIED RICE

(4 servings)

INGREDIENTS

4½ cups cold cooked rice

¾ cup cooked meat, poultry, or seafood (see possibilities
   below)

5 tablespoons mild, light-flavored olive oil

¼ cup minced scallions

2 cups diced vegetables and fruits (see possibilities below)

2 tablespoons light soy sauce

1 teaspoon dry sherry (optional)

2 egg whites and 1 egg yolk, beaten

1. Break up the cold cooked rice so that the grains separate.
2. Dice or shred meat, poultry, or seafood.
3. Heat half of the olive oil in a large skillet or wok. Add scallions and stir-fry for 30 seconds. Add fresh vegetables and fruits. Stir-fry for 2 minutes.
4. Add meat, poultry, or seafood and any canned vegetables and fruits. Stir-fry for 2 more minutes.
5. Remove meat, poultry, or seafood and vegetables from the skillet or wok.
6. Add the remaining oil.
7. Add the cold rice. Turn it with a spatula to keep it from sticking.
8. When rice is heated through, return meat, poultry, or seafood, and vegetables to skillet or wok.
9. Quickly add soy sauce and sherry.
10. Stir in beaten eggs with spatula and turn off heat as eggs start to set.

MEAT, POULTRY, AND SEAFOOD POSSIBILITIES

Cooked pork	Cooked chicken
Cooked beef	Flaked crab meat
Cooked lamb	Cooked fish
Cooked turkey	Cooked shrimp

VEGETABLE AND FRUIT POSSIBILITIES

Blanched green peas; red bell peppers; scallions; romaine lettuce; celery

Blanched string beans; water chestnuts; scallions; mushrooms

Navel oranges; water chestnuts; bamboo shoots; green bell pepper; peanuts

Pineapple; red bell pepper; zucchini; broccoli

Tomatoes; sautéed eggplant; onions; celery

Bean sprouts; tomatoes; onions; mushrooms; green bell peppers; blanched cauliflower

Nectarines; green bell peppers; zucchini; walnuts

Green peas; tomatoes; green bell peppers; red bell peppers

Shredded romaine; shredded spinach; tomatoes

Broccoli; corn; red pepper; mushrooms; pineapple

QUICK TAKES

APPLE-RAISIN RICE SALAD: Cook 1 cup long-grain white or brown rice according to package directions, substituting apple juice for half the liquid. Cool to room temperature. Toss with 2 tablespoons lemon juice, 2 tablespoons mild, light-flavored olive oil, ¼ cup raisins, 2 teaspoons cider vinegar, 2 tart APPLES, cut into small cubes, 2 scallions, chopped, and ½ cup chopped fresh parsley. Chill before serving. (4 servings)

PEPPER, CHICKEN, AND RICE–STUFFED PEPPERS: Preheat oven to 400 degrees. Combine 1 cup cooked rice, 1 GREEN BELL PEPPER, seeded and chopped, ½ cup chopped cooked chicken or turkey, ¼ cup chopped red onion, 2 tablespoons chopped fresh parsley, and ½ cup grated part-skim mozzarella cheese. Toss with 3 tablespoons mild, light-flavored olive oil and 2 tablespoons red wine vinegar. Cut 4 large RED BELL PEPPERS in half lengthwise; core and remove seeds. Brush pepper halves with mild, light-flavored olive oil. Fill each half with ½ cup of the rice mixture. Sprinkle with grated Parmesan cheese. Cover with foil. Bake for 25 minutes. (4 servings)

RAINBOW RICE SALAD: Combine 3 cups cooked brown rice, 2 cups steamed GREEN PEAS, 2 cups chopped TOMATOES, 1½ cups GREEN BELL PEPPER strips, 1 cup diced part-skim mozzarella cheese, and ⅓ cup chopped scallions. Combine ⅓ cup mild, light-flavored olive oil, ⅓ cup red wine vinegar, 1 teaspoon Dijon mustard, and ¼ teaspoon black pepper. Toss dressing with salad. (4–6 servings)

AT YOUR LEISURE

PEAR VEGETABLE RICE

Ripe pears, carrots, and celery are tossed with brown rice, lemon juice, and ginger.

YIELD: *4 servings*
PREPARATION TIME: *15 minutes*
COOKING TIME: *40 minutes*

1 1/2 cups raw brown rice
3 1/2 cups water
3 tablespoons lemon juice
2 cloves garlic, minced
1/4 teaspoon ground ginger
1/4 teaspoon black pepper
2 large ripe pears, cored and diced
1/2 cup chopped scallion
3/4 cup grated carrots
2 stalks celery, chopped
3 tablespoons mild, light-flavored olive oil

1. Place the rice and water in a medium saucepan. Bring water to a boil. Reduce heat to simmer, cover, and cook for 40 minutes or until rice is tender and fluffy.
2. Combine lemon juice, garlic, ginger, and pepper. Toss with diced pears.
3. When rice is done, remove from heat and stir in scallion, carrots, celery, and olive oil. Combine with pear mixture and serve.

RED AND GREEN RICE

Apples, cabbage, and prunes are mixed with brown rice in this dish that combines fruits, vegetables, and a grain.

YIELD: *4 servings*
PREPARATION TIME: *20 minutes*
COOKING TIME: *40 minutes*

1 cup raw brown rice
2¼ cups water
1 teaspoon ground cumin
2 tablespoons mild, light-flavored olive oil
2 onions, chopped
4 apples, cored and diced
4 cups shredded cabbage
1 tablespoon minced fresh gingerroot
6 large prunes, pitted and chopped
2 cups apple juice

1. Place the rice, water, and cumin in a medium saucepan. Bring water to a boil. Reduce heat to simmer, cover, and cook for 40 minutes or until tender and fluffy.
2. Approximately 10 minutes before the rice is done, heat the olive oil in a skillet over medium heat. Sauté onions for 5 minutes. Add apples and continue to sauté until they start to brown.
3. Add cabbage, gingerroot, prunes, and apple juice. Bring to a boil. Cover and cook for 5 minutes. Remove cover and continue to cook until apple juice is absorbed by the apples and cabbage.
4. When rice is done, remove it from heat and stir in apple-cabbage mixture.

RISOTTO

Imported Italian rice, such as Arborio, should be used for risotto recipes because it is best suited to the technique of cooking risotto. The method involves sautéing the rice in olive oil, then adding liquid, a little at a time, and stirring constantly. After the liquid has all been absorbed, the resulting dish is very creamy. While most American rice becomes mushy when prepared in this way, you can try substituting long-grain Carolina rice if imported Italian rice is not available.

MIXED VEGETABLE RISOTTO

You can vary the mix of vegetables in this dish according to the currently available bounty from the garden.

YIELD: *4 servings*
PREPARATION TIME: *20 minutes*
COOKING TIME: *25 minutes*

3 tablespoons mild, light-flavored olive oil
1 cup finely chopped onion
1½ cups ½-inch pieces of asparagus
1 cup fresh peas
2 cups yellow squash, cut lengthwise, then into ¼-inch-thick slices
2 cups fresh or canned tomatoes, drained
1 teaspoon dried basil leaves
3 cups low-salt chicken broth, heated
1 cup raw Italian Arborio rice
½ cup grated Parmesan cheese
1 tablespoon lemon juice
¼ cup chopped fresh parsley
¼ teaspoon black pepper

1. Heat 2 tablespoons of the olive oil in a heavy saucepan over medium heat. Add onion and sauté for 5 minutes. Add asparagus and sauté for 3 minutes more. Add peas, yellow squash, and tomatoes and sauté for 5 minutes more. Add basil and ⅓ cup of the chicken broth. Cover, reduce heat, and simmer for 10 minutes. Set aside.
2. While vegetables are simmering, heat remaining 1 tablespoon of olive oil in a second heavy saucepan over moderate heat. Add the rice, stirring until it is well coated. Stir in ½ cup of the broth, lower heat, and maintain a gentle boil. Stir constantly with a wooden spoon until the broth is absorbed. Continue adding enough broth to keep the liquid boiling, stirring frequently. By the time most of the broth has been added, the rice should be tender but still firm and quite creamy in texture.
3. Add the reserved vegetables and cook until they are heated through. Remove from heat and stir in the Parmesan cheese, lemon juice, parsley, and black pepper.

GARDEN BIRYANI

Biryani is a form of rice pilaf from northern India. It is a treasure chest of vegetables, spices, and nuts. This version is made with brown rice.

YIELD: *6 servings*
PREPARATION TIME: *20 minutes*
COOKING TIME: *55 minutes*

4 tablespoons mild, light-flavored olive oil
1 onion, chopped
1 clove garlic, minced
1 small red or green bell pepper, seeded and cut into
    1-inch pieces
2 cups raw brown rice
1 teaspoon minced fresh gingerroot
1/4 teaspoon ground cloves
3/4 teaspoon ground cinnamon
1/2 teaspoon ground cumin
4 cups boiling water
1 cup fresh or frozen green beans, cut into 1 1/2-inch pieces
1 cup carrots, cut into 1 1/2-inch strips
3/4 cup broccoli florets
3/4 cup cauliflower florets
1 cup diced potato
1/2 cup fresh or frozen green peas
1/2 cup unsalted peanuts or cashews

1. Heat the 3 tablespoons of the olive oil in a large heavy saucepan over medium heat. Sauté the onion, garlic, and red or green pepper for 4 minutes. Add the rice and stir until the kernels are coated with oil.
2. Add the ginger, cloves, cinnamon, cumin, and stir over medium heat for 2 minutes.
3. Add the boiling water. As soon as the water returns to a boil, add the green beans, carrots, broccoli, cauliflower, potato, and peas. Cover and gently simmer the mixture for 45 minutes, until rice is tender.
4. Immediately before serving, heat the remaining tablespoon olive oil in a skillet over medium heat and sauté the nuts until they are slightly toasted. Sprinkle over biryani.

VARIATIONS

- Use basmati, a long-grain Indian rice with a distinctive nutty flavor, instead of brown rice for a more authentic biryani. Follow package directions for cooking time for biryani.
- For a biryani with a creamier texture, substitute 1½ cups skim or low-fat milk for part of the boiling water.

WILD RICE

Wild rice is an excellent source of fiber, vitamins, and minerals. It adds a hearty flavor to this trio of recipes. Cooked wild rice can be frozen.

MELON AND PAPAYA WILD RICE SALAD

Fresh cantaloupe and papaya are tossed with toasted nuts and wild rice.

YIELD: *4 servings*
PREPARATION TIME: *15 minutes*
COOKING TIME: *1 hour and 10 minutes*

2½ cups low-salt chicken broth
1 cup wild rice
⅓ cup mild, light-flavored olive oil
½ cup chopped walnuts or pecans
¼ teaspoon black pepper
1 cup fresh cantaloupe chunks
1 cup fresh papaya chunks
8 romaine lettuce leaves

1. Bring chicken broth to boil in a medium saucepan. Stir in wild rice. Reduce heat, cover, and simmer for 1 hour or until rice is tender and kernels are slightly open. Drain rice.
2. Heat olive oil in a medium skillet and sauté walnuts until lightly toasted. Sprinkle with black pepper.
3. Toss walnuts with wild rice, cantaloupe chunks, and papaya chunks.
4. Line a serving bowl with romaine lettuce leaves and transfer rice salad to a bowl. Serve at once.

WILD RICE VEGETABLE MEDLEY

Substitute your own choice of fresh vegetables for the garden vegetables in this dish.

YIELD: *4 servings*
PREPARATION TIME: *20 minutes*
COOKING TIME: *1 hour*

2 cups low-salt chicken broth
1 cup wild rice
2 cups broccoli florets
6 asparagus spears, cut into 1-inch pieces
1½ cups sliced fresh green beans
2 carrots, scrubbed and sliced
1 tomato, chopped
¼ cup mild, light-flavored olive oil
2 tablespoons red wine vinegar
¼ teaspoon black pepper

1. Bring chicken broth to boil in a medium saucepan. Stir in wild rice. Reduce heat, cover, and simmer for 1 hour or until rice is tender and kernels are slightly open. Drain rice.
2. While rice is cooking, fill a large pot with water and bring to a boil. Drop in broccoli, asparagus, green beans, and carrots. Bring water back to a boil. Remove vegetables with a slotted spoon after 5 minutes. Plunge into ice water to stop cooking and drain.
3. When rice is done, toss in a salad bowl with blanched vegetables, tomato, olive oil, vinegar, and pepper.

Pastas

The possibilities for combining fruits, vegetables, and pastas in hot and cold main dishes and salads are limitless. Here are a few ideas to get you started!

EASY ACCESS: THE BASICS

If you keep your pantry and freezer stocked with dried and fresh pastas in several sizes and shapes, canned tomato purée, tomato sauce, and whole plum tomatoes, olive oil, mozzarella and Parmesan cheeses, walnuts, and canned chick-peas and white kidney beans, you'll have the basics on hand to whip up a pasta dish.

MULTI-VEGETABLE PASTA

(4 servings)

INGREDIENTS
½ cup mild, light-flavored olive oil
1 medium onion, chopped
1 clove garlic, minced
½ cup chopped fresh parsley
5 cups raw vegetables, cut into ¾-inch pieces (see possibilities below)
1 cup tomato sauce
¼ teaspoon black pepper
½ teaspoon dried basil leaves
½ teaspoon dried oregano leaves
12 ounces tubular pasta, such as penne, or small rigatoni, cooked and drained
2 tablespoons extra-virgin olive oil (optional)
Grated Parmesan cheese

1. Heat olive oil in a heavy saucepan over medium heat. Add onion, garlic, and parsley. Cook and stir for 4 minutes.
2. Add denser textured vegetables first and cook over medium-high heat, stirring constantly, for 3–4 minutes.

3. Add remaining vegetables and tomato sauce and cook, stirring, for 3–4 more minutes.
4. Add pepper, basil, and oregano.
5. Toss with cooked pasta, olive oil, and Parmesan cheese.

VEGETABLE POSSIBILITIES
Leeks; red bell peppers; carrots; celery; sliced artichoke; turnip
Shelled peas; radishes; zucchini; mushrooms
Broccoli; zucchini; snow peas; asparagus; pine nuts; mushrooms
Asparagus; carrots; celery; mushrooms
Zucchini; eggplant; green pepper; spinach
Leeks; cabbage; radishes; carrots; zucchini
Asparagus; broccoli; snow peas; pine nuts; mushrooms
Spinach; carrots; mushrooms; zucchini
Broccoli; cauliflower; carrots; frozen green peas; olives
Yellow summer squash; jalapeño pepper; red bell pepper; peas; zucchini
Broccoli; zucchini; green beans; snow peas; mushrooms; pine nuts
Scallions; yellow summer squash; red bell pepper; Brussels sprouts;
    broccoli; snow peas; carrots
Green beans; carrots; yellow summer squash; eggplant
Red and yellow bell peppers; eggplant; olives; pine nuts
Shredded sweet potato; green beans; yellow bell pepper; pumpkin seeds

VEGETABLE PASTA SALAD

(4 servings)

INGREDIENTS
1/2 cup diced part-skim mozzarella or feta cheese
1/2 cup diced fresh tomatoes or cherry tomatoes, cut in half
1/2 cup halved pitted olives
1 1/2 cups raw or blanched fresh vegetables, cut into bite-
    sized pieces (see possibilities below)
12 ounces small shells, penne, or ziti, cooked and drained
1/2 cup extra-virgin olive oil
1/2 cup lemon juice
2 cloves garlic, minced
1/2 teaspoon black pepper
1/2 cup chopped fresh parsley

1. Toss cheese, tomatoes, olives, vegetables, and pasta together in a large salad bowl.

2. Combine olive oil, lemon juice, garlic, pepper, and parsley in a jar with a tight-fitting lid and shake to blend.

3. Toss dressing with salad. Chill before serving.

VEGETABLE POSSIBILITIES

Broccoli; carrots; red bell pepper; blanched tiny frozen peas

Blanched green beans; green bell pepper; mushrooms; zucchini

Onions; cauliflower; blanched peas; carrots; zucchini; red bell pepper

Red cabbage; turnips; green bell pepper

Broccoli; carrots; zucchini; blanched peas; blanched green beans;
    scallions; radishes

Chopped raw spinach leaves; carrots; mushrooms

Blanched peas; carrots; blanched asparagus; mushrooms

Carrots; zucchini; radishes; cabbage; drained canned white cannellini beans

Red bell pepper; mushrooms; peas; zucchini; radishes; celery; turnips;
    carrots; artichokes

Red and yellow bell peppers; sugar snap peas; cucumber

Red and green bell peppers; corn; tomatoes; celery; carrots

OTHER EASY ACCESS ADD-INS: Julienned turkey breast; Swiss cheese; cooked chicken; flaked canned tuna; flaked canned salmon.

QUICK TAKES: WARM PASTA DISHES

APPLE AND SHRIMP PASTA SALAD: Combine 1 cup blanched BROCCOLI florets, 24 medium cooked peeled shrimp, 2 APPLES, diced, ½ cup raisins, 1 cup cherry TOMATOES, halved, ½ red onion, chopped, ½ cup chopped PINEAPPLE, ½ cup nonfat or low-fat plain yogurt, ½ cup reduced-calorie mayonnaise, 1 tablespoon curry powder, ½ tablespoon ground cumin, ¼ teaspoon ground cloves, and ⅛ teaspoon cayenne pepper. Toss with 12 ounces of cooked pasta. (4 servings)

ZITI WITH BROCCOLI AND CHICKEN: Heat 2 tablespoons mild, light-flavored olive oil in a heavy skillet over medium heat. Add 1 pound boneless chicken breast, cut into thin strips, and stir-fry for 2 minutes. Add ¼ teaspoon black pepper and 1 clove garlic, minced. Stir-fry for 2 more minutes. Add 1 teaspoon dried rosemary leaves, 1 teaspoon dried oregano leaves, and 3 TOMATOES, chopped. Cook, stirring, for 1 minute. Add ¾ cup skim or low-fat milk, bring to a boil, reduce heat, and simmer for 2 minutes. Toss with 12 ounces cooked ziti, 4 cups chopped steamed BROCCOLI, and ¼ cup grated Parmesan cheese. (4 servings)

CAULIFLOWER AND SHELLS: Heat ¼ cup mild, light-flavored olive oil in a large skillet over medium heat. Add ½ teaspoon dried thyme leaves, 1 medium onion, sliced, and 1 CARROT, shredded. Stir-fry for 5 minutes. Stir in 2 cloves garlic, minced, 4 cups fresh or canned chopped TOMATOES, and ½ cup dry white wine or water. Bring to a boil. Reduce heat and simmer for 10 minutes, covered. Remove cover and raise heat to medium. Add 2 cups chopped CAULIFLOWER and cook for 10 more minutes. Toss with 12 ounces cooked small pasta shells, ½ cup chopped fresh parsley, and ½ cup grated Parmesan cheese. (4 servings)

CARROT ZUCCHINI PASTA: Heat 1 tablespoon mild, light-flavored olive oil in a large skillet over medium heat. Add 4 medium CARROTS, scrubbed and cut into thin julienne strips, and stir-fry for 2 minutes. Add 2 medium ZUCCHINI, thinly sliced, 4 scallions minced, ½ teaspoon minced fresh gingerroot, and 1 clove garlic, minced. Cover and cook for 2 minutes. Add 1 pound fresh bean sprouts, rinsed and drained. Cover and cook for 2 minutes. Stir in ½ cup light soy sauce, ¼ cup water, and 1 teaspoon sesame oil. Toss with 12 ounces hot thin spaghetti and garnish with strips of raw cucumber. Pass with hot chili oil. (4 servings)

CORN AND TOMATO PASTA: Combine 1 clove garlic, minced, 4 ounces nonfat or low-fat cheese, cut into ½-inch cubes, 1 pound ripe TOMA-TOES, cored and cut into ½-inch cubes, the kernels from 2 ears of CORN, ¼ cup sliced scallions, ½ teaspoon dried basil leaves, and 2 tablespoons of mild, light-flavored olive oil in a salad bowl. Toss with 12 ounces hot medium-size shells or other pasta and sprinkle with grated part-skim mozzarella cheese. (4 servings)

EGGPLANT AND GREEN PEPPER PASTA: Heat ¼ cup mild, light-flavored olive oil in a large skillet over medium heat. Add 1 onion, sliced, and ½ cup pine nuts (optional). Cook and stir until onion is transparent and pine nuts are lightly toasted. Add 2 medium EGGPLANTS, cut into ¼-inch-thick slices, and 1 GREEN BELL PEPPER, seeded and thinly sliced. Cook for 10 minutes. Add 3 cups sliced fresh or canned TOMATOES and ¼ teaspoon black pepper. Simmer for 10 minutes, uncovered. Cover and simmer for 10 more minutes. Remove from heat and sprinkle with the juice of 1 lemon. Serve over 12 ounces hot spaghetti. (4 servings)

PASTA WITH SNOW PEAS AND RED PEPPER: Stir-fry 1 clove garlic, minced, 1 large CARROT, scrubbed and julienned, 2 medium ZUCCHINI, cut into ¼-inch slices, ½ pound SNOW PEAS, ends snipped, 1 small RED BELL PEPPER, seeded and cut into thin strips, and 1½ cups fresh sliced mushrooms in 4 tablespoons mild, light-flavored olive oil. Stir in 1 cup halved cherry TOMATOES and 3 tablespoons low-salt soy sauce. Serve over 12 ounces linguine or other pasta and sprinkle with chopped fresh parsley. (4 servings)

UNCOOKED TOMATO SAUCE AND PASTA: Place 1 pound fresh TOMATOES, chopped, 2 tablespoons mild, light-flavored olive oil, 1 tablespoon chopped scallions, 1 clove garlic, minced, ¼ teaspoon black pepper, and 1 teaspoon dried basil leaves in the workbowl of a food processor or in a blender. Blend until puréed. Serve at once over 12 ounces hot cooked pasta that has been tossed with ½ cup grated part-skim mozzarella cheese and ½ cup grated Parmesan cheese. Garnish with grated raw red onion and chopped black olives. (4 servings)

COLD PASTA DISHES

ASPARAGUS AND SCALLOP PASTA SALAD: Heat 1 tablespoon mild, light-flavored olive oil in a heavy skillet. Stir 1 pound ASPARAGUS spears, cut into 2-inch-long slices, in the oil. Add 3 tablespoons water. Cover and cook for 3 minutes. Remove asparagus from skillet and set aside. Add 2 more tablespoons olive oil and sauté 1 clove garlic, minced, and 1 tablespoon fresh minced gingerroot for 1 minute. Add ½ pound bay scallops. Stir-fry for 3 minutes. Stir in ½ cup rice vinegar, 1 teaspoon sesame oil, and 1 teaspoon light soy sauce. Toss scallop mixture with 12 ounces cooked capellini or vermicelli and the asparagus. Serve chilled. (4 servings)

CARROT AND MUSHROOM PASTA SALAD: Combine 4 cups sliced mushrooms, 4 medium TOMATOES, sliced, 1 cup grated CARROTS, ½ cup chopped fresh parsley, and ½ cup grated Parmesan cheese in a large salad bowl with 12 ounces cooked macaroni. Toss with ¾ cup extra-virgin olive oil, ¼ cup red wine vinegar, 3 cloves garlic, minced, ½ teaspoon black pepper, and 1 teaspoon dried thyme leaves. Serve chilled. (4 servings)

BEAN AND PASTA SALAD: Combine 1½ cups cooked lima beans, 2 cups cooked cut GREEN BEANS, 1½ cups drained canned red kidney beans, and ½ cup sliced scallions with 12 ounces cooked ziti or elbow macaroni. Place 1 clove garlic, minced, 1 tablespoon dried oregano leaves, ½ teaspoon paprika, 1 teaspoon dry mustard, 1 cup mild, light-flavored olive oil, ¼ cup lemon juice, ¼ teaspoon black pepper, and ¼ cup grated Parmesan cheese in a jar with a tight-fitting lid and shake to blend. Toss with beans, scallions, and pasta. Serve chilled. (4 servings)

PINEAPPLE CHICKEN PASTA SALAD: Toss together 4 halved cooked chicken breasts, cut into bite-sized pieces, 1 stalk celery, chopped, ½ cup chopped RED or GREEN BELL PEPPER, ¼ cup sliced scallions, ½ cup chopped almonds, 1 cup canned juice-packed pineapple chunks (juice reserved), 1 cup seedless grapes, and 12 ounces cooked pasta twists. Chill until ready to serve. Toss with a dressing made of 1 cup reduced-calorie mayonnaise, 2 tablespoons pineapple juice, 1 teaspoon lemon juice, and ¼ teaspoon black pepper. (4 servings)

VEGETABLE AND TUNA PASTA SALAD: Toss 1 7½-ounce can tuna, packed in olive oil, with 3 tablespoons red wine vinegar, 1 teaspoon Dijon mustard, ¼ teaspoon black pepper, 1½ cups steamed GREEN BEANS, cut in ½-inch pieces, 2 stalks celery, sliced, 1 RED BELL PEPPER, seeded and sliced, ¼ cup chopped fresh parsley, and 12 ounces cooked small pasta shells. Chill before serving. (4 servings)

AT YOUR LEISURE

BAKED MACARONI AND CHEESE AND VEGETABLES

Macaroni and cheese is a favorite "security blanket" food that's perfect for those occasions when a trying day has left you in need of something simple and soothing for dinner. With the addition of vegetables, it's not only comforting, but healthy as well.

YIELD: *6 servings*
PREPARATION TIME: *20 minutes + macaroni cooking time*
COOKING TIME: *30 minutes*

1 cup chopped broccoli
1 cup chopped carrots
1 cup chopped cauliflower
3 tablespoons mild, light-flavored olive oil
2 scallions, sliced

3 tablespoons unbleached all-purpose flour
2 cups skim or low-fat milk
¼ cup chopped fresh parsley
½ teaspoon black pepper
¼ teaspoon dried basil leaves
¼ teaspoon dried thyme leaves
1 cup nonfat or low-fat cottage cheese
4 cups elbow macaroni, cooked according to package
    directions and well drained in a colander
1 cup grated part-skim mozzarella cheese
⅓ cup grated Parmesan cheese
⅔ cup whole-grain bread crumbs

1. Place 1 inch of water in the bottom of a steamer pot and bring to a boil. Place broccoli, carrots, and cauliflower in a colander or steamer basket over the boiling water and steam, covered, for 4–6 minutes or until vegetables are just tender. Run cold water over vegetables, drain, and set aside.

2. Preheat oven to 350 degrees. Lightly oil a 2½-quart baking dish.

3. Heat olive oil in a heavy medium saucepan over medium heat. Sauté scallions for 3 minutes. Add flour to saucepan and cook for several minutes, stirring constantly. Add milk slowly and continue to stir. Add parsley, pepper, basil, thyme, and cottage cheese. Cook until sauce thickens.

4. Combine cooked macaroni, steamed vegetables, and cheese sauce in a large bowl. Pour into baking dish. Top with mozzarella cheese, Parmesan cheese, and bread crumbs. Bake for 20 minutes or until heated through.

LINGUINE WITH ORANGE, CHICKEN, AND SPINACH

Oranges, chicken breast, and spinach are tossed with hot linguine and Parmesan cheese.

YIELD: *4 servings*
PREPARATION TIME: *15 minutes + pasta cooking time*
COOKING TIME: *20 minutes*

½ cup mild, light-flavored olive oil
1 onion, sliced
1 clove garlic, minced
1 teaspoon dried basil leaves
1 pound boneless skinless chicken breast, cut into 1-inch
    strips
2 10-ounce packages frozen and thawed chopped
    spinach, squeezed dry
¼ teaspoon black pepper
8 ounces linguine, cooked according to package
    directions and well drained in a colander
1 cup seedless orange chunks
1 cup grated Parmesan cheese

1. Heat the olive oil in a skillet over medium heat. Sauté onion and garlic for 5 minutes.
2. Stir in basil leaves. Add chicken and cook, stirring, for 10 minutes.
3. Add spinach and black pepper and cook for 5 more minutes.
4. Toss hot cooked linguine in a bowl with chicken-spinach mixture, the orange chunks and the Parmesan cheese.

PASTA SALAD PRIMAVERA

Avocados top a salad of penne, peas, broccoli, carrots, green pepper, mushrooms, and asparagus.

YIELD: *4 servings*
PREPARATION TIME: *20 minutes*
COOKING TIME: *6 minutes + pasta cooking time*

½ cup broccoli florets
½ cup sliced carrots
½ cup extra-virgin olive oil
2 tablespoons red wine vinegar
¼ teaspoon dried basil leaves
¼ teaspoon black pepper
8 ounces penne or mostaccioli pasta, cooked according to
   package directions and well drained in a colander
½ cup green bell pepper strips
½ cup fresh mushroom slices
½ cup asparagus tips
½ cup diced low-fat mozzarella cheese
½ cup sliced red onion
½ cup fresh or frozen and thawed green peas
1 avocado, peeled and sliced

1. Place 1 inch of water in the bottom of a steamer pot and bring to a boil. Place broccoli and carrots in a colander or steamer basket over the boiling water and steam, covered, for 6 minutes or until just tender. Run cold water over vegetables, drain, and set aside.
2. Combine olive oil, vinegar, basil, and pepper in a small jar. Cover and shake well.
3. Toss cooked pasta with olive oil dressing in a large salad bowl.
4. Add broccoli, carrots, peppers, mushrooms, asparagus tips, mozzarella cheese, red onion, and green peas. Toss again.
5. Divide among 4 serving plates and top each serving with avocado slices.

PASTA SHELLS WITH GROUND TURKEY AND EGGPLANT

Lean ground turkey makes a great substitute for ground beef in pasta sauce recipes. This eggplant sauce features ground turkey, carrots, peppers, and tomatoes.

YIELD: *4 servings*
PREPARATION TIME: *20 minutes + pasta cooking time*
COOKING TIME: *25 minutes*

½ pound ground turkey
¼ cup mild, light-flavored olive oil
1 12-ounce eggplant, cut into 1-inch cubes
1 medium onion, chopped
½ cup chopped green bell pepper
2 carrots, scrubbed and finely chopped
1 clove garlic, minced
1½ cups chopped fresh or canned tomatoes
½ teaspoon dried basil leaves
½ teaspoon black pepper
8 ounces medium-size pasta shells, cooked according to
    package directions and well drained in a colander
¼ cup grated Parmesan cheese
2 tablespoons chopped fresh parsley

1. Sauté ground turkey in a skillet over medium heat until lightly browned. Remove from skillet with a slotted spoon and set aside. Drain fat from skillet.
2. Heat olive oil in the skillet over medium heat. Add eggplant and stir-fry for 10 minutes. Remove from skillet with the slotted spoon and set aside.
3. Sauté onion, pepper, carrots, and garlic in skillet for 5 minutes. Return ground turkey and eggplant to skillet.
4. Stir in tomatoes, basil, and pepper. Simmer for 5 minutes.
5. In a large bowl, toss cooked pasta with the eggplant-ground turkey sauce. Garnish with Parmesan cheese and parsley before serving.

Sauces, Relishes, Chutneys, and Fruit Butters

EASY ACCESS: THE BASICS

Yogurt Fruit Sauce   Hot Jam and Fruit Sauce   Basic Vegetable Sauce
Tomato Salsa   Vegetable Relish
Sweet and Pungent Vegetable Sauce for Meat or Fish

QUICK TAKES

Nectarine Sauce   Iced Cantaloupe Sauce   Pineapple-Banana Sauce
Instant Fruit Sauce   Easy Fresh Raspberry Sauce
Honey-Blueberry Sauce   Mixed Berry Coulis   Fruit Foam
Speedy Fresh Pear Topping   Lemon, Mango, and Papaya Sauce
Tropical Salsa   Avocado Salsa   Raspberry Salsa   Raw Cranberry Salsa
Mango Salsa   Strawberry Relish   Raspberry-Cranberry Relish
Tropical Yogurt Sauce   Passover Fruit and Nut Charoses
Fruit and Vegetable Relish   Raw Cranberry–Pineapple Relish
Instant Cranberry Orange Relish   Refrigerated Corn Relish
Spicy Paradise Chutney   Crunchy Vegetable Topping
Fresh Tomato Sauce   Vegetable Sauce

AT YOUR LEISURE

Apple-Blueberry Sauce   Pineapple Sauce   Banana Fluff Sauce
Apple-Nectarine Sauce   Apple-Maple-Walnut Sauce
Cranberry-Citrus Sauce   Melon Sauce   Eggplant Sauce
Asparagus Sauce   Spinach Sauce   Cauliflower Sauce
Tomato-Jalapeño Sauce   Pepper-Apple Relish   Harvest Chutney
Carrot Chutney   Apple Butter   Pear Butter   Pumpkin Butter

S auces, relishes, chutneys, raitas, salsas, and fruit butters can add a triumphant finishing touch to soups and salads, grilled dishes, and roasts. The light and easy recipes in this section are a great substitute for heavy sauces. They can perk up both vegetarian meals and chicken, seafood, pork, and beef selections. They are simple to fix and can be made well in advance of meal time. Learning to mix and match them with your favorite dishes will instantly expand your repertoire of tempting, healthy menus.

EASY ACCESS: THE BASICS

YOGURT FRUIT SAUCE

(4 servings)

INGREDIENTS
2 cups chopped fruit (see possibilities below)
1 teaspoon grated orange rind
1 tablespoon lemon juice
2 tablespoons honey
1 cup nonfat or low-fat plain yogurt

1. Place chopped fruit, orange rind, lemon juice, honey, and yogurt in the workbowl of a food processor or in a blender and blend until smooth.
2. Chill until ready to serve.

FRUIT POSSIBILITIES
Oranges and blueberries
Apples and pears
Apricots and blackberries
Raspberries and honeydew
Mango and kiwi
Seeded tangerines and bananas
Nectarines or peaches and strawberries

HOT JAM AND FRUIT SAUCE

(2¾ cups)

INGREDIENTS
¾ cup all-fruit jam (see possibilities below)
2 teaspoons lemon juice
2 cups diced fresh or frozen fruit (see possibilities below)

1. Rub jam through a fine strainer into a bowl.
2. Combine strained jam with lemon juice in a medium saucepan and stir over low heat until mixture comes to a boil.
3. Add fruit and continue to stir until it is warmed through. Serve hot.

JAM AND FRUIT POSSIBILITIES

Blueberry jam and fresh or frozen blueberries, pears, and seeded tangerine chunks
Strawberry jam and fresh or frozen strawberries and bananas
Apricot jam and fresh apricots and blueberries
Blackberry jam and fresh or frozen blackberries, and apples
Raspberry jam and fresh or frozen raspberries and nectarines
Orange marmalade and fresh orange chunks and kiwi

BASIC VEGETABLE SAUCE

(Approximately 6 cups)

INGREDIENTS
6 cups sliced vegetables (see possibilities below)
1 tablespoon sugar (optional)
4 tablespoons diet or reduced-calorie margarine, containing no more than 1 gram of saturated fat per tablespoon
⅛ teaspoon cayenne pepper
Low-fat milk or low-salt chicken broth

1. Place the vegetables in a wide saucepan and add enough water to cover them by 1 inch. Add sugar and 1 tablespoon of the margarine. Place over medium heat and cook, uncovered, for 25 minutes or until vegetables are tender. Increase heat and cook, stirring, until all the water has evaporated.

2. Transfer the vegetables to the workbowl of a food processor or to a blender. Process until smooth.

3. Return the purée to the saucepan and stir it continuously over medium heat until it is heated through.

4. Whisk in enough milk or chicken broth to give the sauce a pouring consistency. Add the remaining margarine and the cayenne. Stir until the margarine is melted and absorbed. Serve immediately.

VEGETABLE POSSIBILITIES

Asparagus	Peas
Broccoli	Green or red bell peppers
Carrots	Spinach
Cauliflower	Winter squash
Eggplant	Pumpkin
Green beans	Avocado

TOMATO SALSA

(4 cups)

INGREDIENTS
2 fresh tomatoes, diced
1 green bell pepper, seeded and diced (see possibilities below)
1 medium onion, diced
2 cloves garlic, minced
2 teaspoons lime or lemon juice
1 teaspoon ground cumin
1 teaspoon ground oregano
¼ teaspoon black pepper
¼ teaspoon cayenne pepper
2 cups crushed canned tomatoes

1. Combine fresh tomatoes, bell pepper, onion, garlic, lime juice, cumin, oregano, black pepper, and cayenne pepper in a bowl and stir.

2. Place tomato mixture in the workbowl of a food processor or in a blender and process until well mashed.

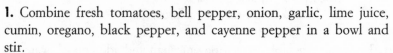

3. Return to bowl and stir in crushed tomatoes.

4. Cover with plastic wrap and chill for 2 hours.

VARIATIONS

- Add 2 jalapeño peppers, seeded and finely chopped, in Step 1 and ½ cup fresh, frozen, or canned corn kernels in Step 3.
- Add ½ cup chopped red bell pepper and ½ cup chopped green bell pepper in Step 3.
- Add ¾ cup diced carrot in Step 3.
- Add 1 medium avocado, peeled and cut into ½-inch pieces, 1 jalapeño pepper, seeded and finely chopped, ½ green bell pepper, seeded and diced, ¼ cup minced red onion, and ½ cup cooked black beans in Step 3. Reduce the crushed tomatoes to 1 cup.

VEGETABLE RELISH

(3 cups)

INGREDIENTS

4 tablespoons mild, light-flavored olive oil

3 cups thinly sliced vegetables (see possibilities below)

2 cloves garlic, minced

2 tablespoons chopped fresh parsley

¼ teaspoon dried oregano leaves

2 tablespoons red wine vinegar

¼ teaspoon black pepper

1. Heat olive oil in a skillet over medium heat. Add the vegetables and sauté for 2 minutes.

2. Add garlic and sauté for 1 minute.

3. Transfer contents of skillet to a large bowl. Stir in parsley, oregano, vinegar, and black pepper. Cool and serve at room temperature.

VEGETABLE POSSIBILITIES

Green bell peppers; red bell peppers; yellow bell peppers; onion

Zucchini; scallions; tomatoes; green pepper

Eggplant; yellow summer squash; carrot; onion

Cauliflower; fresh, frozen, or canned corn kernels; tomatoes; red onion

Eggplant; tomatoes; onion

SWEET AND PUNGENT VEGETABLE SAUCE FOR MEAT OR FISH

(2½ cups)

INGREDIENTS
½ cup sugar
½ cup vinegar
½ cup pineapple juice
2 tablespoons light soy sauce
2 tablespoons mild, light-flavored olive oil
1 clove garlic, minced
1 cup diced vegetables and/or fruit (see possibilities below)
1½ tablespoons cornstarch (optional)

1. Combine sugar, vinegar, pineapple juice, and soy sauce.
2. Heat olive oil in a large skillet or wok. Add garlic and stir-fry for 30 seconds.
3. Add vegetables and stir-fry for 2–3 minutes.
4. Pour vinegar-soy sauce over vegetables.
5. If you want a thicker sauce, mix cornstarch with ½ cup water. Add to skillet and stir to thicken sauce.
6. Serve over meat or fish.

VEGETABLE AND/OR FRUIT POSSIBILITIES
Green bell pepper; onions; carrots; bamboo shoots
Red and green bell pepper; mushrooms; bamboo shoots; pineapple
Carrots; mushrooms; bamboo shoots; snow peas
Green bell peppers; pineapple; carrots; green peas
Turnips; red bell peppers; carrots; onions.

QUICK TAKES

NECTARINE SAUCE: Combine 2 NECTARINES, pitted and cut into chunks, 1 banana, sliced, and ½ cup orange juice in a blender and purée.
ICED CANTALOUPE SAUCE: Place ¼ CANTALOUPE, cut into wedges and frozen, and ¼ cup orange juice in the workbowl of a food processor and process until smooth. Serve on fruit salads.
PINEAPPLE-BANANA SAUCE: Combine 1 cup canned juice-packed PINE-APPLE chunks with 1 BANANA, sliced, and ¼ cup orange juice in the workbowl of a food processor and process.

INSTANT FRUIT SAUCE: Combine 1 ripe medium NECTARINE, peeled, or ¾ cup STRAWBERRIES with 1 teaspoon lemon juice, ⅛ teaspoon ground ginger, and ⅛ teaspoon ground cinnamon in the workbowl of a food processor or in a blender and purée. Serve over fruit desserts.

EASY FRESH RASPBERRY SAUCE: Combine 2 cups RASPBERRIES, 1 tablespoon sugar, and 1 tablespoon lime juice in a bowl. Mash the berries slightly with a fork and let stand, covered, at room temperature for 1 hour. Serve over angel food cake.

HONEY-BLUEBERRY SAUCE: Combine 2 cups fresh BLUEBERRIES with ¼ cup honey and 1 tablespoon lemon juice in a small saucepan over medium heat. Bring to a boil and reduce heat. Simmer for 5 minutes. Transfer to the workbowl of a food processor or to a blender and process until smooth. Serve over fruit salad or grilled chicken.

MIXED BERRY COULIS: Combine ⅔ cup BLUEBERRIES, ⅔ cup STRAWBERRIES, and ⅔ cup RASPBERRIES with 2 teaspoons sugar, 1 tablespoon lemon juice, and 1 strip of lemon zest. Place in the workbowl of a food processor or in a blender and purée. Strain to remove seeds. Serve garnished with whole berries.

FRUIT FOAM: Combine 1 cup STRAWBERRY, NECTARINE, or plum purée with ½ cup sugar, 1 teaspoon lemon juice, and 1 large egg white. Beat until it forms a foam and serve immediately as a thin fruit purée spooned over cake, frozen desserts, or fresh fruit.

SPEEDY FRESH PEAR TOPPING: Combine 4 PEARS, sliced, 1 cup reduced-calorie maple syrup, ⅓ cup skim or low-fat milk, and ¾ teaspoon vanilla extract in a saucepan. Heat until bubbly. Serve with waffles, pancakes, or cereal. For a chunkier pear topping, place 6 pears, peeled and cored, and 1 teaspoon ground ginger in the workbowl of a food processor or in a blender and process until thick. Chill before serving.

LEMON, MANGO, AND PAPAYA SAUCE: Seed and chop 1 ripe MANGO and 1 ripe PAPAYA. Add ½ jalapeño pepper, seeded and minced, 1 teaspoon light soy sauce, 1½ tablespoons lemon juice, and 1 tablespoon chopped scallions. Stir to blend and chill.

TROPICAL SALSA: Combine 1 ripe PAPAYA, peeled, seeded, and diced, 1 RED BELL PEPPER, seeded and chopped, 1 small BANANA, peeled and chopped, 1 scallion, sliced, 1 small jalapeño pepper, seeded and minced, and 3 tablespoons lime juice. Serve with fish.

AVOCADO SALSA: Toss 2 ripe AVOCADOS, peeled and cubed, in ½-inch squares, 2 large TOMATOES, chopped, 1 medium red onion, chopped, 1 GREEN BELL PEPPER, seeded and chopped, 1 jalapeño pepper, seeded and chopped, 2 tablespoons lime juice, ¼ teaspoon black pepper and 3 tablespoons minced fresh parsley. Serve at once with chicken fajitas or wrap, pressing plastic wrap directly on surface to prevent darkening.

RASPBERRY SALSA: Combine 2 cups fresh or frozen RASPBERRIES, 2 jalapeño peppers, seeded and finely minced, 2 tablespoons minced red onion, and 2 tablespoons red wine vinegar in a mixing bowl and chill for 2 hours. Serve with grilled trout or spooned over steamed asparagus, winter squash, or carrots.

RAW CRANBERRY SALSA: Combine ½ cup orange juice, 1 cup chopped raw CRANBERRIES, 2 RED BELL PEPPERS, seeded and chopped, 1 chili pepper, seeded and chopped, 1 red onion, chopped, 1 clove garlic, minced, ½ cup chopped fresh parsley, and ¼ teaspoon ground cumin. Store in the refrigerator until serving time. Serve with stuffed tortillas.

MANGO SALSA: Combine 2 ripe MANGOES, peeled, seeded, and diced, 1 cucumber, peeled and cut in half lengthwise, 1 jalapeño pepper, seeded and minced, 2 slices fresh gingerroot, minced, 2 scallions, chopped, the juice of 2 limes, ¼ teaspoon black pepper, and 1 teaspoon brown sugar. Serve with grilled bluefish.

STRAWBERRY RELISH: Combine 1 pint STRAWBERRIES, chopped, 3 cups seedless raisins, ½ teaspoon ground ginger, 2 tablespoons fresh lime juice, 2 tablespoons honey, 1 tablespoon chopped scallion, and ¼ teaspoon black pepper. Toss in a glass bowl. Allow flavors to combine at room temperature for 1 hour. Refrigerate until serving time. Serve with roast chicken or grilled fish.

RASPBERRY-CRANBERRY RELISH: Bring 1 cup CRANBERRIES to a boil in 1 cup orange juice. Add ½ cup sugar and stir until dissolved. Add 2 cups fresh or frozen RASPBERRIES. Simmer for 3 minutes. Serve with chicken, fish, pork, or turkey.

TROPICAL YOGURT SAUCE: Combine 1 cup nonfat or low-fat plain yogurt, 1 cup diced PAPAYA or MANGO, 1 cup PINEAPPLE chunks, 2 tablespoons honey, and ⅛ teaspoon ground nutmeg in the workbowl of a food processor or in a blender. Combine until the fruit is in tiny pieces.

PASSOVER FRUIT AND NUT CHAROSES: Squeeze the juice of ½ lemon over 2 chopped red APPLES. Combine with rind of ½ lemon, grated, 1 cup chopped walnuts, ¼ cup chopped raisins, 2 teaspoons honey, 1 teaspoon ground cinnamon, and 1 teaspoon sweet red wine.

FRUIT AND VEGETABLE RELISH: Combine ¼ medium HONEYDEW, peeled and diced, ½ cucumber, peeled, seeded, and diced, ½ PAPAYA, peeled and diced, 1 small TOMATO, seeded and diced, ¼ red pepper, seeded and diced, 1 small jalapeño pepper, seeded and diced, 1 teaspoon lime juice, 1 teaspoon lemon juice, ½ teaspoon dried mint leaves, ¼ teaspoon white pepper, ½ teaspoon Dijon mustard, 1 tablespoon orange juice, and 2 tablespoons mild, light-flavored olive oil.

RAW CRANBERRY–PINEAPPLE RELISH: Coarsely chop 12 ounces raw CRANBERRIES in the workbowl of a food processor or in a blender. Transfer to a medium bowl and stir in 16 ounces unsweetened canned crushed PINEAPPLE, drained, 2 tablespoons reserved pineapple juice, 1 tablespoon sugar, and ½ cup chopped walnuts. More sugar can be added to taste. Cover and chill for at least 1 hour. Can be stored in the refrigerator for 1 day. Serve with roast poultry.

INSTANT CRANBERRY-ORANGE RELISH: Place 3 seedless ORANGES, quartered, 2 cups fresh CRANBERRIES, and 1 tablespoon sugar in the workbowl of a food processor or in a blender and process until finely chopped. Add more sugar if desired. Chill before serving. Use as a condiment on cold chicken sandwiches.

REFRIGERATED CORN RELISH: Combine ½ cup vinegar, ¼ cup lemon juice, ½ cup sugar, ½ teaspoon black pepper, and ½ teaspoon celery seed in a small saucepan. Bring to a boil and simmer for 3 minutes. Pour over 1 large GREEN BELL PEPPER, seeded and diced, ½ cup chopped scallions, and 4½ cups fresh, frozen and thawed, or canned CORN kernels. Toss to combine and keep in the refrigerator overnight before serving. Serve with broiled turkey burgers.

SPICY PARADISE CHUTNEY: Combine 1 medium ripe PAPAYA, peeled, seeded, and diced, 2 ripe KIWIS, peeled and diced, ½ small red chili pepper, minced, and 1 teaspoon lime juice. Serve immediately or refrigerate until ready to serve. Serve with curried dishes, red meat, or baked pumpkin or pumpkin muffins.

CRUNCHY VEGETABLE TOPPING: Combine ½ cup chopped zucchini, ¼ cup chopped GREEN BELL PEPPER, ¼ cup chopped TOMATO, 1 tablespoon chopped fresh parsley, 1 teaspoon chopped garlic, 1 teaspoon extra-virgin olive oil, and ¼ teaspoon black pepper. Serve with hot baked potatoes.

FRESH TOMATO SAUCE: Place 3 cups chopped fresh TOMATOES, 2 cloves garlic, minced, ¼ cup chopped fresh parsley, ½ teaspoon dried mint leaves, ¼ cup extra-virgin olive oil, and ¼ teaspoon black pepper in the workbowl of a food processor or in a blender and purée.

VEGETABLE SAUCE: To make 3 quarts of all-purpose vegetable sauce, heat ¼ cup olive oil in a large skillet over medium heat. Sauté 3 cups chopped onions, 3 cups sliced CARROTS, 3 cups sliced GREEN BELL

PEPPER, and 3 cloves garlic, minced, for 10 minutes. Add 2 cups sliced zucchini and 2 cups sliced mushrooms and sauté for 5 more minutes. Stir in 6 cups TOMATO sauce, ½ cup apple juice, 1 tablespoon dried oregano leaves, 1 tablespoon dried thyme leaves, and ½ teaspoon black pepper. Simmer for 20–25 minutes. Serve over pasta, rice, or couscous.

AT YOUR LEISURE

APPLE-BLUEBERRY SAUCE

Fruit combinations can be used to create great-tasting sauces to serve with meat, poultry, and fish.

YIELD: *3 cups*
PREPARATION TIME: *20 minutes*
COOKING TIME: *10 minutes + chilling time*

2 cups blueberries, washed and stemmed
½ cup water
¼ cup brown sugar
1 apple, peeled, cored, and chopped
1 seedless orange, peeled and chopped
¼ teaspoon ground cinnamon
½ cup chopped pecans

1. Combine berries and water in medium saucepan and bring to a boil.
2. Add brown sugar, apple, orange, and cinnamon and cook over medium heat for 10 minutes.
3. Remove from heat and stir in pecans.
4. Place in a bowl, cover, and chill.

PINEAPPLE SAUCE

Fresh pineapple is simmered in pineapple and lemon juice. Serve this warm.

YIELD: *2 cups*
PREPARATION TIME: *15 minutes*
COOKING TIME: *15 minutes*

¾ cup unsweetened pineapple juice
2 tablespoons brown sugar
1 teaspoon lemon juice
1 cup chopped fresh pineapple

1. Bring pineapple juice and sugar to a boil in a small saucepan with a heavy bottom.
2. Add the lemon juice and pineapple and stir until heated through.

BANANA FLUFF SAUCE

Use this sauce over strawberries, peaches, or cake.

YIELD: *2 cups*
PREPARATION TIME: *20 minutes*

2 bananas
½ teaspoon lemon juice
2 large egg whites
Pinch of salt
2 drops of vanilla extract

1. Mash bananas with lemon juice.
2. Beat egg whites until they are frothy. Add salt and keep beating until peaks form.
3. Beat mashed bananas until they are smooth. Gradually add bananas to egg whites.
4. Add vanilla and beat until the banana and egg whites are well combined.

APPLE-NECTARINE SAUCE

Serve this sauce with fruit salad that is accented with fresh mint and lemon juice.

YIELD: *6 servings*
PREPARATION TIME: *15 minutes + 1 hour chilling time*
COOKING TIME: *3 cups*

1 cup apple juice
1 tablespoon sugar
2 slices fresh gingerroot, peeled
5 ripe nectarines, peeled, pitted, and sliced

1. Place apple juice in a medium saucepan with sugar and ginger. Bring to a boil, lower heat, and simmer for 5 minutes.
2. Add nectarine slices and simmer for 7 minutes.
3. Allow sauce to cool for 10 minutes and purée in the workbowl of a food processor or in a blender.
4. Return sauce to saucepan and simmer for 10 minutes. Cover and chill for 1 hour before serving.

APPLE-MAPLE-WALNUT SAUCE

This sauce is a fine accompaniment to breakfast pancakes, waffles, or French toast.

YIELD: *2 cups*
PREPARATION TIME: *15 minutes*
COOKING TIME: *18 minutes*

3 tablespoons diet or reduced-calorie margarine, containing not
more than 1 gram of saturated fat per
tablespoon
¼ cup chopped walnuts or pecans
1 cup reduced-calorie maple syrup
½ teaspoon ground cinnamon
2 cups thinly sliced peeled apples

1. Heat margarine in a skillet over medium heat. Add nuts and brown lightly. Remove nuts with a slotted spoon and set aside.
2. Add maple syrup, cinnamon, and apples to margarine in skillet. Cover and simmer for 10 minutes. Remove cover and simmer for 3 minutes.
3. Remove from heat and stir in nuts. Serve at once.

CRANBERRY-CITRUS SAUCE

Lemon, cinnamon, tangerine, and cranberries are jumbled in this easy-to fix sauce that will make any meal seem special.

YIELD: *2 cups*
PREPARATION TIME: *15 minutes + 2 hours chilling time*
COOKING TIME: *10 minutes*

1 cup raw cranberries
1 small cinnamon stick
½ cup water
½ cup sugar
2 tangerines, peeled, separated into sections, seeded, and
    cut into bite-sized pieces
1 teaspoon lemon zest
2 teaspoons lemon juice

1. Combine cranberries, cinnamon stick, and water in a saucepan. Bring to a boil and cook over medium heat for 3–4 minutes until the cranberries are tender.
2. Stir in the sugar and cook over low heat for 3–5 minutes until the mixture reaches the consistency of thick jam.
3. Stir the tangerine pieces, lemon zest, and lemon juice into the cranberries. Remove pan from heat and let cool to room temperature.
4. Place in a covered glass container and chill for 2 hours before serving.

MELON SAUCE

This curried melon sauce is a great dip for poultry and seafood.

YIELD: *2 cups*
PREPARATION TIME: *20 minutes*
COOKING TIME: *20 minutes*

2 tablespoons mild, light-flavored olive oil
½ onion, chopped
1 ripe cantaloupe, peeled, seeded, and chopped
2 teaspoons minced fresh gingerroot
1 teaspoon curry powder
1 tablespoon cider vinegar
⅛ teaspoon cayenne pepper
1 tablespoon seedless raisins

1. Heat olive oil in a skillet over medium heat. Sauté onion for 3 minutes.
2. Stir in chopped cantaloupe and ginger. Sauté for 2 minutes.
3. Add curry powder and sauté for 2 minutes.
4. Stir in vinegar, cayenne, and raisins. Simmer for 3 minutes. Cool for 10 minutes.
5. Transfer sauce to the workbowl of a food processor or to a blender and purée.

EGGPLANT SAUCE

This sauce of eggplant, tomatoes, green pepper, and onion can be served hot with meat or fish.

YIELD: *2–3 cups*
PREPARATION TIME: *15 minutes*
COOKING TIME: *22 minutes*

4 tablespoons mild, light-flavored olive oil
1 onion, chopped
1 green bell pepper, seeded and cut into strips
1 eggplant, cut into strips
3 tomatoes, chopped

1. Heat olive oil in a skillet over medium heat. Sauté onion for 5 minutes.
2. Add green pepper and cook for 7 minutes.
3. Stir in eggplant. Cook for 5 minutes.
4. Add the tomatoes and cook for 5 more minutes.

ASPARAGUS SAUCE

Try this spring-like sauce with chicken or pasta.

YIELD: *2 cups*
PREPARATION TIME: *15 minutes*
COOKING TIME: *35 minutes*

4 tablespoons regular stick margarine, containing no more
    than 2 grams of saturated fat per tablespoon
1 clove garlic, minced
4 tablespoons unbleached all-purpose flour
4 cups low-salt chicken broth
4 tablespoons chopped fresh parsley
1 cup fresh or frozen asparagus tips
1 cup fresh or frozen green peas
½ cup skim or low-fat milk

1. Melt margarine in a medium saucepan with a heavy bottom over medium heat. Sauté garlic for 2 minutes. Sprinkle the flour over the margarine and garlic and cook, stirring, over low heat for 1 minute.
2. Remove pan from heat and stir 1 cup of the chicken broth into the mixture until smooth. Return to heat and add the remaining broth and the parsley. Bring to a boil, stirring. Let sauce simmer for 30 minutes or until it is reduced by half.
3. If asparagus is fresh, add it after 15 minutes of simmering time; if asparagus is frozen, add it after 20 minutes of simmering time.
4. If peas are fresh, add them after 20 minutes of simmering time; if they are frozen, add them after 25 minutes of simmering time.
5. Stir in milk, heat until warmed through, and serve.

SPINACH SAUCE

This spinach sauce can be used as a dressing for hot or cold vegetables, fish, and poultry.

YIELD: *3 cups*
PREPARATION TIME: *20 minutes*
COOKING TIME: *8 minutes*

1 cup fresh spinach leaves, rinsed and stemmed
2 cloves garlic, minced
4 tablespoons chopped scallions
1/2 teaspoon dried dill leaves
1/4 teaspoon dried tarragon leaves
1/2 cup chopped fresh parsley
1 1/2 cups nonfat or low-fat plain yogurt
4 tablespoons lemon juice
1/2 cup reduced-calorie mayonnaise
1/4 teaspoon black pepper

1. Place the spinach leaves in a pot of boiling water and boil for 3 minutes. Remove at once and run under cold water. Drain and squeeze the spinach to get rid of as much liquid as possible.
2. Chop the spinach and place it in the workbowl of a food processor or in a blender with the garlic, scallions, dill, tarragon, parsley, yogurt, and lemon juice. Process until smooth.
3. Stir in the mayonnaise and black pepper.

CAULIFLOWER SAUCE

Use this sauce as a healthy alternative to fattening white sauces.

YIELD: *3 cups*
PREPARATION TIME: *15 minutes*
COOKING TIME: *15 minutes*

1 1/2 cups skim or low-fat milk
2 cups cauliflower florets
1/4 teaspoon ground nutmeg

1. Heat milk in a saucepan over low heat until it simmers. Add cauliflower florets. Simmer until cauliflower is tender.

2. Transfer milk, cauliflower, and nutmeg to the workbowl of a food processor or to a blender. Process until smooth.

TOMATO-JALAPEÑO SAUCE

This sauce can be made with the hot peppers of your choice. Serve it with poultry or beef. It can also be added to soups.

> **YIELD:** *3 cups*
> **PREPARATION TIME:** *20 minutes*
> **COOKING TIME:** *45 minutes*
>
> 1 cup chopped jalapeño peppers
> 1 clove garlic
> 2 cups chopped fresh tomatoes
> 1 tablespoon red wine vinegar
> 1 tablespoon mild, light-flavored olive oil
> ½ cup chopped onions
> 1 cup low-salt chicken broth

1. Place peppers, garlic, tomatoes, and vinegar in the workbowl of a food processor or in a blender and purée.

2. Heat olive oil in a skillet over medium heat. Sauté onions for 5 minutes.

3. Add the pepper purée and the chicken broth to the skillet. Cover and cook for 5 minutes. Uncover and boil gently for 30 minutes until sauce has thickened.

PEPPER-APPLE RELISH

Pass this unusual fruit and vegetable relish with fish, pork, or poultry dishes.

YIELD: *8 servings*
PREPARATION TIME: *20 minutes + 1 hour chilling time*

6 large tart apples, peeled, cored, and diced
1 medium onion, minced
1 green bell pepper, seeded and minced
1 red bell pepper, seeded and minced
¼ cup reduced-calorie sour cream
¼ teaspoon black pepper

Combine apples, onion, green pepper, red pepper, sour cream, and black pepper. Chill for 1 hour.

HARVEST CHUTNEY

Chutneys are Indian side dishes made from spiced fruits and vegetables. Chutney is an essential element in a meal featuring a curried main course. You can either serve this tangy chutney warm or spoon it into clean jars. It can be stored for several weeks in the refrigerator.

YIELD: *8 servings*
PREPARATION TIME: *20 minutes*
COOKING TIME: *25 minutes*

¼ cup chopped onion
2 teaspoons minced fresh gingerroot
½ cup cider vinegar
½ cup sugar
½ cup orange juice
1 clove garlic, minced
½ teaspoon ground cinnamon
½ teaspoon black pepper
¼ teaspoon ground nutmeg
¼ teaspoon ground cloves
⅛ teaspoon cayenne pepper
1 large apple, peeled, cored, and chopped

1 large pear, peeled, cored, and chopped
¾ pound fresh cranberries
¼ cup water

1. In a large nonaluminum saucepan combine onion, ginger, vinegar, sugar, orange juice, garlic, cinnamon, black pepper, nutmeg, cloves, and cayenne. Bring to a boil and cook over medium-low heat for 5 minutes.
2. Add the apple and cook for 5 minutes.
3. Add the pear and cook for 5 minutes.
4. Add the cranberries, bring to a boil, and cook until they pop their skins, about 5 minutes.
5. Stir in the water and remove from heat.
6. If not serving warm, pour chutney into jars and let cool. Cover and refrigerate.

CARROT CHUTNEY

This chutney tastes particularly good with curried chicken dishes. Make it close to serving time.

YIELD: *6 servings*
PREPARATION TIME: *20 minutes*
COOKING TIME: *25 minutes*

1 pound carrots, scrubbed and diced
1 onion, diced
½ cup diced celery
½ cup diced green bell pepper
½ cup diced red bell pepper
½ cup seedless raisins
¼ cup sugar
¼ teaspoon dry mustard
1 tablespoon unbleached all-purpose flour
½ cup vinegar

1. Place carrots in ½ cup water in a medium saucepan. Bring to a boil and cool for 10 minutes. Drain water from saucepan.
2. Add the onion, celery, green pepper, red pepper, and raisins to the pan.
3. Combine the sugar, mustard, flour, and vinegar in a small bowl.

4. Add sugar mixture to the pan.

5. Cook over medium heat until carrot mixture begins to bubble. Reduce heat and simmer, stirring often, for 15 minutes.

PEAR BUTTER

Pear butter can be stored in the refrigerator for several weeks. Use it as a spread instead of margarine.

YIELD: *9 servings*
PREPARATION TIME: *20 minutes*
COOKING TIME: *1 hour and 20 minutes*

3 pounds ripe pears, peeled, quartered, cored, and cut in
    1-inch chunks
2 tablespoons water
2 cups unsweetened applesauce
¼ cup sugar
1 tablespoon lemon juice
1 teaspoon vanilla extract
1 teaspoon ground nutmeg

1. Place pears and water in a large heavy saucepan. Cover and simmer over medium-low heat about 20 minutes or until pears are tender. Drain.

2. Purée pears in the workbowl of a food processor or in a blender.

3. Return pear purée to saucepan with applesauce, sugar, lemon juice, vanilla, and nutmeg. Bring to a simmer over medium heat and reduce heat to low. Simmer, covered but with lid slightly ajar, for 1 hour.

4. Spoon into jars and cover tightly. Let cool and refrigerate.

VARIATION

- Use 4 16-ounce cans of water-packed pear halves, drained, instead of fresh pears. Omit Step 1.

APPLE BUTTER

Apple butter is a perfect heart-healthy substitute for margarine and butter on bread, muffins, and rolls. Keep a supply in your refrigerator and get in the habit of putting it on the table instead of other spreads.

YIELD: *6 servings*
PREPARATION TIME: *20 minutes*
COOKING TIME: *1½ hours*

2 pounds apples, cored and sliced
¾ cup apple juice
¼ cup sugar
1 teaspoon ground cinnamon
½ teaspoon ground nutmeg
¼ teaspoon ground cloves

1. Put half of the apples and half of the apple juice in the workbowl of a food processor or in a blender and process until smooth. Empty blender into heavy saucepan.
2. Repeat Step 1 with remaining apples and apple juice.
3. Add sugar, cinnamon, nutmeg, and ground cloves to apple purée.
4. Cook apples over low heat for 1½ hours. Spoon at once into a heatproof container. Cool. Cover and refrigerate.

PUMPKIN BUTTER

Pumpkin butter is a great change of pace from traditional apple butter. You can store pumpkin butter in the refrigerator for several weeks or freeze it for several months.

YIELD: *8 servings (½ cup each)*
PREPARATION TIME: *10 minutes*
COOKING TIME: *45 minutes*

4 cups puréed pumpkin
½ cup honey
1 tablespoon ground cinnamon
¼ teaspoon ground ginger
¼ teaspoon ground cloves
2 tablespoons lemon juice

1. Combine pumpkin, honey, cinnamon, ginger, cloves, and lemon juice in a large heavy saucepan. Cook over low heat for 45 minutes, stirring frequently.
2. Pour into large jars and cover tightly. Let cool and refrigerate.

Breads and Muffins

EASY ACCESS: THE BASICS

Basic Fruit or Vegetable Muffins   Basic Fruit Bread   Basic Fruit Coffee Cake

QUICK TAKES

Lemon-Cranberry Muffins   Blackberry Cornmeal Muffins
Carrot-Pineapple Muffins   Simple Banana Bread   Simple Tomato Bread

AT YOUR LEISURE

Pumpkin Bread   Tex-Mex Corn Bread   Apple-Oat Morning Cake
Easy Pineapple Upside-Down Cake

lease note that regular stick margarine, which has under two grams of saturated fat per tablespoon is suggested in some of the recipes in this grouping. Soft margarines do not work well in recipes that call for margarine to be creamed. The water content of diet and reduced-calorie margarines may also have a negative impact on baked goods. However, if controlling saturated fat intake and calories is a specific concern, you can substitute diet or reduced-calorie soft tub or liquid margarine, with the understanding that they may not perform as well as a baking ingredient.

If you are on a sugar-restricted diet, you may also wish to replace the sugar in some of these recipes with the equivalent amount of sugar substitute or to choose recipes not requiring sugar.

Due to the nature of baked goods, the proportion of fruits and vegetables to other ingredients per serving is often not quite as high in the following recipes as in most of the other recipes in this book.

EASY ACCESS: THE BASICS

BASIC FRUIT OR VEGETABLE MUFFINS

(12 muffins)

INGREDIENTS
1 cup unbleached all-purpose flour
1 cup whole-wheat flour
2$\frac{1}{2}$ teaspoons baking powder
1 teaspoon ground cinnamon
$\frac{1}{2}$ teaspoon baking soda
$\frac{1}{4}$ teaspoon salt
1 cup coarsely shredded vegetables or fruits (see possibilities below)
$\frac{1}{2}$ cup seedless raisins
$\frac{3}{4}$ cup skim or low-fat milk
$\frac{1}{4}$ cup mild, light-flavored olive oil
$\frac{1}{4}$ cup honey
1 egg

1. Preheat oven to 400 degrees. Lightly oil 12 muffins cups or line with paper liners.
2. Combine all-purpose flour, whole-wheat flour, baking powder, cinnamon, baking soda, and salt in a large bowl with a fork.

3. Stir in fruits or vegetables and raisins.

4. In a separate bowl combine milk, oil, honey, and egg.

5. Stir the wet ingredients into the dry ingredients until just moistened. Divide the lumpy batter among the muffin cups.

6. Bake for 20 to 25 minutes or until a toothpick comes out clean. Remove from muffin cups and serve warm.

FRUIT AND VEGETABLE POSSIBILITIES

Carrots	Pears
Zucchini	Apricots
Sweet potato	Pineapple
Apple	Nectarines
Blueberries or raspberries	

BASIC FRUIT BREAD

INGREDIENTS

2 cups chopped fruit (see possibilities below)
½ cup sugar
3 cups unbleached all-purpose flour
3 teaspoons baking powder
¼ teaspoon salt
1 egg, beaten
1 cup skim or low-fat milk
2 tablespoons mild, light-flavored olive oil
2 tablespoons grated orange peel

1. Preheat oven to 350 degrees. Lightly oil a 9- by 5-inch loaf pan.

2. Toss fruit and ¼ cup of the sugar and set aside.

3. Sift flour, remaining sugar, baking powder, and salt into a bowl.

4. Combine beaten egg, milk, and oil in another bowl.

5. Pour wet ingredients into dry ingredients.

6. Stir in orange peel and fruit.

7. Bake for 1 hour or until a wooden pick inserted in center comes out clean.

8. Let bread stand for 10 minutes before turning out on a wire rack.

FRUIT POSSIBILITIES

Apples and apricots	Pears and pineapple
Blueberries and cranberries	Blackberries and nectarines

BASIC FRUIT COFFEE CAKE

INGREDIENTS
1 cup unbleached all-purpose flour
½ teaspoon salt
1 teaspoon baking soda
2 cups peeled diced fruit (see possibilities below)
1 egg
¼ cup mild, light-flavored olive oil
1 cup sugar
1 teaspoon ground cinnamon
¼ teaspoon ground nutmeg
½ cup chopped nuts

1. Preheat oven to 350 degrees.
2. Sift flour, salt, and baking soda together into a large bowl. Set aside.
3. Place fruit in a separate bowl. Add egg, oil, sugar, cinnamon, nutmeg, and nuts. Combine well.
4. Add fruit mixture to flour mixture. Combine only until flour is slightly moist.
5. Spread in a greased 8-inch square baking pan.
6. Bake for 40–45 minutes or until a wooden pick inserted in center of cake comes out clean.
7. Let cake stand in pan for 10 minutes before turning out onto a wire rack.

FRUIT POSSIBILITIES

Apples	Blueberries
Cranberries	Raspberries
Pears	Nectarines
Strawberries	Apricots

QUICK TAKES

LEMON-CRANBERRY MUFFINS: Preheat oven to 400 degrees. Sift 1¼ cups unbleached all-purpose flour, 2 tablespoons sugar, 1 teaspoon baking powder, and 1 teaspoon baking soda into a large bowl. In a second bowl beat 1 cup nonfat or low-fat plain yogurt, 3 tablespoons mild, light-flavored olive oil or regular stick margarine, containing less than 2 grams of fat per tablespoon, melted, 1 teaspoon grated lemon peel, 1 teaspoon lemon juice, and 2 egg whites together until smooth. Add wet ingredients to dry ingredients and stir until moistened. Stir in ⅔ cup fresh CRANBERRIES, chopped. Use a 12-cup nonstick muffin tin or line cups with paper liners. Spoon batter into muffin tin, filling tins about ¾ full. Bake for 20 minutes until a wooden pick inserted in the center of the muffins comes out clean.

BLACKBERRY CORNMEAL MUFFINS: Preheat oven to 400 degrees. Stir 1 cup cornmeal, 1 cup all-purpose flour, 1 tablespoon baking powder, and ½ teaspoon baking soda in a large bowl. In a second bowl beat ⅓ cup honey, ⅓ cup mild, light-flavored olive oil, ¾ cup apple juice, and 3 egg whites plus 1 egg yolk together until smooth. Add wet ingredients to dry ingredients and stir until moistened. Stir in 1 cup fresh or frozen unsweetened BLACKBERRIES. Use a nonstick muffin tin or line cups with paper liners. Spoon batter into muffin tin, filling tins about ¾ full. Bake for 25 minutes, until a wooden pick inserted in the center of the muffins comes out clean.

CARROT-PINEAPPLE MUFFINS: Preheat oven to 350 degrees. Stir 1 cup whole-wheat flour, ½ cup all-purpose flour, ½ cup brown sugar, 1 teaspoon baking powder, 1 teaspoon baking soda, ½ teaspoon ground nutmeg, and 1 teaspoon ground cinnamon in a large bowl. In a separate bowl mix 2 tablespoons mild, light-flavored olive oil, 2 egg whites, ¼ cup skim or low-fat milk, 1 cup grated CARROT, and 1 8-ounce can juice-packed crushed PINEAPPLE with juice. Add wet ingredients to dry ingredients until flour mixture is just moistened. Use a nonstick muffin tin or line tin with paper liners. Spoon batter into muffin tin. Bake for 20–25 minutes until a wooden pick inserted in the center of the muffins comes out clean.

SIMPLE BANANA BREAD: Preheat oven to 325 degrees. Stir together 1½ cups unbleached all-purpose flour, ½ teaspoon salt, and 1 teaspoon baking soda in a large bowl. In a second bowl combine 1 cup mashed ripe BANANAS and 1 cup sugar. Add 1 egg and ¼ cup mild, light-flavored olive oil or melted regular stick margarine containing less than 2 grams of saturated fat per tablespoon. Stir to blend. Pour banana mixture into flour mixture. Mix until dry ingredients are just moistened. Pour batter into an oiled 8½- by 4½-inch loaf pan. Bake for 55 minutes or until a wooden pick inserted in the center of the loaf comes out clean. Cool in pan for 10 minutes. Remove and cool bread on rack before slicing.

SIMPLE TOMATO BREAD: Combine 3 cups unbleached all-purpose flour, 1 teaspoon salt, 1 teaspoon baking soda, ½ teaspoon baking powder, and 2 teaspoons ground cinnamon. In a second bowl beat 4 egg whites and 2 egg yolks with a whisk. Add 1½ cups sugar, 1 cup mild, light-flavored olive oil, 1 teaspoon vanilla extract, and 2 cups seeded chopped TOMATOES. Combine wet and dry ingredients until dry ingredients are moistened. Transfer to 2 greased 4½- by 8½-inch baking pans. Bake for 50 minutes or until a wooden pick inserted in the center of the bread comes out dry. Cool in pans for 10 minutes, then transfer to wire racks. Let cool. Wrap and refrigerate overnight before cutting and serving.

AT YOUR LEISURE

PUMPKIN BREAD

Fresh or canned pumpkin and walnuts are the key ingredients in this versatile bread that can double as a dessert.

YIELD: *6 servings (2 slices each)*
PREPARATION TIME: *15 minutes*
COOKING TIME: *50 minutes*

1½ cups unbleached all-purpose flour
1 cup cornmeal
2 teaspoons baking powder
1 teaspoon baking soda
2 teaspoons ground cinnamon
¼ teaspoon ground cloves
½ cup honey
¼ cup mild, light-flavored olive oil
½ cup apple juice
3 egg whites and 1 egg yolk
1 cup pumpkin purée
½ cup chopped walnuts

1. Preheat oven to 350 degrees. Lightly oil a 9- by 5-inch pan.
2. Combine flour, cornmeal, baking powder, baking soda, cinnamon, and cloves in a large bowl.
3. Beat the honey, oil, apple juice, eggs, and pumpkin purée together in another bowl.
4. Stir the wet ingredients into the dry ingredients until slightly moistened. Stir in nuts.
5. Bake for 50 minutes or until a wooden pick inserted in the center comes out clean.
6. Cool in the pan for 10 minutes. Remove and finish cooling on a wire rack.

TEX-MEX CORN BREAD

Serve this bread, which features whole corn kernels, cheese, and bits of red bell pepper, warm from the oven.

YIELD: *6 servings (2 slices each)*
PREPARATION TIME: *15 minutes*
COOKING TIME: *30 minutes*

1¼ cups unbleached all-purpose flour
¾ cup cornmeal
2 teaspoons baking powder
1 teaspoon baking soda
1 teaspoon sugar
¾ cup skim or low-fat milk
¼ cup mild, light-flavored olive oil
1 egg, beaten
½ cup chopped red bell pepper
¾ cup grated reduced-calorie cheddar cheese
1 cup fresh, canned, or frozen corn kernels

1. Preheat oven to 400 degrees. Lightly oil an 8-inch square baking pan.
2. Mix flour, cornmeal, baking powder, baking soda, and sugar in a large bowl.
3. Combine milk, olive oil, egg, red pepper, cheese, and corn in a separate bowl.

4. Stir the wet ingredients into the dry ingredients until slightly moistened.

5. Transfer batter to the baking pan and bake for 30 minutes or until a wooden pick inserted in the center comes out clean.

6. Cool for 10 minutes before turning out on a wire rack.

7. Serve warm or store in refrigerator, wrapped in foil or plastic wrap.

APPLE-OAT MORNING CAKE

Although it's just about impossible to make a totally guilt-free cake, this one comes close! It's made without egg yolks and with skim milk and old-fashioned, good-for-your-cholesterol oats.

YIELD: *8 servings*
PREPARATION TIME: *20 minutes*
COOKING TIME: *30 minutes*

CAKE
2 egg whites
¼ cup sugar
1 cup unbleached all-purpose flour
1 teaspoon baking powder
¼ teaspoon salt
½ cup skim or low-fat milk
1 cup old-fashioned rolled oats
¼ cup mild, light-flavored olive oil or melted regular stick
    margarine, containing less than 2 grams of saturated fat
    per tablespoon
2 large apples, peeled, cored, and cut into ¼-inch slices

TOPPING
¼ cup sugar
½ teaspoon ground cinnamon
½ teaspoon ground nutmeg
2 tablespoons regular stick margarine, containing less
    than 2 grams of saturated fat per tablespoon

1. Preheat oven to 375 degrees.

2. To make the cake, beat egg whites and sugar together in a large mixing bowl until creamy.

3. Sift flour, baking powder, and salt together in a separate mixing bowl.

4. Alternate adding milk and flour mixture to egg mixture.

5. Stir in oats and oil or margarine.

6. Spread half the batter in a lightly oiled 9-inch round baking pan.

7. Arrange the apple slices over the batter.

8. Spread remaining batter over the apple slices.

9. To make the topping, combine the sugar, cinnamon, nutmeg, and margarine. Sprinkle over top of batter.

10. Bake for 25 to 30 minutes.

EASY PINEAPPLE UPSIDE-DOWN CAKE

Pineapple upside-down cake is simple to make and can be served for brunch, at snack time, or for dessert.

> **YIELD:** *8 servings*
> **PREPARATION TIME:** *20 minutes*
> **COOKING TIME:** *30 minutes*
>
> 1 20-ounce can juice-packed crushed pineapple, drained
>   and juice reserved
> ³/₄ teaspoon ground cinnamon
> 1 tablespoon melted regular stick margarine, containing
>   less than 2 grams of saturated fat per tablespoon
> 1½ cups unbleached all-purpose flour
> ½ teaspoon baking soda
> 1 teaspoon baking powder
> ½ cup reserved pineapple juice
> 2 tablespoons skim or low-fat milk
> 2 egg whites

1. Preheat oven to 350 degrees. Lightly oil an 8-inch round cake pan.

2. Mix pineapple with cinnamon.

3. Add margarine to pineapple and cinnamon.

4. Spread pineapple mixture in bottom of the cake pan.

5. Combine flour, baking soda, and baking powder.

6. Combine pineapple juice, milk, and egg whites. Add to flour mixture and mix well.

7. Pour cake batter over pineapple in cake pan. Bake for 30 minutes.

8. Cool for 20 minutes in pan and invert on serving plate.

Desserts

Frozen Fruit Desserts

EASY ACCESS: THE BASICS

Easy Canned Fruit Frost   Canned Fruit Yogurt Ice
Frozen Fruit Maple Sorbet

QUICK TAKES

Frozen Fruit   Frozen Oranges   Strawberry Freezes
Frozen Pineapple on a Stick   Peanut Banana Pop

AT YOUR LEISURE

Banana Ice Cream   Nectarine Raspberry Sorbet
Strawberry-Banana Buttermilk Freeze
Cantaloupe Freeze with Blueberry Garnish
Fresh Strawberry Sorbet (Ice-Cream Maker)
Honey and Melon Sherbet (Ice-Cream Maker)
Apple Berry Sherbet (Ice-Cream Maker)
Frozen Blueberry Yogurt (Ice-Cream Maker)

Fruit Desserts

EASY ACCESS: THE BASICS

Single-Serving Yogurt-Fruit Parfait   Fresh Fruit Tart   Fruit Crunch

QUICK TAKES

Honeydew, Kiwi, and Grape Dessert   Fruit Medley
Strawberries with Raspberry Sauce   Spiced Pears   Simply Papaya
Strawberry Dippers   Curried Raspberries, Pineapple, and Apricots
Fresh Fruit Bake with Frozen Yogurt   Fruit Plates

AT YOUR LEISURE

Papaya Supreme   Winter Compote   Banana Apricot Mousse
Orange Carrot Pudding   Pumpkin Ricotta Dessert   Spicy Carrot Cookies
Cranberry-Pumpkin Snacks

Frozen Fruit Desserts

When making frozen fruit desserts, be sure to start with ripe, full-tasting, unblemished fruit. If you are puréeing fruit that has small seeds, such as blackberries or raspberries, or those with thick skins, such as blueberries or grapes, you may wish to strain them. Although mechanical or electric ice cream freezers produce smoother results, delicious frozen desserts can be simply frozen in a pan in the freezer. While automatic ice-cream makers aerate frozen dessert mixtures by constant agitation during the freezing period, if you are relying on your home freezer, you need to whip, stir, or whisk air into your frozen dessert preparations several times during the freezing period. Specific instructions for aerating desserts are given with each recipe.

Frozen fruit desserts taste best when fresh, so plan to use them as soon after they are made as possible. If a frozen fruit dessert has frozen too hard to eat immediately, place in the refrigerator from 20 to 45 minutes to allow it to soften slightly before serving. You can also cut hard frozen fruit desserts into chunks and process in a food processor or heavy-duty electric mixer until they are barely slushy.

While many of the following recipes do not use sugar at all, those that do require only a small amount. Use extra-fine granulated sugar, which dissolves rapidly.

EASY CANNED FRUIT FROST

(4 servings)

INGREDIENTS

1 16-ounce can unsweetened juice-packed or water-
 packed fruit, drained and frozen (see possibilities
 below)
¼ cup orange juice
1 tablespoon honey

1. Fifteen minutes before serving time, remove frozen canned fruit from freezer and allow to thaw slightly at room temperature.
2. Immediately before serving time, place fruit, orange juice, and honey in the workbowl of a food processor or in a blender. Purée and serve.

FRUIT POSSIBILITIES

Juice-packed canned apricots
Juice-packed canned grapefruit
Juice-packed canned pineapple
Juice-packed canned peaches
Juice-packed canned pears
A mixture of any of the fruits listed above

CANNED FRUIT YOGURT ICE

(4 servings)

INGREDIENTS

1 16-ounce can unsweetened juice-packed fruit, drained
 and chopped, juice reserved (see possibilities below)
2 teaspoons honey
1 tablespoon lemon juice
1 cup nonfat or low-fat plain yogurt
¼ cup chopped almonds

1. Pour the reserved juice from the fruit into a saucepan over low heat. Add honey and lemon juice and stir until mixed. Remove from heat. Allow to cool to room temperature.

2. Add yogurt to juice-honey mixture. Pour into a shallow metal pan, such as an ice-cube tray or baking tin or other freezer-safe bowl. Freeze until mixture becomes slushy.

3. Stir in chopped fruit and almonds. Continue freezing. Stir frequently to evenly mix solid and soft areas until mixture is frozen firm, but not hard.

FRUIT POSSIBILITIES

Juice-packed canned apricots
Juice-packed canned grapefruit
Juice-packed canned pineapple
Juice-packed canned peaches
Juice-packed canned pears
A mixture of any of the fruits listed above

FROZEN FRUIT MAPLE SORBET

(6 servings)

INGREDIENTS
3¾ cups fresh or unsweetened frozen and thawed fruit
    (see possibilities below)
¼ cup reduced-calorie maple syrup
½ cup evaporated skim milk, well chilled

1. Place the fruit in the workbowl of a food processor or in a blender and purée until smooth. If using seeded berries, pass them through a fine sieve to remove the skins and seeds.

2. Add maple syrup to the fruit in the workbowl. Process for 30 seconds. Pour mixture into a shallow metal pan, such as an ice-cube tray or baking tin or other freezer-safe bowl. Freeze uncovered. Stir frequently to evenly mix solid and soft areas.

3. When the edges of the fruit mixture are firm, beat the evaporated milk in an electric mixer until soft peaks form. Scrape the fruit mixture into the mixer bowl and mix for 30 seconds. Return to dish and stir frequently, freezing until firm, but not hard. This should take between 1 and 2 hours.

4. Return sorbet to the mixer bowl and mix for 30 seconds. Serve at once.

FRUIT POSSIBILITIES

Fresh apricots
Fresh nectarines
Fresh or frozen blueberries, strawberries, blackberries, or raspberries
Bananas
A mixture of any of the fruits listed above

QUICK TAKES

FROZEN FRUIT: Rinse off stemmed grapes, hulled STRAWBERRIES, BLUE-BERRIES, and PINEAPPLE, or peach chunks. Place them in plastic bags and pop them in the freezer for an hour or two. Munch frozen or use instead of ice cubes in lemonade and other summer drinks.

FROZEN ORANGES: Put small whole seedless ORANGES in the freezer and leave them for 6 hours or overnight. Remove and thaw for 30 minutes before serving. Slice off the tops and serve with small sharp spoons.

STRAWBERRY FREEZES: Purée 1 pint of STRAWBERRIES, hulled, in the workbowl of a food processor. Pour purée into small paper cups, insert a wooden stick in each, and freeze.

FROZEN PINEAPPLE ON A STICK: Insert pop sticks in the ends of PINEAP-PLE wedges (each wedge should be ⅛ of a peeled and trimmed pine-apple. Roll each wedge in 2 tablespoons ground walnuts. Stand upright in an empty jar and freeze.

PEANUT BANANA POP: Stick pop sticks in the cut end of each of 6 BANANA halves. Stand banana halves upright in an empty jar and freeze for 1 hour. Melt 3 tablespoons natural peanut butter in a saucepan over low heat. Place crushed unsalted peanuts in a small flat dish. Roll bananas in melted peanut butter, then in crushed peanuts. Stand in jar and return to freezer until hard.

AT YOUR LEISURE

BANANA ICE CREAM

Adding whipped evaporated skim milk gives frozen fruit desserts a creamy texture without adding lots of fat. Garnish this lemon-flavored banana treat with strawberries and almond slices.

YIELD: *4 servings*
PREPARATION TIME: *15 minutes + freezing time*

4 large bananas, peeled
½ cup extra-fine granulated sugar
Juice of ½ lemon
1 cup evaporated skim milk, well chilled

1. Mash the bananas in a medium mixing bowl and combine with sugar and lemon juice.
2. Beat the chilled evaporated milk in an electric mixer until soft peaks form.
3. Fold the banana mixture into the whipped milk.
4. Pour into a shallow metal pan, such as an ice-cube tray or baking tin or other freezer-safe bowl, and freeze. Stir frequently during the freezing period to evenly mix solid and soft areas until mixture is frozen firm, but not hard.

NECTARINE RASPBERRY SORBET

This elegant sorbet is made with plain gelatin, another popular method of preparing fresh fruit frozen desserts.

YIELD: *4 servings*
PREPARATION TIME: *15 minutes + freezing time*

½ cup water
1 envelope plain gelatin
½ cup nonalcoholic white wine or dry white wine
⅓ cup extra-fine granulated sugar
10 ounces unsweetened frozen and thawed raspberries
4 peaches, pitted and cut into chunks
1 teaspoon lemon zest
¼ cup lemon juice

1. Place water and gelatin in a saucepan and stir over medium heat until gelatin is dissolved.
2. Add wine and sugar and stir until sugar is dissolved.
3. Remove saucepan from heat.
4. Place raspberries, peaches, lemon zest, and lemon juice in the workbowl of a food processor or in a blender. Pour in wine-gelatin mixture. Blend until smooth.
5. Pour into a shallow metal pan, such as an ice-cube tray or baking tin or other freezer-safe bowl, and freeze, uncovered. Stir frequently to evenly mix solid and soft areas, freezing until firm, but not hard. Allow to soften slightly and transfer to the large bowl of an electric mixer. Beat at medium speed until smooth. Serve.

STRAWBERRY-BANANA BUTTERMILK FREEZE

Buttermilk adds a special flavor to this strawberry and banana combination. Try using all-fruit jams instead of honey or sugar to sweeten other frozen desserts.

YIELD: *4 servings*
PREPARATION TIME: *15 minutes + 4 hours freezing time*

1 pint fresh or unsweetened frozen and thawed
    strawberries
1 ripe banana, peeled and cut into 1-inch slices
2 tablespoons all-fruit strawberry jam
½ cup low-fat buttermilk

1. Place strawberries and banana in the workbowl of a food processor or in a blender and purée. Add jam and buttermilk and process until blended.
2. Pour into a shallow metal pan, such as an ice-cube tray or baking tin or other freezer-safe bowl.
3. Freeze for about 2 hours, until edges are firm. Stir frequently to evenly mix solid and soft areas.
4. Transfer to the large bowl of an electric mixer and beat on medium-high speed until smooth. Return to pan.
5. Freeze for 2 more hours, again stirring frequently. Beat in electric mixer again. Serve.

CANTALOUPE FREEZE WITH BLUEBERRY GARNISH

This tempting "double-fruit" dessert is low in sugar and fat and high on taste. The addition of a beaten egg white gives it a fluffy texture.

YIELD: *4 servings*
PREPARATION TIME: *15 minutes + 4 hours freezing time*

2 cups ripe cantaloupe, cut into cubes
1 egg white
⅓ cup extra-fine granulated sugar
2 tablespoons lemon juice
1 tablespoon fresh mint leaves (or ½ teaspoon dried)
1 cup fresh or unsweetened frozen and thawed
blueberries

1. Process cantaloupe, egg white, sugar, and lemon juice in the workbowl of a food processor or in a blender until smooth.
2. Transfer to a shallow metal pan, such as an ice-cube tray or baking tin or other freezer-safe bowl, and freeze for 2 hours. Stir mixture frequently to evenly mix solid and soft areas.
3. After 2 hours, process mixture in the workbowl of the food processor or blender for 10 seconds or until smooth. Pour mixture back into pan, cover with plastic wrap, and freeze for 2 more hours, again stirring frequently.
4. Serve with mint leaves and blueberries sprinkled over the melon freeze.

ICE-CREAM MAKER RECIPES

While most of the frozen dessert mixtures described above can also be processed in ice-cream makers, here are a group of recipes especially designed for that purpose. Sorbet and sherbet mixtures need a lower ratio of salt to ice than ice creams do. Use 1 cup plus 2 tablespoons of salt for 6 pounds of ice cubes, or ¾ cup rock salt for 6 pounds crushed ice.

FRESH STRAWBERRY SORBET

Use firm ripe strawberries that have been chilled in the refrigerator for this sorbet.

YIELD: *6 servings*
PREPARATION TIME: *15 minutes + freezing time*

2 pints fresh strawberries, hulled and halved
½ cup extra-fine granulated sugar
3 tablespoons lemon juice

1. Place strawberries in the workbowl of a food processor or in a blender and purée. Add sugar and lemon juice. Blend well.
2. Process in an ice-cream maker according to manufacturer's instructions.

HONEY AND MELON SHERBET

This sherbet can also be prepared with honeydew melon.

YIELD: *4 servings*
PREPARATION TIME: *20 minutes + freezing time*

1 medium cantaloupe, halved, seeded, and diced
⅓ cup extra-fine granulated sugar
⅓ cup honey
2 tablespoons lemon juice
1 teaspoon vanilla extract
2½ cups cold skim or low-fat milk
2 egg whites

1. Place cantaloupe with sugar, honey, lemon juice, and vanilla in the workbowl of a food processor or in a blender. Purée until smooth.
2. Pour purée into a large mixing bowl and add milk.
3. Beat egg whites until stiff and fold into purée-milk mixture.

4. Pour purée into freezer can of an ice-cream maker and process according to manufacturer's instructions.

5. After processing, remove sherbet from freezer can and place in a plastic bowl with a tight cover. Keep in freezer several hours before serving.

APPLE BERRY SHERBET

Serve this treat with fresh blackberries as a topping. Enjoy as dessert after a dinner of Pasta Shells with Ground Turkey and Eggplant (page 268).

YIELD: *4 servings*
PREPARATION TIME: *15 minutes + freezing time*
COOKING TIME: *10 minutes*

½ cup water
2 cups apple chunks
¼ cup honey
¼ cup fresh crushed blackberries
2 tablespoons orange juice
½ cup skim or low-fat milk
2 cups fresh whole blackberries

1. Combine water, apples, and honey in a saucepan and bring to a boil. Reduce heat to low and add crushed blackberries, orange juice, and milk. Cook for 10 minutes, remove from heat, and allow to cool to room temperature.

2. Freeze in an ice-cream maker according to the manufacturer's instructions.

3. Serve topped with remaining whole blackberries.

FROZEN BLUEBERRY YOGURT

Serve this blueberry yogurt, slightly softened, with thinly sliced peeled fresh peaches as a topping. Serve with Baked Macaroni and Cheese and Vegetables (page 264).

YIELD: *4 servings*
PREPARATION TIME: *10 minutes + freezing time*

2 cups nonfat or low-fat plain yogurt
2 cups fresh blueberries
2 tablespoons orange juice
2 tablespoons honey

1. Stir the yogurt, 1 cup of blueberries, orange juice, and honey together, crushing the berries slightly as you stir.
2. Freeze in an ice-cream maker according to the manufacturer's instructions.
3. Top frozen yogurt with remaining 1 cup of fresh blueberries before serving.

Fruit Desserts

When choosing ingredients for these desserts, look for fruit at the peak of perfection. In most cases, frozen fruit can be substituted when fresh fruit is out of season.

Simple fruit desserts can be greatly enhanced by serving them in attractive bowls and garnishing them with sprigs of fresh mint or other fresh herbs, such as tarragon and thyme; slices of fresh lemon, lime, orange, and tangerine; black or golden raisins; chopped dates; whole, halved, chopped, or ground nuts; whole grapes, cherries, or berries; sunflower, sesame, or pumpkin seeds.

Please note that regular stick margarine, which has under two grams of saturated fat per tablespoon, is suggested in some of the recipes in this grouping. Soft margarines do not work well in recipes that call for margarine to be creamed. The water content of diet and reduced-calorie margarines may also have a negative impact on baked goods. However, if controlling saturated fat intake and calories is a specific concern, you can substitute diet or reduced-calorie soft tub or liquid margarine with the understanding that they may not perform as well as a baking ingredient.

If you are on a sugar-restricted diet, you may also wish to replace the sugar in some of these recipes with the equivalent amount of sugar substitute or to choose recipes not requiring sugar.

Due to the nature of baked goods, the proportion of fruits and vegetables to other ingredients per serving is often not quite as high in the following recipes as in most of the other recipes in this book.

EASY ACCESS: THE BASICS

SINGLE-SERVING YOGURT FRUIT PARFAIT

INGREDIENTS
8 ounces nonfat or low-fat plain yogurt
1 cup sliced fresh or juice-packed canned fruit, drained
  (see possibilities below)

1. Place ¼ of the yogurt in a long-stemmed glass. Top with ¼ of the fruit.
2. Continue to add layers of yogurt and fruit, ending with a final layer of fruit.
3. Chill until ready to serve.

FRUIT POSSIBILITIES

Apricots	Cantaloupe
Banana	Honeydew
Blueberries	Mango
Strawberries	Nectarines
Blackberries	Pineapple
Raspberries	Pears

FRESH FRUIT TART

(6 servings)

INGREDIENTS
1 cup granola
1 cup graham cracker crumbs
½ teaspoon ground cinnamon
¼ cup sugar
½ cup regular stick margarine, containing less than
    2 grams of saturated fat per tablespoon, melted
¼ cup skim or low-fat milk
5 cups sliced fresh fruit (see possibilities below)
1 cup nonfat or low-fat plain yogurt

1. Preheat oven to 350 degrees.
2. Combine granola, crumbs, cinnamon, sugar, margarine, and milk and blend.
3. Press the mixture onto bottom and sides of a 9-inch pie pan and bake for 25 minutes.
4. Remove from oven and cool for 20 minutes. Fill shell with sliced fruit. Top with the yogurt.
5. Chill for several hours before serving.

FRUIT POSSIBILITIES
Blueberries and peaches
Strawberries
Apricots and blackberries
Nectarines and raspberries

FRUIT CRUNCH

(6 servings)

INGREDIENTS
5 cups sliced fruit, rinsed and dried (see possibilities below)
½ cup brown sugar
½ cup + 1 tablespoon unbleached all-purpose flour
1 cup quick rolled oats
½ teaspoon ground cinnamon
½ cup cold regular stick margarine, containing less than
     2 grams of saturated fat per tablespoon, cut into small
     pieces

1. Preheat oven to 375 degrees. Lightly oil a 9-inch square baking dish.
2. Toss fruit with ¼ cup of the brown sugar and 1 tablespoon flour. Transfer to baking dish.
3. Combine oats, cinnamon, remaining brown sugar, and remaining flour. Cut in margarine with pastry blender or 2 knives until coarse crumbs are formed. Sprinkle topping over fruit.
4. Bake for 30 minutes. Serve warm.

FRUIT POSSIBILITIES

Nectarines and pitted red cherries
Apricots and raspberries
Plums and bananas
Apples and cranberries
Blueberries and strawberries
Pears and blackberries

QUICK TAKES

HONEYDEW, KIWI, AND GRAPE DESSERT: Combine the chunks from 1 medium HONEYDEW melon, ½ pound seedless green grapes, and 6 KIWIS, peeled and cut in ¼-inch slices. Fill wine glasses with the mixture and top with nonfat or low-fat plain yogurt. (4 servings)
FRUIT MEDLEY: Combine 2 cups sliced peaches, 2 cups sliced plums, ¼ cup seedless grapes, 1 pint STRAWBERRIES, hulled and halved, 1½ cups BLUEBERRIES, 4 KIWIS, sliced, 1 teaspoon sugar, and 1 table-

spoon lemon juice. Let fruit stand, covered, at room temperature for 1 hour. Stir together 2 cups nonfat or low-fat plain yogurt, 2 tablespoons honey, and 1 teaspoon vanilla. Serve fruit medley in dessert bowls and top with sauce. (6 servings)

STRAWBERRIES WITH RASPBERRY SAUCE: Place 6 cups fresh RASPBERRIES in the workbowl of a food processor or in a blender with ¼ cup lemon juice and 2 tablespoons sugar. Purée. Chill purée. Serve sauc over 6 cups fresh STRAWBERRIES, hulled, in glass dessert bowls. (6 servings)

SPICED PEARS: Core and halve 2 PEARS. Place them in a medium saucepan with 1 cup cranberry juice, 1 tablespoon sugar, ⅛ teaspoon ground cloves, ⅛ teaspoon ground cinnamon, and ½ teaspoon grated orange rind. Bring to a boil, reduce heat, and simmer, covered, for 15 minutes or until pears are tender. (4 servings)

SIMPLY PAPAYA: Slice a ripe PAPAYA and serve it simply with a squeeze of lime.

STRAWBERRY DIPPERS: Dip STRAWBERRIES first in nonfat or low-fat plain yogurt, then in brown sugar.

CURRIED RASPBERRIES, PINEAPPLE, AND APRICOTS: Preheat oven to 350 degrees. Place 2 cups RASPBERRIES, 3 cups drained juice-packed canned PINEAPPLE chunks, and 4 cups drained juice-packed canned APRICOT chunks in a 2-quart casserole. Combine ¼ cup melted regular stick margarine, ¼ cup brown sugar, and 1 teaspoon curry powder. Pour over fruit. Bake for 30 minutes. (6 servings)

FRESH FRUIT BAKE WITH FROZEN YOGURT: Preheat oven to 325 degrees. Place 1 cup hulled halved STRAWBERRIES, ⅔ cup BLUEBERRIES, 2 plums, pitted and sliced, and 1 NECTARINE, pitted and sliced, in an 8-inch square baking dish. Sprinkle with 1 tablespoon brown sugar. Pour ½ cup white grape juice or dry white wine over fruit and bake for 20 minutes. Serve warm with vanilla frozen yogurt. (4 servings)

FRUIT PLATES: Serve fruit combinations arranged on attractive dessert plates topped with one of the Fruit Sauces. Some possible combinations include:

Navel orange slices; red grapefruit slices; and avocado slices
Papaya slices; avocado slices; and banana slices
Cubed mango; sliced papaya; sliced avocado; and pineapple spears
Honeydew slices; cantaloupe slices; watermelon slices
Honeydew slices; nectarine slices; apricot slices; and blueberries
Navel orange slices; banana slices; sliced strawberries; kiwi slices
Mango chunks; papaya slices; kiwi slices; pear slices; strawberries

PAPAYA SUPREME

A lemon-accented yogurt honey sauce tops a tempting array of fruits in this tropical delight. Serve with Scallop-Vegetable Bisque (page 131).

YIELD: *4 servings*
PREPARATION TIME: *15 minutes + 1 hour chilling time*

1½ cups nonfat or low-fat plain yogurt
¼ cup honey
1 tablespoon grated lemon peel
½ teaspoon ground nutmeg
1 large ripe papaya, peeled, seeded, and sliced
8 spears of fresh pineapple or slices of juice-packed
    canned pineapple
2 cups strawberries, hulled
4 bananas, peeled and sliced

1. Combine yogurt, honey, lemon peel, and nutmeg 1 hour in advance of serving and chill in refrigerator.
2. Immediately before serving, arrange papaya, pineapple, strawberries, and bananas on a serving platter and top with yogurt sauce.

WINTER COMPOTE

Fruit compotes make soul-warming winter desserts when served solo or superb toppings when served with pancakes. Serve with Dijon Rosemary Pork (page 204).

YIELD: *6 servings*
PREPARATION TIME: *20 minutes*
COOKING TIME: *20 minutes*

1 pound seedless red grapes
2 large ripe pears, peeled, cored, and chopped

2 large apples, peeled, cored, and chopped
1 small lemon, cut into quarters
½ cup orange juice
¼ teaspoon ground cinnamon
¼ teaspoon ground allspice
2 teaspoons sugar

1. Combine grapes, pears, apples, lemon, orange juice, cinnamon, allspice, and sugar in a large heavy nonaluminum saucepan and place over medium-high heat.

2. When the compote begins to bubble, reduce the heat to a simmer and cook for 20 minutes or until the pears are soft and the mixture is quite thick.

BANANA APRICOT MOUSSE

This mousse is not molded, but simply blended and chilled.

YIELD: *4 servings*
PREPARATION TIME: *15 minutes + chilling time*

4 fresh apricots, peeled, halved, and pitted
2 overripe bananas, peeled and cut in 1-inch slices
2 tablespoons lemon juice
2 tablespoons grated orange rind
¾ cup blackberries, blueberries, or sliced hulled
    strawberries

1. Combine apricots, bananas, lemon juice, and orange rind in the workbowl of a food processor or in a blender. Process for 1 minute at high speed.

2. Stir in berries and pour into 4 glass dessert dishes.

3. Chill in the refrigerator until ready to serve.

VARIATION
- Substitute 3 overripe small pears or plums for the apricots and an overripe avocado for the bananas.

ORANGE CARROT PUDDING

This unusual pudding is packed with spices, oranges, and carrots.

YIELD: *6 servings*
PREPARATION TIME: *20 minutes*
COOKING TIME: *55 minutes*

3 large seedless oranges, peeled and separated into
    sections
½ cup grated carrots
1 teaspoon orange zest
1 large egg
½ cup sugar
1 cup unbleached all-purpose flour
½ teaspoon baking soda
½ teaspoon ground cinnamon
¼ teaspoon ground ginger
¾ cup skim or low-fat milk
¼ cup melted diet or reduced-calorie margarine,
    containing less than one gram of saturated fat per
    tablespoon

1. Preheat oven to 325 degrees.
2. Purée orange sections in the container or a blender or food processor.
3. Combine orange purée, carrots, and orange zest in a large mixing bowl. Beat in the egg and the sugar.
4. In a separate bowl combine the flour, baking soda, cinnamon, ginger, milk, and margarine.
5. Add the flour mixture to the orange mixture and blend well.
6. Pour into a buttered 1½-quart baking dish.
7. Bake for 50–55 minutes until a knife inserted in the center comes out clean.

PUMPKIN RICOTTA DESSERT

Puréed pumpkin and part-skim ricotta cheese are combined to make a cheesecake-style dessert. Serve topped with fresh blackberries or blueberries.

YIELD: *8 servings*
PREPARATION TIME: *15 minutes*
COOKING TIME: *1½ hours + 2 hours sitting time*

8 graham cracker squares
½ cup walnuts
2 cups mashed pumpkin
2½ pounds part-skim ricotta cheese
½ cup sugar
1 egg white
1 teaspoon mild, light-flavored olive oil
3 tablespoons unbleached all-purpose flour
2 teaspoons ground cinnamon
½ teaspoon ground cloves
1 teaspoon ground ginger
¾ cup canned evaporated skim milk
1 tablespoon vanilla extract

1. Oil the bottom and sides of a 9-inch springform pan. Place the graham cracker crumbs and walnuts in the container of a blender and crush. Press crumbs into the pan to coat sides and bottom evenly.
2. Combine the pumpkin, ricotta cheese, sugar, egg white, oil, flour, cinnamon, cloves, ginger, skim milk, and vanilla extract in a blender, food processor, or electric mixer, and process until smooth, working in batches, if necessary.
3. Pour pumpkin-ricotta mixture into springform pan. Bake for 15 minutes.
4. Reduce temperature to 275 degrees and bake for 1 hour and 15 minutes.
5. Turn off oven and leave cake in oven for 2 hours.
6. Remove cake from oven, cover, and refrigerate until ready to serve.

SPICY CARROT COOKIES

These oatmeal cookies feature carrots, raisins, cinnamon, and cloves.

YIELD: *3 dozen cookies*
PREPARATION TIME: *20 minutes*
COOKING TIME: *11 minutes*

¾ cup softened regular stick margarine, containing less
    than 2 grams of saturated fat per tablespoon
2 cups unbleached all-purpose flour
½ cup brown sugar
2 egg whites
1 teaspoon baking powder
½ teaspoon ground cinnamon
¼ teaspoon baking soda
¼ teaspoon ground cloves
1 teaspoon vanilla extract
2¼ cups rolled oats
1 cup finely shredded carrots
½ cup raisins

1. Preheat oven to 375 degrees.
2. Place softened margarine, 1 cup of the flour, brown sugar, egg whites, baking powder, cinnamon, baking soda, cloves, and vanilla extract in a large bowl. Beat until combined, scraping the sides of the bowl.
3. Stir in remaining 1 cup flour, the oats, carrots, and raisins.
4. Drop dough by rounded teaspoons onto an ungreased cookie sheet, leaving 2 inches between cookies. Bake for 11 minutes or until edges are lightly browned. Remove from oven and transfer cookies to a rack to cool.

CRANBERRY-PUMPKIN SNACKS

These soft cookies are a blend of cranberries, pumpkin, cinnamon, orange peel, and walnuts. Enjoy for lunch with Grilled Chicken Citrus Sandwiches (page 90).

YIELD: *3 dozen cookies*
PREPARATION TIME: *20 minutes*
COOKING TIME: *11 minutes*

½ cup softened regular stick margarine, containing no
     more than 2 grams of saturated fat per tablespoon
¾ cup sugar
1 teaspoon vanilla extract
2 egg whites
1 cup puréed cooked pumpkin
2½ cups all-purpose flour
2 teaspoons baking powder
1 teaspoon baking soda
¼ teaspoon salt
1 teaspoon ground cinnamon
1 cup raw cranberries, chopped
1 tablespoon grated orange peel
½ cup chopped walnuts

1. Preheat oven to 375 degrees. Lightly oil a baking sheet.
2. Combine margarine and sugar until light and fluffy. Beat in vanilla, egg whites, and puréed pumpkin.
3. Sift flour, baking powder, baking soda, salt, and cinnamon together.
4. Combine dry ingredients and wet ingredients. Stir in cranberries, orange peel, and walnuts.
5. Drop dough by rounded teaspoons onto baking sheet, leaving 2 inches between cookies. Bake for 11 minutes or until edges are lightly browned. Remove from oven and transfer cookies to a rack to cool.

Microwave

EASY ACCESS: THE BASICS
Microwaving Vegetables   Microwaving Fruit

QUICK TAKES
Eggplant-Stuffed Celery   Broccoli Dip   Microwave Pumpkin Soup
Microwave Pea Soup   Vegetable Stock   Microwave Zucchini Sandwich
Chicken with Peppers   Lemon Flounder with Broccoli
Green Beans and Fresh Tuna   Microwave Ratatouille   Squash Bake
Vegetable Stew   Pears and Carrots   Sweet Potatoes with Peanuts
Chili Corn with Tomatoes   Maple Baked Fruit
Grapefruit and Tangerine Bake   Nectarines with Apricot Sauce
Baked Apples   Raspberry Crisp   Blueberry Sauce   Cranberry Sauce
Pear Chutney   Mango Chutney

Microwave cooking times may vary from one manufacturer's product to another, depending on power and size configurations. Therefore, you should be sure to use the instructions that accompanied your particular microwave oven as your specific frame of reference and treat the times given in these recipes as general guidelines.

EASY ACCESS: THE BASICS

MICROWAVING VEGETABLES

Vegetables cooked in the microwave retain their color, shape, and nutrients because they can be cooked quickly without water.

MICROWAVE COOKING TIPS

- Rinse fruits and vegetables before microwaving them to supply moisture for cooking.
- Prepare fruits and vegetables so the pieces are uniform in size to promote even cooking.
- When microwaving two or more kinds of fruits and vegetables at once, choose those with a similar texture. Otherwise those that are more delicate will become tough as the denser ones continue to cook.
- Pierce whole unpeeled fruits and vegetables before cooking to prevent skins from bursting.
- Lay the denser sections of a fruit or vegetable toward the outside edge of the dish so that they are first to be hit by the microwaves.
- When cooking several vegetables together on a plate, place slower-cooking vegetables toward the outside. Slower-cooking vegetables include broccoli, cauliflower, green beans, red cabbage, carrots, peas, and cherry tomatoes. Quicker-cooking vegetables include asparagus, red onions, mushrooms, summer squash, and red and green bell peppers.
- Try to cook fruits and vegetables in their serving dish, covered with vented plastic wrap or a tight-fitting lid.
- Cook on 100% HIGH until a specific recipe directs you to do otherwise.

ASPARAGUS: To microwave asparagus spears, cut tough ends from 1 pound of asparagus. Measure ¼ cup water into a shallow microwave-safe dish. Stir in ¼ teaspoon honey. Arrange asparagus so that tips are toward the center. Cover with vented plastic wrap, and cook 3–4 minutes. Rearrange the spears from the outside to the middle of the dish, keeping tips in the center. Cover again and microwave for 3–4 more minutes. Let stand, covered, for 3 minutes. To microwave 1 pound of cut asparagus pieces, place in a 2-quart covered casserole with ¼ cup water and microwave for 5–7 minutes. Let stand, covered, for 3 minutes.

AVOCADO: You can use your microwave to soften a hard avocado. Cut the avocado in half lengthwise and remove the pit. Wrap each half in vented plastic and microwave at 100% HIGH for 1 minute. Remove immediately, run under cold water, and unwrap.

GREEN BEANS: Place ½ pound trimmed beans with ½ cup water in a 1½-quart covered microwave-safe casserole. Microwave for 3 minutes. Stir and microwave for 3 more minutes or until tender crisp. Let stand, covered, for 3 minutes.

BROCCOLI: To microwave 1 pound broccoli spears, remove woody ends and peel stems with a vegetable peeler if desired. Pour ½ cup water into a microwave-safe baking dish. Arrange spears with florets toward center. Cover with vented plastic wrap. Microwave for 4–6 minutes and rotate dish. Microwave for 4–6 more minutes until stalks are tender. Let stand, covered, for 3 minutes. To microwave 1 pound broccoli pieces, cut off florets and slice stems into 1-inch lengths. Place in 2-quart microwave-safe casserole with ½ cup water. Cover with vented plastic wrap. Microwave for 4 minutes. Stir. Microwave for 4–5 more minutes until tender. Let stand, covered, for 3 minutes.

BRUSSELS SPROUTS: Trim stems from 1 pound Brussels sprouts and cut a cross in stem end of each sprout to speed up cooking process. Place in microwave-safe baking dish. Cover with vented plastic wrap. Microwave for 4 minutes. Stir. Microwave for 4 minutes more or until tender. Let stand, covered, for 3 minutes.

CABBAGE: To cook green or red cabbage wedges, cut 1 pound cabbage into quarters. Place in a microwave-safe baking dish and add ¼ cup water. Add 2 teaspoons vinegar if using red cabbage. Cover with vented plastic wrap. Microwave for 8 minutes. Rearrange cabbage and rotate dish. Microwave for 5 more minutes. Let stand, covered, for 3 minutes. To microwave shredded green cabbage, place 1 pound cabbage and 2 tablespoons water in a microwave-safe covered casserole. Microwave for 8 minutes. Stir. Microwave for 5 more minutes. Let stand, covered, for 3 minutes. To microwave 1 pound shredded red cabbage, place cabbage, ¼ cup water, 2 teaspoons sugar, and 2 teaspoons vinegar in a microwave-safe covered casserole. Microwave for 8 minutes. Stir. Microwave for 5 more minutes. Let stand, covered, for 3 minutes.

CARROTS: Place 2 cups thick-sliced (¼ inch thick) carrots in a microwave-safe 1-quart casserole with 2 tablespoons water. Cover. Microwave for 3 minutes. Stir. Microwave for 3 more minutes. If preparing 10 carrots, cut into 2-inch pieces, place in a 1-quart microwave-safe casserole with 2 tablespoons water. Cover and microwave for 4 minutes. Stir. Microwave for 4 more minutes. Let stand, covered, for 3 minutes.

CAULIFLOWER FLORETS: Place 2 cups florets in a 1½-quart microwave-safe covered casserole with 2 tablespoons water. Microwave for 4 minutes. Stir. Microwave for 3 more minutes. Let stand, covered, for 3 minutes.

CORN: Husk 4 ears of corn and wrap in vented plastic wrap. Microwave for 4 minutes. Turn over and rearrange. Microwave for 4 more minutes, turn over, and rearrange. Microwave for 4 more minutes. If corn is still not tender, turn over, rearrange, and cook for 4 more minutes. Let stand 5 minutes. (You can also place ears in a microwave-safe baking dish with ¼ cup water, leaving space between ears. Cover with plastic wrap, leaving one corner loose so steam can escape. Microwave for 4 minutes. Turn over and rearrange. Microwave for 4 more minutes, turn over, and rearrange. Microwave for 4 more minutes. If corn is still not tender, turn over, rearrange, and cook for 4 more minutes. Let stand 5 minutes.) To microwave corn kernels, place 2 cups kernels in a microwave-safe baking dish with 2 tablespoons water. Cover and microwave on 100% HIGH for 5 minutes.

EGGPLANT: Place 1½ pounds ¾-inch eggplant cubes in a 2-quart microwave-safe casserole with 2 tablespoons diet or reduced-calorie margarine. Cover and microwave for 8–10 minutes, stirring every 2 minutes. Microwave on 100% HIGH for 3–5 minutes or until tender. Let stand, covered, for 3 minutes.

ONIONS: Place 2 medium onions, sliced, in a 1-quart microwave-safe casserole with ¼ cup water. Microwave, uncovered, to minimize cooking odors for 3 minutes. Stir. Microwave for 3 more minutes. Cover. Let stand for 5 minutes.

PEAS: Place 2 cups fresh peas in a 1½-quart microwave-safe casserole with ¼ cup water. Cover. Microwave for 3 minutes. Stir. Microwave for 3 more minutes. Let stand, covered, for 3 minutes.

POTATOES: To bake 4 medium baking potatoes, pierce each with a fork. Arrange potatoes on a paper towel, 1 inch apart. Microwave for 6 minutes. Turn potatoes over and rearrange. Microwave for 6 more minutes. Wrap in foil to retain heat and let stand for 5 minutes. To boil 8 whole potatoes, pierce with fork and place in 1½-quart microwave-safe casserole with 2 tablespoons water. Microwave for 8 minutes. To boil 4 medium potatoes, cut into ¼-inch slices, place in casserole with ¼ cup water. Cover. Microwave for 4 minutes. Stir. Microwave for 4 more minutes. Let stand, covered, for 3 minutes.

SPINACH: Cook 1 pound rinsed trimmed spinach in a 3-quart covered microwave-safe casserole for 4 minutes. Stir. Cook for 3 more minutes. Let stand, covered, for 3 minutes.

SUMMER SQUASH: Place 2 cups of ¼-inch-thick zucchini slices in a microwave-safe 2-quart casserole with 2 tablespoons diet or reduced-calorie margarine. Cover. Microwave for 2 minutes. Stir. Microwave for 2 more minutes. Check for tenderness. Let stand, covered, 2 minutes. Place 2 cups of ¼-inch-thick yellow squash slices in a 2-quart microwave-safe casserole with 2 tablespoons diet or reduced-calorie margarine. Cover. Microwave for 3½ minutes. Stir. Microwave for 3 more minutes. Check for tenderness. Let stand, covered, 2 minutes.

WINTER SQUASH: Cut whole 1½-pound acorn squash in half. Scoop out seeds and fibers. Cover halves with vented plastic wrap and place in microwave with space between halves. Microwave for 5½ minutes. Rotate and rearrange. Microwave for 5 more minutes. Let stand, covered, for 5 minutes. Cut butternut or Hubbard squash lengthwise, then cut into ½-pound pieces, removing seeds and fibers. Place 4 pieces in a microwave-safe baking dish. Cover with plastic wrap, leaving one corner loose so that steam can escape. Microwave for 6 minutes. Rearrange pieces. Microwave for 6 more minutes. Let stand, covered, for 5 minutes.

SWEET POTATOES: Prick 4 sweet potatoes with a fork. Place in oven on paper towel, leaving space between potatoes. Microwave for 6 minutes. Rearrange. Microwave for 6 more minutes. Let stand, covered, for 3 minutes.

TURNIPS: Place 4 medium turnips, cut into ¼-inch slices, in a 1-quart covered microwave-safe casserole with ¼ cup water. Microwave for 5 minutes. Stir. Microwave for 4 more minutes. Let stand, covered, for 3 minutes.

MICROWAVING FRUIT

CHUNKY MICROWAVE APPLESAUCE: Place 2 apples, peeled, cored, and chopped, ¼ cup orange juice, 2 tablespoons honey, and ¼ teaspoon ground cinnamon in a 9-inch microwave-safe glass pie dish. Cover with vented plastic wrap and microwave for 8 minutes at 100% HIGH. Let stand, covered, for 3 minutes.

MICROWAVE APRICOTS: Place 8 fresh apricots, pitted and halved, 2 tablespoons lemon juice, and ¼ cup water in a large glass microwave-safe measure and cover with vented plastic wrap. Microwave at 100% HIGH for 10 minutes. To microwave dried apricots, place 1½ cups dried apricots, 1½ cups water, ¼ teaspoon vanilla extract, and 1 tablespoon sugar in a large microwave-safe glass measure. Cover with vented plastic wrap. Cook at 100% HIGH for 7 minutes. Remove from microwave and drain.

MICROWAVE BANANAS: Peel and slice lengthwise one banana per person. Lay the bananas, cut sides up, on a microwave-safe platter. Sprinkle with brown sugar and microwave at 100% HIGH until the sugar has melted.

MICROWAVE GRAPEFRUIT: Cut a grapefruit in half and section it with a serrated knife so it will be easy to eat. Place each grapefruit half in a microwave-safe bowl. Sprinkle each half with ½ teaspoon brown sugar and ¼ teaspoon ground cinnamon. Microwave at 100% HIGH for 2–3 minutes.

MICROWAVE ORANGES: Cut large navel oranges in half and section with a serrated knife. Place each orange half in a microwave-safe bowl. Top with 2 tablespoons reduced-calorie maple syrup. Microwave at 100% HIGH for 2½ minutes.

MICROWAVE NECTARINES (or PEACHES): These can be poached in a microwave in a simple syrup. To make syrup, combine 2 cups sugar and 1 cup water in an 8-cup microwave-safe glass measure. Cover with vented plastic wrap and microwave at 100% HIGH for 15 minutes, stirring twice. Place 2¼ pounds small pierced nectarines or peaches with 2 cups syrup in a microwave-safe covered casserole. Microwave at 100% HIGH for 5 minutes. (To make nectarine or peach butter, place 1½ pounds quartered nectarines or peaches in a 2-quart microwave-safe casserole with ½ cup water and ½ cup sugar. Cover and microwave at 100% HIGH for 15 minutes.)

MICROWAVE PEARS: Peel, halve, and core 2 pears. Place them, cut sides down, on a 9-inch microwave-safe pie dish. Sprinkle with 2 tablespoons lemon juice. Cover with vented plastic wrap and microwave at 100% HIGH for 2½ minutes. Let stand, covered, for 2 minutes.

MICROWAVE PINEAPPLE: Trim, peel, core, and quarter a ripe pineapple and microwave in a covered microwave-safe baking dish at 100% HIGH for 8 minutes.

QUICK TAKES

EGGPLANT-STUFFED CELERY: Prick 1 medium EGGPLANT in a few places with a fork. Place on 2 layers of paper toweling in microwave oven. Microwave, uncovered, at 100% HIGH for 12 minutes until eggplant is soft. Remove from oven. Let cool in the refrigerator for 30 minutes. Cut the eggplant in half lengthwise and scoop out the inside. Discard the shell. Place the eggplant pulp in a medium bowl and chop lightly, using a fork. Add 1 clove garlic, minced, 3 tablespoons mild, light-flavored olive oil, 1 tablespoon lemon juice, 3 tablespoons chopped fresh parsley, 1 teaspoon paprika, 1 teaspoon ground cumin, and ¼ teaspoon black pepper. Stuff 12 stalks celery with eggplant mixture. Cut into 3-inch lengths.

BROCCOLI DIP: Place 1½ cups BROCCOLI florets in a single layer on a microwave-safe dish just large enough to hold them. Sprinkle with 1½ tablespoons water. Cover with vented plastic wrap and cook at 100% HIGH for 4–5 minutes. Remove from oven. Remove plastic wrap with care. Place the broccoli under cold running water immediately. Drain, pat dry, and chop. Place broccoli, ½ cup nonfat or low-fat plain yogurt, ¼ cup skim or low-fat milk, 1 tablespoon lemon juice, 1 teaspoon curry powder, and ¼ teaspoon black pepper in the workbowl of a food processor or in a blender and process just until blended.

MICROWAVE PUMPKIN SOUP: Place 5 scallions, sliced, and 2 tablespoons mild, light-flavored olive oil in a 3-quart microwave-safe casserole. Microwave at 100% HIGH for 3 minutes or until scallions are tender. Stir once. Add to casserole 1 16-ounce can cooked PUMPKIN, ¼ teaspoon ground ginger, 1 cup evaporated skim milk, 1 cup skim or low-fat milk, 2 cups hot water, and 1 teaspoon reduced-calorie maple syrup. Microwave at 100% HIGH for 6–7 minutes or until heated through. Stir every 2 minutes. (6 servings)

MICROWAVE PEA SOUP: Defrost 1 10-ounce package frozen PEAS under warm running water. Place peas, ½ teaspoon dried thyme leaves, 1½ cups low-salt chicken broth, and ¼ cup skim or low-fat milk, in a large glass microwave-safe measure. Cover with vented plastic wrap. Microwave at 100% HIGH for 8 minutes. Remove from microwave and let stand for 2 minutes. Transfer contents to the workbowl of a food processor or to a blender. Purée. Return to glass measure. Microwave, uncovered, for 1½ minutes. Stir. Microwave for 1½ more minutes. Season with ¼ teaspoon black pepper and ½ teaspoon lemon juice. Serve. (4 servings)

VEGETABLE STOCK: Place 1 clove garlic, minced, ½ cup chopped celery, 1 medium onion, chopped, 1 cup zucchini, chopped, 1 CARROT, scrubbed and sliced, 1 medium RED BELL PEPPER, seeded and chopped, 1 bay leaf, and 4 cups water in a 2½-quart microwave-safe casserole and cover with a lid. Cook at 100% HIGH for 20 minutes. Remove from oven and strain. Remove vegetables. Use as a soup base or freeze to use at another time. (4 servings)

MICROWAVE ZUCCHINI SANDWICH: Combine 1 cup shredded zucchini and ½ cup sliced mushrooms in a microwave-safe bowl and microwave at 100% HIGH for 2–3 minutes. Remove from microwave and drain liquid. Add 1 cup chopped TOMATO, ½ teaspoon dried basil leaves, 1 clove garlic, minced, and 2 tablespoons grated Parmesan cheese. Fill each of 4 pita bread halves with ¼ of the zucchini mixture.

CHICKEN WITH PEPPERS: Heat ¼ cup mild, light-flavored olive oil in a microwave-safe baking dish at 100% HIGH for 2 minutes. Add 1 large onion, sliced, and stir. Cook without a cover at 100% HIGH for 2 minutes. Add 1 RED BELL PEPPER, seeded and cut into 1-inch strips, 1 GREEN BELL PEPPER, seeded and cut into 1-inch strips, 3 medium TOMATOES, sliced, ¼ teaspoon dried basil leaves, ¼ teaspoon dried oregano leaves, and ¼ teaspoon black pepper. Stir to coat with olive oil. Push vegetables to center of dish. Arrange 2 chicken breasts, skinned, boned, and halved, around vegetables, with thicker portions toward the edge of the dish. Cover with vented plastic wrap. Cook at 100% HIGH for 8 minutes. (4 servings)

LEMON FLOUNDER WITH BROCCOLI: Arrange 1 pound flounder or sole fillets, cut into 4 pieces, and 4 cups BROCCOLI florets on a round microwave-safe plate, leaving center empty. Sprinkle with 2 tablespoons fresh lemon juice, 1 tablespoon mild, light-flavored olive oil, ½ teaspoon grated lemon peel, and ¼ teaspoon black pepper. Cover with vented plastic wrap. Microwave at 100% HIGH for 3 minutes. Rotate plate. Microwave at 100% HIGH for 3 more minutes. (4 servings)

GREEN BEANS AND FRESH TUNA: Toss 2 cups sliced GREEN BEANS, 1 TOMATO, diced, 4 scallions, chopped, 2 tablespoons light soy sauce, 1 teaspoon grated fresh gingerroot, 1 clove garlic, minced, and 1 teaspoon sesame oil together in a bowl. Transfer to the center of a microwave-safe baking dish. Arrange 1 pound tuna steaks, cut into 4 pieces, around the vegetables. Cover with vented plastic wrap and cook at 100% HIGH for 4 minutes. (4 servings)

MICROWAVE RATATOUILLE: Combine ½ pound EGGPLANT, cut into ½-

inch cubes, 1 clove garlic, minced, 1 small onion, sliced and separated into rings, 1 small zucchini, thinly sliced, 1 medium GREEN BELL PEPPER, seeded and cut into thin strips, 1 stalk celery, sliced, 1 TOMATO, cut in wedges, ¼ teaspoon black pepper, ¼ teaspoon dried basil leaves, ¼ teaspoon dried oregano leaves, ⅛ teaspoon dried thyme leaves, and 1 tablespoon grated Parmesan cheese in a 2-quart microwave-safe casserole and cover. Microwave at 100% HIGH for 7–10 minutes or until eggplant is translucent. Stir 2 or 3 times. (4 servings)

SQUASH BAKE: Microwave 2 small ACORN SQUASH at 100% HIGH for 2 minutes. Remove from microwave and cut in half. Scoop out seeds. Place squash halves, cut sides up, in a 13- by 9-inch microwave-safe dish. Cover and microwave at 100% HIGH for 10 minutes. Brush each squash half with maple syrup and sprinkle with chopped walnuts. Microwave, uncovered, at 100% HIGH for 2 more minutes. (4 servings)

VEGETABLE STEW: Combine 4 cups low-salt tomato juice, 2 cloves garlic, minced, 1 teaspoon ground cumin, ¼ teaspoon ground ginger, ¼ teaspoon ground nutmeg, ¼ teaspoon cayenne pepper, ½ teaspoon black pepper, ¼ teaspoon ground cinnamon, and 2 tablespoons mild, light-flavored olive oil in a large microwave-safe baking dish. Add 2 CARROTS, scrubbed and cut into 1-inch slices, 4 small TURNIPS, peeled and cut into 1-inch chunks, 3 cups CAULIFLOWER florets, 1 cup fresh or frozen CORN kernels, 2 cups sliced TOMATOES, 4 cups cubed EGGPLANT, 1 large onion, sliced, and 3 cups sliced asparagus spears. Cover with vented plastic wrap and cook at 100% HIGH for 20 minutes. Uncover and cook for 10 more minutes. Sprinkle with 3 tablespoons lemon juice before serving. (4 servings)

PEARS AND CARROTS: Place ¼ cup apple juice and ¾ pound CARROTS, sliced, in a 1-quart microwave-safe dish and cover with wax paper. Microwave at 100% HIGH for 5 minutes. Remove from microwave and drain. Place 2 tablespoons diet or reduced-calorie margarine, containing no more than 1 gram of saturated fat per tablespoon, 1 tablespoon honey, 1 tablespoon lemon juice, and 1 tablespoon grated fresh gingerroot in 1 cup microwave-safe measure. Microwave at 100% HIGH for 1 minute. Remove from microwave. Add 2 cups juice-packed canned PEARS to carrots in dish. Pour honey mixture over pears and carrots. Microwave at 100% HIGH for 2 minutes. (4 servings)

SWEET POTATOES WITH PEANUTS: Combine 3 medium SWEET POTA-TOES, cut into 1- by 2-inch chunks, and 3 tablespoons low-salt chicken broth in a 9-inch microwave-safe glass pie dish. Cover with vented plastic wrap and microwave at 100% HIGH for 6 minutes. Stir every 2 minutes. Remove from microwave and let stand 5 minutes. Combine 1 tablespoon maple syrup, 2 tablespoons lemon juice, 1 teaspoon mild, light-flavored olive oil, 1 tablespoon minced scallions, and ¼ cup crushed roasted, unsalted peanuts. Toss with sweet potato chunks. (4 servings)

CHILI CORN WITH TOMATOES: Place ⅔ cup fresh, canned, or frozen and thawed CORN kernels, 1 scallion, chopped, and 1 onion, chopped, in the workbowl of a food processor or in a blender and process until smooth. Place in a microwave-safe casserole with 2 cups crushed TOMATOES, 1 cup low-salt chicken broth, ½ teaspoon dried oregano leaves, 1 teaspoon chili powder, 2 cloves garlic, minced, 1 jalapeño pepper, seeded and minced, and 2 bay leaves. Cover and microwave at 100% HIGH for 3 minutes. Stir and microwave for 3 more minutes. Remove bay leaves and sprinkle with grated reduced-calorie cheddar cheese before serving. (4 servings)

MAPLE BAKED FRUIT: Combine the juice from 1 ORANGE, 1 tablespoon reduced-calorie maple syrup, 2 tablespoons regular stick margarine, containing no more than 2 grams of saturated fat per tablespoon, and ¼ teaspoon ground cinnamon in a 9-inch microwave-safe glass pie dish and cover with vented plastic wrap. Microwave at 100% HIGH for 1½ minutes. Add 2 BANANAS, sliced, and 2 PINEAPPLE spears, diced, to the pie dish and cover again. Microwave at 100% HIGH for 4 minutes. Serve sprinkled with chopped walnuts. (4 servings)

GRAPEFRUIT AND TANGERINE BAKE: Combine the sections from 2 PINK GRAPEFRUIT, the sections from 2 TANGERINES, 1 tablespoon lime juice, and 1 tablespoon reduced-calorie maple syrup in a 9-inch microwave-safe glass pie dish. Cover with vented plastic wrap and microwave at 100% HIGH for 2 minutes. Stir and microwave at 100% HIGH for 2 more minutes. Remove from microwave and let stand for 2 minutes. (4 servings)

NECTARINES WITH APRICOT SAUCE: Combine 2 tablespoons lemon juice, 1 tablespoon maple syrup, 2 tablespoons apricot all-fruit jam, and ⅛ teaspoon ground nutmeg in a small microwave-safe bowl. Cover with vented plastic wrap and microwave at 100% HIGH for 40 seconds. Place 4 fresh NECTARINES, peeled, pitted, and halved, cut sides down, in a 9-inch glass pie dish. Spoon apricot-maple sauce over them. Cover with vented plastic wrap and microwave at 100% HIGH for 3 minutes. Let stand for 2 minutes. Serve nectarines with the sauce over frozen yogurt. (4 servings)

BAKED APPLES: Core 4 baking APPLES, being careful not to cut all the way through the bottoms. Pare skin ⅓ of the way down from the top of the apples. Place in an 8-inch round microwave-safe dish. Combine 1 tablespoon reduced-calorie or diet tub or liquid margarine, containing no more than 1 gram of saturated fat per tablespoon, 1 tablespoon brown sugar, 3 tablespoons raisins, and 3 tablespoons chopped walnuts. Stuff into cavity of apples. Combine ¼ cup apple juice, ¼ cup water, ½ teaspoon ground cinnamon, and ¼ teaspoon ground nutmeg. Pour over apples. Microwave at 100% HIGH, uncovered, 10–12 minutes. Rotate dish and baste every 4 minutes. Cooking time may vary according to size and variety of apple. (4 servings)

RASPBERRY CRISP: Place 3 cups fresh or frozen RASPBERRIES in an 8-inch square microwave-safe baking dish. Sprinkle with 2 tablespoons lemon juice. Combine 2 tablespoons brown sugar, ½ cup unbleached all-purpose flour, ⅔ cup quick-cooking rolled oats, ⅓ cup diet or reduced-calorie tub or liquid margarine, containing no more than 1 gram of saturated fat per tablespoon, and 1 teaspoon cinnamon. Sprinkle over berries. Microwave, uncovered, at 100% HIGH for 10 minutes. (4 servings)

BLUEBERRY SAUCE: Mix 2 teaspoons cornstarch with 2 tablespoons water in a 1-quart microwave-safe glass bowl. Stir until smooth and add ½ cup water, ¾ cup fresh or frozen BLUEBERRIES, and 2 tablespoons honey. Microwave on 100% HIGH for 2 minutes. Stir well. Microwave for 2 additional minutes or until mixture comes to a full boil. Remove and stir in 2 tablespoons lemon juice.

CRANBERRY SAUCE: Combine 12 ounces fresh or frozen CRANBERRIES, ¾ cup sugar, and 3 tablespoons orange juice in a 2-quart microwave-safe bowl. Cover with wax paper and microwave at 100% HIGH for 4–5 minutes or until berries have popped. Stir after 2 minutes.

PEAR CHUTNEY: Combine ½ teaspoon sugar; ½ cup seedless raisins, ½ teaspoon ground ginger, 1 tablespoon grated orange peel, and ½ teaspoon ground cinnamon in a 2-quart microwave-safe container. Cover with wax paper and microwave at 100% HIGH for 3 minutes. Stir in 4 cups juice-packed canned PEARS, drained and diced, and ¼ cup of their liquid, 1 seedless ORANGE, peeled and diced, and 2 tablespoons chopped green chiles. Microwave, uncovered, at 100% HIGH for 10 minutes, stirring several times. Remove from microwave and stir in ½ cup chopped almonds. Serve warm or transfer to a glass jar with a tight-fitting lid and refrigerate.

MANGO CHUTNEY: Combine 2 ripe MANGOES, peeled, seeded, and cut into ½-inch-thick slices, 1 clove garlic, minced, ½ cup minced onion,

2 tablespoons brown sugar, 2 teaspoons minced fresh gingerroot, ½ cup seedless raisins, 1 TOMATO, chopped, ½ cup chopped almonds, ½ teaspoon ground cinnamon, ⅛ teaspoon ground cloves, and ⅛ teaspoon cayenne pepper in a high-sided 3-quart microwave-safe casserole. Cover with wax paper and microwave at 100% HIGH for 3 minutes. Stir. Remove wax paper and microwave on 100% HIGH for 7 minutes or until fruit is soft and mixture is thickened. Stir in 2 tablespoons lime juice. Served warm or store in a glass jar with a tight-fitting lid in the refrigerator.

Bibliography

A to Z of Favorite Fruits. New York: Arco, 1985.

Ballantine, Rudolph. *Diet and Nutrition: A Holistic Approach.* Honesdale, Pennsylvania: The Himalayan Institute, 1978.

Bland, Jeffrey. *Your Health Under Siege: Using Nutrition to Fight Back.* Brattleboro, Vermont: The Stephen Greene Press, 1981.

Black, Dana Yuen. *The Banana Book.* Hilo, Hawaii: Petroglyph Press, 1988.

Brody, Jane. "Three Promising Weapons Against Disease," *The New York Times* (September 24, 1991), Section C, p. 18.

Brooks, Jeffree Sapp. *The Art of Accompaniment.* San Francisco: North Point Press, 1988.

Burkitt, Denis. *Eat Right to Stay Healthy and Enjoy Life More.* New York: Arco Publishers, 1979.

Cheraskin, Emanuel; Ringsdorf, W. Marshall; and Sisley, Emily L. *The Vitamin C Connection.* New York: Harper & Row, 1983.

Colgan, Dr. Michael. *Prevent Cancer Now: Your Guide to Self-Protection.* San Diego: CI Publications, 1990.

The Columbia Encyclopedia of Nutrition. Myron Winnick, Editor. New York: Perigee, 1988.

Cooper, Kenneth H., M.D. *Preventing Osteoporosis.* New York: Bantam, 1989.

Diet, Nutrition, and Cancer. Committee on Diet, Nutrition, and Cancer of the Assembly of Life Sciences of the National Research Council. Washington, D.C.: National Academy Press, 1982.

Diet, Nutrition, and Cancer Prevention: The Good News. Bethesda, Maryland: National Cancer Institute, 1989.

Dreher, Henry. *Your Defense Against Cancer.* New York: Harper & Row, 1989.

Garland, Cedric, M.D.; and Garland, Frank M.D., with Thro, Ellen. *The Calcium Connection.* New York: G. P. Putnam's Sons, 1989.

Goldbeck, Nikki and David. *The Goldbeck's Guide to Good Food.* New York: New American Library, 1987.

Grigson, Jane. *Jane Grigson's Fruit Book.* New York: Atheneum, 1982.

———. *Jane Grigson's Vegetable Book.* New York: Atheneum, 1979.

Hausman, Patricia and Hurley, Judith Benn. *The Healing Foods.* Emmaus, Pennsylvania: Rodale Press, 1989.

Hendler, Sheldon Saul. *The Doctor's Vitamin and Mineral Encyclopedia.* New York: Simon and Schuster, 1990.

Heriteau, Jacqueline. *The Cook's Almanac.* New York: Stonesong Press, 1983.

Kahn, Frederick E., M.D. *The Sandwich Cookbook.* New York: Nautilus Communications, 1984.

Kamen, Betty, Ph.D. *Osteoporosis.* New York: Pinnacle Books, 1989.

Nutritive Value of America Foods, Agricultural Handbook No. 456. United States Department of Agriculture, Washington, D.C.: Government Printing Office, 1975.

Kobren, Gerri. "In The Battle Against Cancer, Food Could Be the Ultimate Drug." *The Baltimore Sun* (July 24, 1990), To Your Health, p. 4.

———. "Vitamin A Keeps Us Safe from a Host of Ills." *The Baltimore Sun.* (October 17, 1989), To Your Health, p. 5.

Pauling, Linus. *How to Live Longer and Feel Better.* New York: W.H. Freeman and Company, 1986.

Pauling, Linus and Cameron, Ewan. *Cancer and Vitamin C.* New York: Warner Books, 1979.

Quillin, Patrick, Ph.D. *Healing Nutrients.* New York: Vintage, 1989.

Radecka, Helene. *Fruit and Nut Book.* New York: McGraw Hill, 1984.

Schindler, Roana and Gene. *Hawaiian Cookbook.* New York: Dover, 1970.

Simone, Charles B. *Cancer and Nutrition.* New York: McGraw-Hill Book Company, 1983.

Spodnik, Jean Perry and Cogan, David P. *The 35-Plus Good Health Guide for Women.* New York: Harper & Row. 1989.

Standard, Stella. *The Art of Fruit Cookery.* Garden City, N.Y.: Doubleday, 1964.

The Surgeon General's Report on Nutrition and Health. United States Department of Health and Human Services. Government Printing Office, Washington, D.C.: 1988.

Index

About the Author

SARAH SCHLESINGER began researching and writing about healthful cooking in response to her husband's ongoing battle against coronary-artery disease. She is the co-author of *The Low-Cholesterol Oat Plan, The Low-Cholesterol Olive Oil Cookbook,* and author of *500 Fat-Free Recipes.* She also wrote *The Pointe Book,* a book that focuses on health issues for dancers. Ms. Schlesinger is on the faculty of the Graduate Musical Theatre Writing Program at the Tisch School of the Arts, New York University, New York.